SuperF...
Su...

...please...
...online...
...ur loc...
...incit...
...ns

...nath
...b

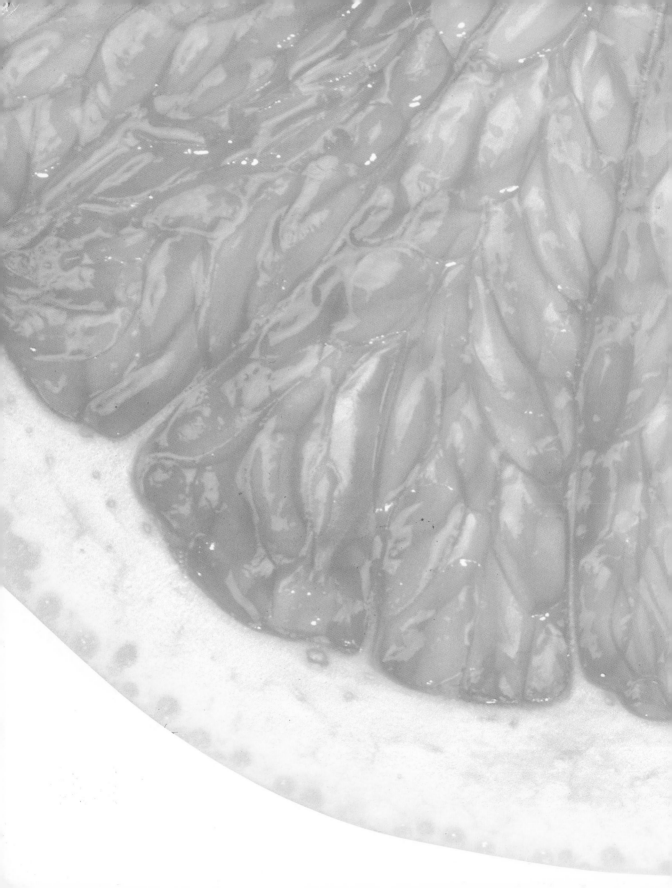

Super**Foods**,
Super**Fast**

Eat your way to superhealth

Michael van Straten
& Barbara Griggs

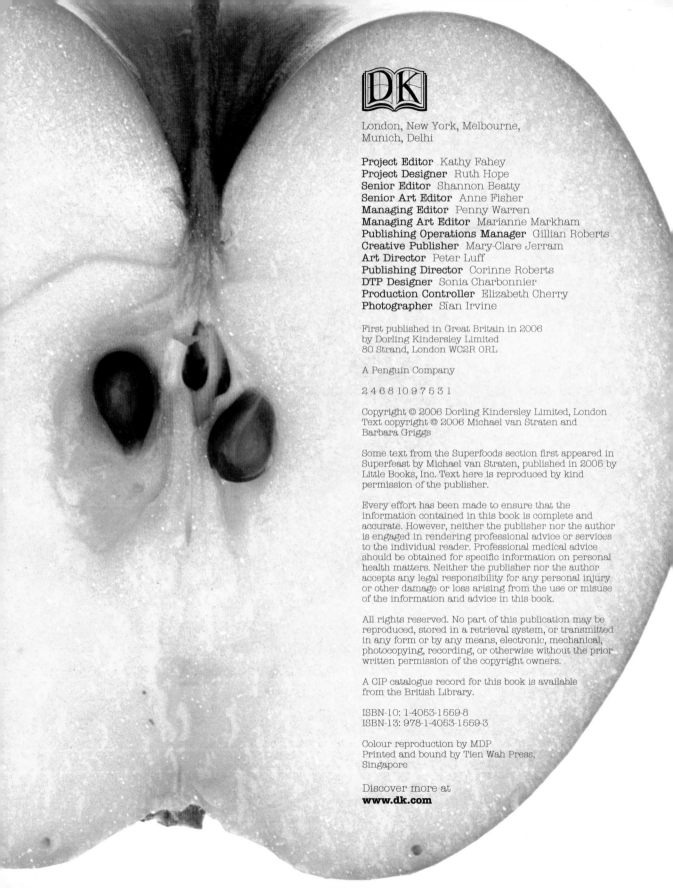

DK

London, New York, Melbourne,
Munich, Delhi

Project Editor Kathy Fahey
Project Designer Ruth Hope
Senior Editor Shannon Beatty
Senior Art Editor Anne Fisher
Managing Editor Penny Warren
Managing Art Editor Marianne Markham
Publishing Operations Manager Gillian Roberts
Creative Publisher Mary-Clare Jerram
Art Director Peter Luff
Publishing Director Corinne Roberts
DTP Designer Sonia Charbonnier
Production Controller Elizabeth Cherry
Photographer Sian Irvine

First published in Great Britain in 2006
by Dorling Kindersley Limited
80 Strand, London WC2R 0RL

A Penguin Company

2 4 6 8 10 9 7 5 3 1

A CIP catalogue record for this book is available
from the British Library.

ISBN-10: 1-4053-1559-8
ISBN-13: 978-1-4053-1559-3

Colour reproduction by MDP
Printed and bound by Tien Wah Press,
Singapore

Discover more at
www.dk.com

Contents

A cookery book with a difference

The purpose of this book is to help people suffering from specific ailments in the simplest, most effective way – by teaching them to eat and enjoy those foods that will promote the healing process, and to avoid those that aggravate the condition, or indeed, may have caused it in the first place.

Equally, you can use this book to help promote the health and improve the resistance of yourself and your whole family by serving up a daily diet of Superfoods.

Your health problem may be a disabling bout of flu or a crippling case of arthritis; you may be coping with an annual visitation of bronchitis, or chronic digestive discomfort, or even a diagnosis of cancer. Whatever the problem, turn to the appropriate section and follow the nutritional guidelines.

Each of the ailments sections of the book deals with disorders of a bodily system, such as the heart and circulation, the respiratory system, the digestive apparatus, the nervous system, the skin, and so on. Each section has an introduction explaining how the wrong diet may have contributed to your problems in the first place, and how eating the right foods can help restore you to good health.

A complete list of the Superfoods, including the potent **Four-Star Superfoods**, which we specifically recommend for your case, appears on p.20. Some of them have a centuries-long history of successful kitchen medicine, such as sauerkraut for digestive problems. However, we certainly do not imply that any fruit, vegetable, or other food not named in the relevant section is without value to you and should be avoided. On the contrary, we always urge that you eat from as wide a range of foodstuffs as possible. So whatever your health problem, choose freely (unless a particular recipe features a food on your danger-list).

The **Danger foods** – listed immediately after the Superfoods – should be avoided wherever possible for those with the health problem specified. For example, avoid tea and coffee if you're suffering from anxiety or fatigue; steer clear of dishes that drip animal fat if you have a heart condition. Explanations are given to detail why a particular food is ill-advised in specific health problems.

The **eating plan** in each section spells out the broad guidelines you'll be following, and gives a week's menus.

How can you get the most out of this book?

Study the Superfoods in the sections that are relevant for you, and master the list of Danger foods too. In the recipe section you'll find dozens of other dishes that feature your Superfoods, while avoiding your Danger foods. All of the recipes are beneficial for many of the ailments, but the ailments for which a recipe is *most* effective are listed under its title.

The menus for specific ailments are for your guidance only. Obviously you don't have to keep eating the same dishes week after week. However, after using them you may find it easier, and certainly cheaper, to plan a whole week's eating ahead in the same way, balancing starch and protein, and including two or three Superfoods at almost every meal.

How carefully should you stick to the eating plan in the section relevant for you?

If you are seriously or chronically ill, if a doctor or specialist has recently given you a diagnosis of bad news, the more closely you stay with the eating plan, and the more you build the appropriate Superfoods into your daily menu, the more dramatic will be the improvement in your condition,

and the sooner you may return to health. Superfoods cannot always guarantee full recovery, but they can always reduce painful symptoms and increase wellbeing.

Some people may choose to stick with a particular eating plan as a form of insurance. If you have high cholesterol levels or high blood pressure, for instance, obviously you would be sensible to follow the recommendations in the section on circulatory problems, however well you feel at present. If you have had problems in the past with indigestion, constipation, or stomach ulcers, you might discover a digestive comfort and efficiency you never knew was possible by following the guidelines in the digestive section. If your workload is backbreaking – and there isn't a lot you can off-load – following the fatigue eating plan will help you cope.

If you wonder just how much "healthy eating" can do for you, follow the **Seven-Day Alimentary Plan** (*p.287*) and find out! The Three-Day Elimination Diet – the first three days of the Alimentary Plan – is recommended for those suffering from digestive problems, but it also works as a gentle cleansing and detoxifying diet after any season of rich eating and general overindulgence, such as Christmas or holiday-time.

Over the last half-century, hundreds of thousands of people have recovered from serious health problems on no other treatment but following the eating plan devised by Dr William Howard Hay in the 1920s, variously known as the Hay Diet or Food Combining, described on p.344. While it is not essential to recovery, there is no doubt at all that **Harmonious Eating**, as we call it, can revolutionize your health, in some cases almost overnight. Whatever your ailments, we strongly recommend that you give it a serious trial for at least a week, as your first step towards super-health.

In our present state of ignorance, it would be foolhardy and irresponsible to claim that dietary changes alone can produce cures, but there can be no doubt that the right food will maximize the body's ability to fight back against many diseases. The extraordinary healing power of nature operates best in the well-nourished organism, whether it is a single cell or a complex human being.

Recent studies show the importance of nutritional factors in the amelioration of many diseases. For this reason we would urge all sufferers from such conditions as AIDS, myalgic encephalopathy (ME), Parkinson's disease, Alzheimer's disease, multiple sclerosis, motor neurone disease, cancer, lupus, rheumatoid arthritis, epilepsy, and schizophrenia to contact the relevant self-help and research organizations for the most up-to-date information and advice.

Whatever your illness, study the chapter on Harmonious Eating, together with those chapters most appropriate to your symptoms. Pick the recipes that take your fancy, enjoy them, and know that every mouthful enhances your health. As doctors are at last beginning to acknowledge, only nature heals.

However, Superfoods was designed to maintain wellbeing, as well as help restore it, and you certainly don't need to be ill or out of condition to enjoy and benefit from the recipes in this book.

It's a rare household these days where all the family sits down to meals together in the evening, let alone at midday. So the menus are planned for breakfast, a light meal needing minimal preparation (which can often be turned into a packed lunch or prepared in advance), and for the main meal of the day, which may or may not be eaten in the evening.

In suggesting main-meal menus, there is always either a starter or a pudding as well as the principal dish. This is certainly not because we expect readers to prepare or eat a multi-course meal every day. Many of the recipes, including several presented as starters (such as Brown rice and celery soup), make a perfectly good meal in themselves, needing only the addition of a wholemeal roll and a salad. However, when this is the only substantial meal of the day, or if it's the only time the family gathers and relaxes together, either starters, puddings, or occasionally both, may well be called for. So we've made appropriate suggestions that preserve the balance of the meal. For those planning a lavish meal, the Sunday menu provides for a three-course feast, which could equally serve as a dinner-party menu.

It's a good idea to make a note of your personal Superfoods and Danger foods. By the time you've been consulting it for a few days, you'll probably end up knowing it by heart. Then when you eat out in a restaurant, canteen, or café, you'll be able to skim the menu and tell at a glance what are the good choices and which should be off-limits.

You can have too much of a good thing, even of a Four-Star Superfood. Some of these foods can be used successfully in what is known as the mono-fast – when you eat nothing but apples, or grapes, or plain brown rice for a day or two to help cleanse and regenerate your bodily forces – but few foods are suitable for such frequent consumption. Even ordinary and everyday foods, such as carrots, wholewheat bread, and oranges, should not be overeaten. Some foods, such as pineapples or strawberries, can actually be harmful if eaten to excess. Let common sense be your guide. Eat the Superfoods that are right for you. Eat them often. Eat them daily, but don't overdo it.

Super-resistance

In an ideal world, the food we eat would be organically grown in soil uncontaminated by heavy metals and acid rain; the vegetables we eat would be freshly picked from our own gardens; the water we drink would be spring-pure and the air we breathe mountain-fresh. For the vast majority of us, this ideal is as remote as the Garden of Eden.

Our bodies suffer the daily insult of pollutants and the stress of food that is often deficient in micronutrients. The fact that the human race has evolved at all is remarkable. We survive at what cost?

We are seeing today a dramatic increase in diseases that are linked directly to the failure of the body's immune defence mechanisms. We are seeing diseases never before encountered, such as MRSA and avian flu, against which we appear to have little immunity. Many workers in the field of environmental medicine believe that our new vulnerability is a consequence of our diet of devitalized foods, the product of agribusiness and global contamination.

Even if you eat the healthy diet all the experts advise, vegetables, fresh fruit, salads, wholegrains, nuts, and seeds, you may be short of the vital nutrients that you think you are getting in abundance. US nutrition expert Michael Colgan went shopping for oranges and found that a freshly picked orange contained as much as 180mg of vitamin C, while a supermarket orange, which looked just as fresh and glowing, contained not a single milligram.

In 1985 a survey in Britain indicated that 35 per cent of all men and 67 per cent of all women had an intake of zinc that fell alarmingly short of the 11mg per day recommended by the World Health Organization. These figures were based on the food intake of the subjects and assumed that these foods contained the levels of zinc set out in every nutritionist's calculating tables. However, as early as 1972, a study by the Food and Agriculture Organization reported severe zinc deficiencies in a wide range of soils in Europe and the United States. Fruit and vegetables grown on depleted soils are often low in vital minerals and trace elements, especially zinc, magnesium, and selenium, and there is no sign of any general improvement in farming methods. In fact, intensive farming today relies on ever-increasing amounts of chemical fertilizer and pesticides that linger in our foodstuffs, further depleting our nutritional reserves. Twenty years on, surveys done in 2005 show that average selenium intake has halved and now represents less than 50 per cent of the recommended daily amount.

Today it is not enough simply to rely on the traditional well-balanced mixed diet. To ensure Super-resistance, you must know how to supplement your diet – not with pills and capsules, but with the Superfoods that are extra-rich sources of the natural goodness we need. Together, they will supply the vital bricks that build your body's resistance to stress, disease, and infection. They are foods with the highest ORAC (oxygen radical absorbance capacity) scores – a system developed by the Department of Aging at Tufts University in the US to calculate the protective antioxidant value of a variety of individual foods.

Treat these foods as extra insurance at times of need, whether physical, mental, or emotional: during pregnancy, flu epidemics, periods of overwork or unusually high stress, or after an indulgent holiday. Use them at times of illness to hasten your recovery and always make sure that they feature regularly in your everyday eating. After all, an ounce of prevention really is worth a pound of cure. See p.20, where you will find a list containing all of the Four-Star Superfoods.

Doesn't eating healthily cost a fortune?

Suppose you buy 500g/1lb of fresh new potatoes at the greengrocer, and then buy the same weight of potato crisps. You will find that you pay around 19 times more for the crisps, and for your money you'll be getting an unhealthy dose of fat, salt, and maybe a bunch of chemicals, too. This is the first lesson in understanding food value for money – the less anybody has done to the food you buy, the cheaper it is. A potato is grown and harvested by the farmer and transported to the wholesaler, who distributes it to the retailer where you buy it, all within as little as 24 hours. So four sets of people are making a living from your potato, and you're eating it soon after harvesting, when it is still richly nutritious. Turn the potato into crisps and you not only have the farmer and the transporter to get it to the factory, but you also have to add on to the price of the crisps the cost of manufacture, packaging, delivery to another wholesaler, and delivery to the retailer. What's more, somebody has to pay for all that prime-time television advertising. Guess who?

Eating healthily doesn't have to cost a fortune. In terms of nutrition, more expensive certainly doesn't mean more valuable. The cheapest shin of beef is no less nutritious than a Chateaubriand steak; and common, locally grown vegetables will actually be fresher and more vitamin-rich than expensive, much-travelled, out-of-season alternatives. Try to buy as many fresh, unpackaged, unprocessed foods as possible. Not only will they cost much less than pre-packed foods, they will also be considerably fresher and thus a better buy nutritionally. Befriend your local butcher, greengrocer, and fishmonger. They will be able to advise you on how to cook unfamiliar joints, vegetables, or fish, which may be the cheapest buy of the day. This is even more important if you're shopping just for one person, since many pre-packed foods are designed for a minimum of two people. Get into the habit of planning meals two or three days ahead. Learn to be resourceful with leftovers. Resist the almost-irresistible impulse buys, as you push the supermarket trolley between shelves groaning with tempting delights. Most important of all, learn to be creative and experimental in your kitchen. If you do not have every single

ingredient in a recipe, you can find a substitute – short of total incineration, you have to do something extremely awful to render food inedible. You will soon discover that you don't have to spend a great deal of money to eat healthily. We costed two sets of menus, buying all of the items at the same snack bars or supermarkets. Eating the healthy Superfood menus actually cost us at least 10 per cent less than the equivalent junk food menus.

In the affluent Western world, those struggling to survive on the lowest incomes often spend their food budget in the worst way. Look into their shopping trolleys and you'll find that they buy, for example, white bread because it's cheaper than wholemeal, margarine because it's cheaper than butter, and packets of instant desserts because they think they're cheaper than fresh fruit. People are convinced that they can't afford "real" food, still less healthy food, but the same people regularly spend money at the fish and chip shop, the pie shop, the hamburger restaurant, and the Indian or Chinese take-away. An enormous amount of money is spent on junk food. Among the best-selling foods in Britain, cola drinks, white sugar, potato crisps, and chocolate bars are all in the premier league, raking in well over £500 million a year. Shopping and eating in Sydney in Australia offers an almost unbelievable choice of the finest fish, fruit, and vegetables, and ethnic restaurants from every corner of the world. But if you travel to the Atherton Tablelands – the fruit basket of north Queensland – you'll find that most of the restaurants there are greasy spoons serving pie and chips and fruit salads from syrup-laden tins. Nutritionally, such foods contribute almost nothing but calories. It is the poorest sector of the community that not only eats worst in nutritional terms, but also fares worst in terms of illness and disease. While social deprivation and poor housing are major factors affecting public health, inadequate and unbalanced eating lies at the root of a huge proportion of illnesses affecting the poorest sector of Western societies. Before you say, "My diet is fine", or "I wouldn't feed my family on that rubbish", keep a notebook for one week and faithfully record every single item of food or drink that goes into your mouth. Get your family to do the same. At the end of the week, add up just how much high-fat, high-sugar, and low-nutrient foods and drinks have come your way. Count every biscuit, sweet, chocolate, sweet fizzy drink, greasy take-away, packet of crisps, ice-cream dessert, bag of chips, pork pie, and sausage roll that you have bought. Then work out how much they've cost you.

The more knowledgeable you are about nutrition, the easier it is to make good choices of food for yourself and your family. It's perfectly true that a burger and French fries, or a helping of the best fish and chips in the neighbourhood, are fun food once in a while and will do you no harm if eaten occasionally. Similarly, everybody likes a bar of chocolate now and then. In a heatwave, what can be more delicious than a good ice cream? However, it is when these foods become part of your staple diet, and when they crowd the good, health-building foods

out of your budget, that your health will suffer. This is the price you're paying.

All you'll ever need to know about nutrition

Your great-grandmother may never have heard the word "nutrition". She didn't know a carbohydrate from a protein, a good fat from a bad fat, or a vitamin from a mineral. In spite of this, she raised your grandmother, who raised your mother, who raised you. How on earth did she do it without the help of nutrition experts, with their lists and diagrams? Simple – she used common sense. She served foods that were fresh and in season, and she planned good, square meals with a wide range of ingredients, which the family sat down to, and enjoyed together. Nutritionists have been arguing about exactly what we should be eating ever since the first vitamin was discovered in the early years of the last century. Today, however, there is nearly complete agreement throughout the world. The rules of sound nutrition can be summed up quite simply:

★ **Eat plenty of fresh fruit and vegetables**
★ **Eat a large variety of foods**
★ **Eat more fibre**
★ **Eat less fat**
★ **Eat less sugar**
★ **Eat less salt**

Thirty years ago, a handful of orthodox scientists raised the alarm about links between the diet of Western civilization and the diseases of affluence. They were branded scaremongers by the medical establishment and the food industry. Today, thanks to the weight of the World Health Organization, government bodies, and the avant-garde of the medical world, things are changing, if slowly. If you're worried about your lack of nutritional knowledge, you can relax – here is all you need to know.

What's in food?

CARBOHYDRATES Carbohydrates occur in grains, such as wheat and rice; pulses, such as beans and lentils; and in some root vegetables, such as potatoes, parsnips, and yams. These are often referred to as "complex carbohydrates". All you need to know is that foods such as wholemeal bread, brown rice, certain breakfast cereals (porridge, shredded wheat, unsweetened muesli), pasta, beans, and potatoes, are all wholesome. They are good because they provide slow release energy and a wide range of nutrients. They are generally inexpensive and bulky, and traditional, healthy diets all over the world are based largely on grains and pulses. These "good" carbohydrates tend to have a low GI (glycaemic index) rating. This means they're converted slowly from carbohydrates into sugars without causing a sudden rush of insulin into the bloodstream. Low GI foods protect against diabetes, obesity, bowel cancer, and heart disease. Confusingly, sugars are also carbohydrates, and these are not good for you, especially if they supply most of the energy in your diet. Refined sugars, such as sucrose, glucose, dextrose, and maltose, are used in massive quantities in processed foods, including savoury products, such as baked beans and tomato soup. You can often find three or four of them listed in the ingredients on food packets. These sugars do not need processing by the body and are absorbed straight into the bloodstream, stimulating the pancreas to produce excess insulin. These are high GI foods and excessive consumption may lead to weight gain and a condition called insulin resistance, a forerunner of type 2 diabetes. This condition is known as "adult onset diabetes", as it normally begins in middle age. Tragically, because of the enormous consumption of high GI carbohydrates, doctors are now seeing type 2 diabetes in children as young as eight years old. The sugars that your body produces from low GI carbohydrates do not have this effect.

Honey has been used as a sweetener since the first beehive was found, and, used in sensible amounts, it is far preferable as a sweetener than any form of sugar. Honey also contains traces of many nutrients.

Until the mid-19th century, white, refined wheat flour was unknown, and until early this century, most of the rice eaten around the world was unpolished, brown rice. What is "refined" out of wheat and rice is most of the goodness. In many countries in the West, including Britain, the United States, Canada, Australia, and New Zealand, certain of these nutrients must by law be added back to the flour before it is baked into bread, but many vital nutrients are not.

FAT Fat is a nutritional minefield, with bitter battles raging over it. You are probably hopelessly confused by the conflicting advice you see in the press, in full-page advertisements for certain brands of margarine, or in promotions paid for by the dairy industry. Owing to modern, intensive rearing methods, factory farming, and the vast meat-processing and fast-food industries, most people in the West today consume unacceptably high levels of animal fat. For much the same reasons, most people are not getting enough of the essential fatty acids found in seeds, nuts, whole grains, some vegetables, and oily fish.

Many people, especially women, believe that a low-fat diet means a no-fat diet. Consequently, they are missing out on almost all of the vital fats. Two fat-facts to note: firstly, all fats and oils contain the same number of calories by weight, unless they are fat-reduced factory products. Secondly, the simple division into the "good" polyunsaturated fats and the "bad" saturated fats is highly misleading. Foods that are as simple as nature intended them to be should be the rule rather than

the exception. Most polyunsaturated margarine is a highly processed, unnatural foodstuff that contains trans-fatty acids. These trans-fats are liquid fats that are chemically treated to make them solid at room temperature, and they appear to be decidedly unhealthy. Natural butter, on the other hand, if used in moderation, is a useful source of vitamins A, D, and E.

We now know what every Mediterranean peasant has always known – that extra-virgin olive oil is a wonderful foundation on which to build your daily diet, and it is the best oil for your health, especially if it is combined with plenty of garlic and a glass of red wine a day. This is hardly surprising. Extra-virgin olive oil is obtained by a simple pressure process and contains the natural goodness to be found in the olive. The consumption of vegetable oils (such as sunflower, safflower, and corn oil) for cooking has rocketed this century. Many of them are heavily processed to turn them into the near-tasteless products you buy. Consequently, there is little of the natural goodness of the sunflower, the safflower, or the corn left in them and they have an unhealthy ratio of omega-6 to omega-3 fats.

With Superfoods, your diet will be low in fat. Consequently, you can enjoy the pleasures of real butter, the occasional dollop of cream, and proper whole milk, instead of skimmed milk, which is nutritionally a poor second cousin to the real thing and should never be

14 introduction

given to children under age five. Full fat milk only contains 4 per cent fat, which means it could legally be labelled as a low fat food. You can reduce your fat intake by:

★ Removing all visible fat from meat and poultry before cooking.
★ Saving meat products, such as sausages, pâtés, meat pies, pasties, salami, and bacon, for occasional treats – they provide up to 85 per cent of their calories from fat.
★ Watching out for the hidden fats. When you eat a small packet of potato crisps, up to two-thirds of its weight may be potato; the other third is fat. French fries are approximately 50 per cent fat. Most cakes, pastries, and biscuits are high in fats. A 250g/8oz burger can contain more than 60g/2oz of fat, and a cheeseburger even more.

PROTEIN Estimates of how much protein – body-building components – we need to keep us going have varied wildly, from the hefty 150g/5oz a day proposed by 19th-century nutritionists (equivalent to the protein content of approximately 600g/1¼lb of lean beef) to the more modest 55–90g (2–3½oz) for adults that is recommended today.

How do you know whether you're getting enough protein? Simple. Unless you are following an extreme form of diet, such as a food-exclusion diet, or you are an exceptionally faddy eater or an anorexic, it is almost impossible to be protein-deficient on an average, mixed diet. Quite the reverse is true. If you are eating eggs and bacon for breakfast, a pork pie at lunchtime, and meat and two vegetables in the evening, you may well be consuming far more protein than your body needs, and your kidneys will feel the strain. Furthermore, meat isn't the only good source of protein, as is obvious when you consider the world's millions of healthy vegetarians. For those with high blood pressure, it is useful to know that reducing your animal protein intake helps to bring it down. Fish, chicken, eggs, cheese, milk, beans, peas, nuts, grains, vegetables, and even some fruits all supply varying quantities of protein. The average Western adult gets around 66 per cent of his or her protein from meat, fish, eggs, cheese, and milk; 25 per cent from bread and other cereals; and 10 per cent from vegetables.

In spite of many doctors' opposition to vegetarianism, some of the healthiest cultures in the world never eat meat or animal products. The wisdom of centuries-old eating traditions helps these peoples balance their diets without even thinking about it. The old idea of first-class and second-class proteins, with meat belonging in the executive class, is now, thankfully, dying out. The only imperative for vegetarians is that they should get their protein from mixed sources, as in the traditional rice and peas of the West Indies, for example; the rice and lentils of the Middle East; the pasta and beans of Italy; and the rice and dhal of India.

However, it is virtually impossible to be an adult vegan – someone who avoids eggs and all milk products as well as meat and fish – without supplementing the diet with

B vitamins, and it is irresponsibly risky to bring up a child as a vegan unless you are extremely well-informed and give the child the appropriate dietary supplements.

FIBRE Fibre occurs in whole grains, pulses, vegetables, fruits, and seeds. A hundred years ago nobody needed to worry about fibre, since it was naturally present in their daily bread, cereals, and vegetables. There is now a huge body of evidence to suggest that when your diet is deficient in fibre, you are likely to suffer from a whole range of digestive nasties. As well as benefiting the digestive system, certain forms of fibre, especially the type in oats, barley, and beans, help the body eliminate excess cholesterol, and consequently protect the heart and circulatory system.

VITAMINS AND MINERALS Even a qualified nutritionist would need a computer to work out how many of your daily vitamin and mineral needs will be met by a particular diet or food. Without burdening you with an incomprehensible array of numbers, here are some simple guidelines to ensure that you obtain all of your vitamin and mineral requirements from the food you eat.

★ **The fresher the fruit and vegetables you eat, the better they are for you.** Much of their goodness starts to disappear the moment they are picked. The loss of vitamin C is increased by storage, handling, bruising, and preparation. Heat is the final enemy of vitamin C. The most nutritious way of eating many vegetables and most fruit is raw. Try one meal a day of nothing but raw foods – wonderful fruit, delicious salads, a crunchy carrot or cauliflower, peppers, fennel, celery, and unroasted nuts. Keeping cooked vegetables warm will destroy what little vitamin C may be left. B vitamins and many minerals leach out into the cooking water, so cook vegetables in a minimum of water, for the shortest possible time.

★ **Good, fresh produce is always the first choice when it comes to buying vegetables.** Commercially frozen vegetables are also a good option, since they are harvested and frozen at their best, when their vitamin content is at its highest. They may lose some vitamin C, but they will contain more than vegetables that have spent a long time in transit, in the shop, or in your vegetable rack. Frozen vegetables are handy for the cook who is pressed for time, since they can turn a snack into a nutritious meal.

★ **Discover nuts and seeds – they're not just for the budgie.** Almonds, hazelnuts, walnuts, cashews, and chestnuts, and sunflower, sesame, and pumpkin seeds are all available in supermarkets, and they're delicious. They also happen to be bursting with B vitamins, vitamin E, zinc, iron, protein, and fibre – the nutrients for their future growth into trees, shrubs, and flowers. For suggestions on how to use them, refer to the list of Superfoods (*p.20*).

★ **There are super-nutrients and anti-nutrients.** All the vitamins are essential for life, but some are super-nutrients, such as beta-carotene, which is found in brightly coloured fruits and vegetables and is converted by the body into vitamin A. Vitamin C from fresh produce and vitamin E from nuts seeds are also super-nutrients. Some super-nutrients are antioxidants that mop up excess free radicals, which are the by-products of body chemistry. These are highly destructive to individual cells, and they can trigger cancer, heart disease, and other disorders. Free radicals are also responsible for visible signs of aging, such as wrinkles.

An ever-growing body of research has now established beyond doubt the key role of antioxidants in keeping us healthy. Indeed, conventional nutritionists, who twenty years ago were certain that the "average" diet supplied all our nutritional needs, are now desperately promoting the "five portions of fruit and vegetables a day" message. This confirms the wisdom of the health "cranks", who always maintained that at least one-third of daily food should be fruit, salad, and vegetables. Eat plenty of green leaves, red peppers, grated carrot, radishes, fennel, chopped parsley, and tomatoes, dressed with extra-virgin olive oil, and you're enjoying a mega-helping of the antioxidants.

Anti-nutrients are substances that either interfere with the body's absorption of nutrients or destroy them. The much-touted bran,

lavishly packed into cereals, or sprinkled into soup, can have a disastrous effect on the absorption of calcium, iron, and other minerals. Coffee, tea, and other caffeine-carriers, such as cola and chocolate drinks, can also lower the amount of iron that the body will absorb from food. Vitamin C, on the other hand, will maximize it, so if you must have coffee with your boiled egg (a good source of iron), have some orange juice with it as well.

Refined sugars and alcohol drain the body's vitamin B reserves. Certain drugs also lower nutrient uptake or bodily stores of nutrients, among them antibiotics, the contraceptive pill, antidepressants, antacids, and laxatives. If you are taking any of these regularly, your diet should be especially good, and you should consider taking a simple vitamin supplement.

★ **At least once a day, eat a home-cooked meal (at the table, not in front of the television), and not in a rush.** This way of eating is good for your digestion and results in your body getting more nutrients from the food. This is not to mention the fact that you and your partner, your family, or your friends will gather around the table and talk to one another, something that few people make time to do these days.

If you can't manage a daily gathering around the dining table, why not try resurrecting the traditional Sunday lunch, or making a Friday evening family feast part of your weekly routine? Such gatherings are often among our richest childhood memories, but how many of today's children will be able to look back on them?

introduction 17

18

The Superfoods

★ Fruit

★ Vegetables

★ Grains and pulses

★ Nuts and seeds

★ Eggs and dairy

★ Meat, seafood, and poultry

★ Herbs and spices

★ Miscellaneous

The Superfoods

Fruit

* apples *p.22*
* pears *p.24*
* oranges *p.25*
* grapefruit *p.26*
* lemons and limes *p.27*
* blueberries *p.28*
* cranberries *p.29*
* raspberries *p.30*
* strawberries *p.31*
* apricots *p.32*
* cherries *p.33*
* grapes *p.34*
* kiwifruit *p.36*
* bananas *p.37*
* melon *p.38*
* papayas *p.40*
* mangos *p.41*
* pineapples *p.42*
* pomegranates *p.43*
* dates *p.44*
* figs *p.45*
* raisins *p.46*
* prunes *p.47*

Vegetables

* mushrooms *p.48*
* celery *p.49*
* radishes *p.50*
* watercress *p.51*
* avocados *p.52*
* peppers *p.53*
* tomatoes *p.54*
* pumpkin, squash *p.56*
* carrots *p.57*
* potatoes *p.58*
* sweet potatoes *p.59*
* swedes *p.60*
* turnips *p.61*
* beetroot *p.62*
* parsnips *p.63*
* Jerusalem artichokes *p.64*
* globe artichokes *p.65*
* onions *p.66*
* leeks *p.68*
* spinach *p.69*
* red cabbage *p.70*
* sauerkraut *p.72*
* Oriental greens *p.73*
* asparagus *p.74*
* broccoli *p.75*

Grains and pulses

* barley *p.76*
* brown rice *p.77*
* buckwheat *p.78*
* lentils *p.78*
* beans *p.79*
* millet *p.80*
* maize *p.80*
* oats *p.81*
* soybeans *p.82*
* wheat *p.83*
* pasta *p.84*
* bread *p.85*

★ ★

Nuts and seeds

★ almonds *p.86*
★ cashews *p.87*
★ hazelnuts *p.87*
★ pumpkin seeds *p.88*
★ sesame seeds *p.89*
★ sprouted seeds *p.90*
★ sunflower seeds *p.92*
★ walnuts *p.92*
★ chestnuts *p.93*
★ peanuts *p.93*

Dairy and eggs

★ milk *p.94*
★ eggs *p.95*
★ yoghurt *p.95*
★ butter *p.96*
★ cheese *p.97*

Meat, fish, poultry

★ beef, lamb *p.98*
★ liver *p.98*
★ chicken *p.99*
★ oily fish *p.100*
★ molluscs *p.102*
★ crustaceans *p.103*

Herbs and spices

★ basil *p.104*
★ mint *p.104*
★ oregano *p.105*
★ chives *p.105*
★ sage *p.106*
★ marjoram *p.107*
★ parsley *p.108*
★ rosemary *p.109*
★ savory *p.110*
★ fennel *p.110*
★ tarragon *p.111*
★ thyme *p.111*
★ dill *p.112*
★ dandelion *p.113*
★ bay leaves *p.114*
★ juniper *p.114*
★ nutmeg *p.115*
★ cinnamon *p.115*
★ chilli pepper *p.116*
★ caraway *p.118*
★ cloves *p.119*
★ cumin *p.120*
★ coriander *p.121*
★ garlic *p.122*
★ ginger *p.124*
★ horseradish *p.125*

Miscellaneous

★ brewer's yeast *p.126*
★ oils *p.127*
★ honey *p.128*
★ molasses *p.128*
★ chocolate *p.129*
★ beer *p.130*
★ red wine *p.131*
★ tea *p.132*
★ coffee *p.133*

Apples

★★★★

"If you could plant only one tree in your garden, it should be an apple tree", says famous French herbalist Maurice Messegue. So what's in an apple? A bonus for your heart: the pectin and vitamin C in apples help keep cholesterol levels stable, as US studies have shown; pectin also protects us from the ravages of pollution, binding to heavy metals, such as lead or mercury, in the body and carrying them safely out. The malic and tartaric acids in apples help to neutralize the acid by-products of indigestion and help your body cope with excess protein or rich, fatty foods: apple purée with pork, apples with cheese, or sage and apple stuffing for goose are traditional combinations based on country wisdom.

Because of these qualities, these wonderful autumn fruits are great detoxifiers, and people suffering from arthritis, rheumatism, or gout should eat raw apples regularly. A mono-fast on apples alone, for a day or two, can be warmly recommended for people suffering from food poisoning or inflammatory bowel conditions. It's also a marvellous general pick-me-up after the excesses of a holiday or festive season, or a debilitating bout of flu.

It was observation of an apple cure at work that led Dr Bircher-Benner to his discovery of the healing powers of raw food. On the advice of an old doctor, he fed grated raw apple to a patient whose digestive problems had brought her close to death: it was the first food she was able to take in weeks, and after a few days of the apple cure, she was well on the way to recovery. Apples, as Bircher-Benner realized, are first-class therapy for any digestive problems or infections, being both soothing and antiseptic.

In a French study, eating two apples a day resulted in an average drop in cholesterol levels of up to 10 per cent. That's partly because apples are also a fantastic source of fibre, both soluble and insoluble: one large apple can provide 10 per cent of your daily recommended fibre intake. And we now know that high-fibre foods can be useful in preventing heart disease.

Recommended for:
circulatory *p.278*
digestive *p.284*
joints *p.304*

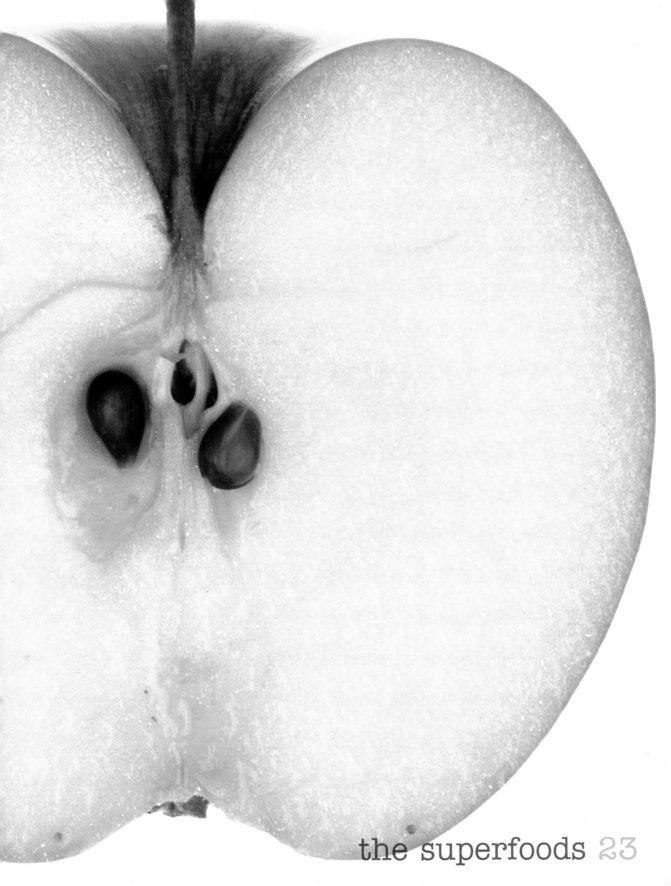

Pears

★★★★

Pears are a good source of pectin, which helps bowel function and increases the amount of cholesterol eliminated by the body. Supplying reasonable vitamin C, some vitamin A and E, and potassium, they're helpful for digestion and convalescence, and are a source of easily accessible good calories. They contain no fat and virtually no sodium, but they do contain fruit sugar, which is easily converted into instantly usable energy.

Pears are one of the foods least likely to cause any type of allergic reaction, so they're ideal puréed for babies and used in exclusion diets where food allergies or intolerances are suspected. However, fresh pears do contain a sugar-based alcohol called sorbitol. While this sugar-free sweetener is tooth-friendly, in large amounts it may cause diarrhoea in a small number of susceptible people.

• • • • • • • • • • • • • • • • • • •

Recommended for:
circulatory *p.278*
digestive *p.284*

Oranges

★★★★

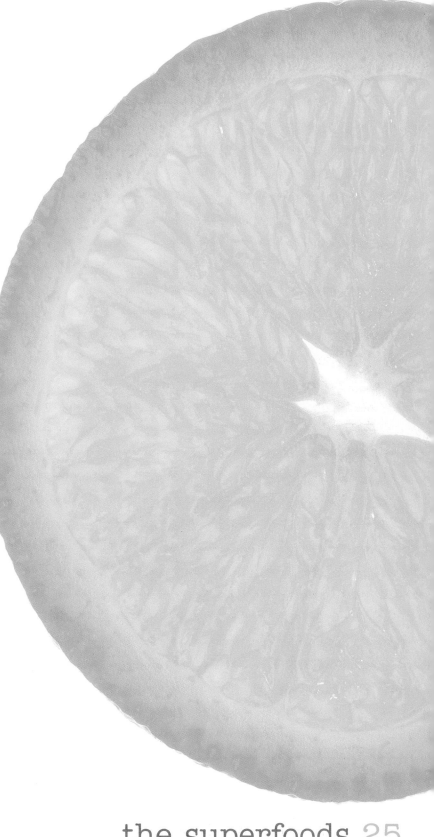

The high vitamin C content of fresh oranges accounts for much of their beneficial influence on our health, given the vital importance of this vitamin in combating infection. Here's one more bonus: in a Swedish study of people eating a Western-style breakfast, orange juice taken at the same meal more than doubled iron absorption. Oranges also contain another antioxidant: the vitamin A precursor beta-carotene.

The pith and segment walls contain bioflavonoids. These are also known as vitamin P factors, or C2 since they appear to make possible the activity of vitamin C. In addition they are known to strengthen the walls of the capillaries. Leslie Kenton points out that in the original plant, these compounds "act as primitive defence systems protecting them from disease...Many studies indicate that various bioflavonoids...actively combat infectious bacteria, viruses and fungi."

Recommended for:
cancer *p.264*
circulatory *p.278*
respiratory *p.312*
skin *p.318*

Grapefruit

★★★★

Grapefruit shares with other citrus fruits a high level of vitamin C and plenty of potassium. It's also well supplied with pectin – a substance recommended to those suffering from circulatory or digestive problems. In addition, grapefruit has high concentrations of bioflavonoids. These plant substances are attracting increasing medical interest. They seem to have the ability to protect the integrity of the blood vessels, particularly the tiny capillaries, and to act against inflammation. Both pectin and bioflavonoids are found in the white pith of grapefruit, and in the membranes dividing the sections, so eat the whole fruit rather than just the juice to ensure maximum benefit.

● ● ● ● ● ● ● ● ● ● ● ● ● ● ● ● ● ● ● ●

Recommended for:
circulatory *p.278*
digestive *p.284*
respiratory *p.312*

Lemons and limes

★★★★

Limes are the most acid of citrus fruits, containing more vitamin C than grapefruit but less than oranges and lemons. Mostly grown for juice used as flavouring, particularly in drinks, limes have a similar chemical composition and medicinal properties to lemon juice. They're also rich in protective bioflavonoids, which are found mostly in the pith.

Royal Navy ships carried barrels of limes to prevent scurvy. This is the origin of the epithet "limey", an American name for an English person.

• • • • • • • • • • • • • • • • • • •

Recommended for:
cancer *p.264*
respiratory *p.312*

Blueberries

★★★★

Blueberries were introduced to early settlers in North America by the Native Americans, for whom they were a staple food. Along with cranberries, the high vitamin C content in blueberries prevented them from dying of scurvy. The pigment, which is mostly in the skin, has a high concentration of antioxidants. Blueberries may even help to prevent Alzheimer's disease and other forms of dementia. Containing more antioxidant chemicals than red wine, blueberries are good for the heart and circulation. Added to breakfast smoothies or sprinkled over your morning cereal, they are a powerful package.

● ● ● ● ● ● ● ● ● ● ● ● ● ●

Recommended for:
cancer *p.264*
circulatory *p.278*
digestive *p.284*
stress *p.292*

Cranberries

★★★★

The Native Americans taught white settlers in North America to eat the tart, bright red berries of the cranberry bush as a remedy for scurvy, and Yankee ships soon routinely carried barrels of cranberries stored in water. The berries are high in vitamin C; but iron, vitamin A, and potassium are among their other nutritional assets.

Worldwide, scientists now accept what Native American medicine men have always known – that cranberry juice both treats and prevents urinary tract infections. It's not the acidity of the cranberries that does the trick, but their natural mucilage, which sticks to the walls of the bladder and its associated structures. This mucilage prevents bacteria from lodging in the tissues and causing chronic and recurrent cystitis. In a number of trials, cranberry juice has been used to treat urinary tract infections over prolonged periods with no marked side effects. There's no evidence of bacterial resistance to the benefits of this amazing juice.

Recommended for:
circulatory *p.278*
fatigue *p.298*
urinary *p.324*

Raspberries

★★★★

Like grapes, raspberries should be on every hospital menu. This tart, delectable fruit supplies not only a fair amount of vitamin C, but useful amounts of calcium, potassium, iron, and magnesium, which are all vital to the convalescent, as well as to those suffering from heart problems, fatigue, or depression. All of the minerals are well absorbed, thanks to the vitamin C.

Herbalists value raspberries for their cooling effect – they are useful in feverish conditions. Naturally astringent, raspberries can do you good the length of your digestive tract, helping to counter spongy, diseased gums, upset stomachs, and diarrhoea along the way.

Recommended for:
circulatory *p.278*
digestive *p.284*
stress *p.292*

Strawberries

★★★★

The great Swedish botanist Linnaeus, whose special interest was in medicinal plants, recommended strawberries as a perfect cure for arthritis, gout, and rheumatism. He spoke from personal experience: he cured himself of gout by eating almost nothing but strawberries morning and night. This agreeable cure probably works because strawberries are admirable cleansers and purifiers of the whole system.

Strawberries also have a confirmed reputation for combating high blood pressure, and they are recommended in European traditional medicine for the elimination of kidney stones. Their high iron content makes them therapeutic for anaemia and fatigue. People with skin problems should enjoy plenty of this wonderful fruit, which cleanses and regenerates the intestinal flora. For full therapeutic effect, strawberries should be eaten on their own, or at the start of a meal.

• • • • • • • • • • • • • • • • • •

Recommended for:

circulatory *p.278*
fatigue *p.298*
joints *p.304*
skin *p.318*

Apricots

★★★★

Apricots, an early summer fruit that originated in China, are loaded with beta-carotene, as their wonderful yellow-orange colour informs us – the brighter the colour, the more beta-carotene a fruit contains. Beta-carotene – a nutrient which is converted by your body in to vitamin A – is one of the most effective antioxidants around, so the ripe, fresh fruit should be eaten whenever possible by those suffering from any infection (especially of the respiratory system) or at risk from cancer or heart disease.

A US study also found that women who had high vitamin A intakes nearly halved their chances of developing cataracts: the more fruit you eat, the better your eyes. Dried apricots supply iron, and they actually have higher antioxidant levels than the fresh fruit. They can be thrown into stews or added to muesli. The sulphur dioxide that preserves their colour can easily be washed off in some warm water.

• • • • • • • • • • • • • • • • • • •

Recommended for:
cancer *p.264*
respiratory *p.312*
skin *p.318*

Cherries

★★★★

Cherries contain plenty of potassium and virtually no sodium, so they're excellent for anyone with high blood pressure or heart disease. They're a reasonable source of vitamin C, but they also contain significant amounts of bioflavonoids and other plant chemicals. This puts them pretty near the top of the list of protective antioxidant foods. Their ellagic acid content adds extra value to their anti-cancer properties.

In folk medicine, cherries have long been used for the relief of arthritis and gout. In addition, dried cherry stones make the most wonderful hot bag for muscular pain, joint disorders, and stomach ache. Although there is no scientific evidence for their effectiveness, the anecdotal stories are legion – and even if cherries don't help, they can't hurt. They taste delicious raw, cooked, juiced, or dried. Of the sour cherries, Morello are wonderful for cooking and Acerola the richest in nutrients.

Recommended for:
cancer *p.264*
circulatory *p.278*
joints *p.304*

Grapes

★★★★

A bunch of grapes is the present that kind people take to their sick friends in hospital: they could do nothing better for them. Grapes are a uniquely nourishing, strengthening, cleansing, and regenerative food, useful in convalescence.

Grapes are also excellent for easing the symptoms of anaemia, fatigue, and disorders such as arthritis, gout, and rheumatism, that may result from poor elimination of waste products, such as urine. The nutritive powers of grapes were confirmed by Mahatma Gandhi, who drank grape juice during his marathon fasts.

In 1926 South African natural healer Johanna Brandt pioneered the grape cure, after claiming to have cured herself of cancer with its help: for weeks on end, she ate nothing but fresh grapes. European nature clinics have obtained excellent results using a grape mono-fast to treat a range of ailments, including skin problems, disorders of the urinary system, arthritis, and gout. A two-day grape mono-fast every ten days is recommended for those wanting to lose weight.

Grapes should be eaten on their own, and not as part of a meal. This is because they ferment rapidly in the stomach. Chewing grapes is also recommended to help alleviate infected gums.

Grapeseed oil, now increasingly seen on supermarket shelves, is rich in polyunsaturated fats and vitamin E. It's also highly heat-stable, even in prolonged cooking at modest temperatures.

It is important to note that most grapes are sprayed incessantly with pesticides during cultivation. Bearing this in mind, it is vital that you wash grapes very carefully indeed before eating them.

. . . .

Recommended for:
cancer *p.264*
stress *p.292*
fatigue *p.298*
joints *p.304*
skin *p.318*
urinary *p.324*

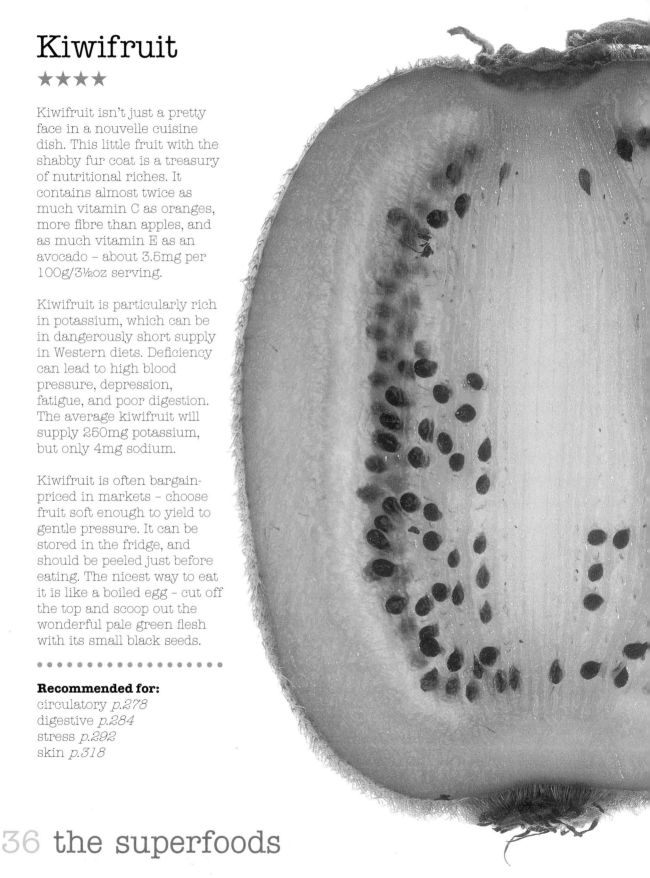

Kiwifruit

★★★★

Kiwifruit isn't just a pretty face in a nouvelle cuisine dish. This little fruit with the shabby fur coat is a treasury of nutritional riches. It contains almost twice as much vitamin C as oranges, more fibre than apples, and as much vitamin E as an avocado – about 3.5mg per 100g/3½oz serving.

Kiwifruit is particularly rich in potassium, which can be in dangerously short supply in Western diets. Deficiency can lead to high blood pressure, depression, fatigue, and poor digestion. The average kiwifruit will supply 250mg potassium, but only 4mg sodium.

Kiwifruit is often bargain-priced in markets – choose fruit soft enough to yield to gentle pressure. It can be stored in the fridge, and should be peeled just before eating. The nicest way to eat it is like a boiled egg – cut off the top and scoop out the wonderful pale green flesh with its small black seeds.

Recommended for:
circulatory *p.278*
digestive *p.284*
stress *p.292*
skin *p.318*

Bananas

One of Nature's most superb fast foods, bananas are unjustly maligned as a high-calorie food; in fact, the average banana contains under 100 calories. Bananas are packed with nourishment, particularly potassium, which is essential to the functioning of every single cell in our bodies. Zinc, iron, folic acid, and calcium are other nutrients that bananas contain. They also contain the useful form of fibre known as pectin, which helps the body to eliminate toxic wastes.

Weight for weight, bananas contain nearly the same amount of vitamin B6 as liver. This important nutrient is chronically undersupplied in the average diet. Bananas are also highly beneficial to the digestive tract, soothing and helping to restore normal function; naturopaths recommend them for both constipation and diarrhoea. They make an ideal energy snack for sporty people, since the potassium helps to prevent cramps. Bananas should be eaten ripe, when they can be easily digested.

Recommended for:
circulatory *p.278*
digestive *p.284*
fatigue *p.298*

Melon

Melons are a cooling, delicious treat in hot weather: a large slice of crunchy pink watermelon – sold from roadside stands all over the Mediterranean – beats any canned fizzy drink for refreshment. Watermelon – or a tea made by simmering its seeds in water for 30 minutes – has long been recommended in traditional medicine as a remedy for kidney and bladder problems. All forms of melon are also mildly stimulating to the kidneys, and are gently laxative, making them useful for those with gout or constipation. A two-day mono-fast on melons of any kind is a delightful summer cleanout of the whole system. Like grapes, melon of all kinds should be eaten on its own, or at least at the start of a meal, since it ferments rapidly in the stomach.

Recommended for:
digestive *p.284*
skin *p.318*
urinary *p.324*

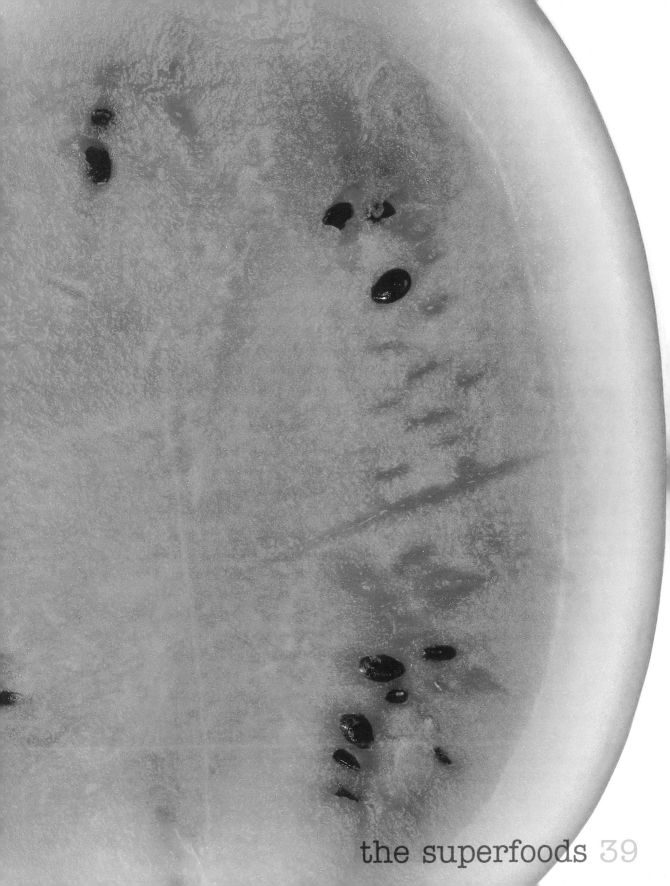

Papayas
★★★★

Papaya contains the enzyme papain, which improves digestion. One fruit provides twice the vitamin C and one-third of the vitamin A you need daily. The medicine men of the South American Mayans used the fruit's sticky latex, its juice, and the flesh as medicine. It's still common today in South America to wrap meat in the leaves of the papaya before cooking to create tender and delectable dishes.

On a less culinary note, the leaves may also be used to improve wound healing and for the treatment of leg ulcers and boils in traditional medicine. Even the seeds of this remarkable fruit are useful. The next time you eat a papaya, try saving the seeds and adding them to olive oil, vinegar, or pickles to impart a unique spicy flavour.

Papayas are particularly good for children because they make great-tasting smoothies. Halve and deseed the fruit, put the flesh into a liquidizer, add a small carton of yoghurt and a cup of milk, and whiz until smooth. For a more sophisticated version for adults, whiz the flesh with a little water and mix half and half with champagne.

Although tinned papaya is widely available, it's not nearly as good for you as the fresh fruit, since most of the vitamin C and more than half the beta-carotene are unfortunately lost in processing.

Recommended for:
digestive *p.284*
respiratory *p.312*
skin *p.318*

Mangos

★★★★

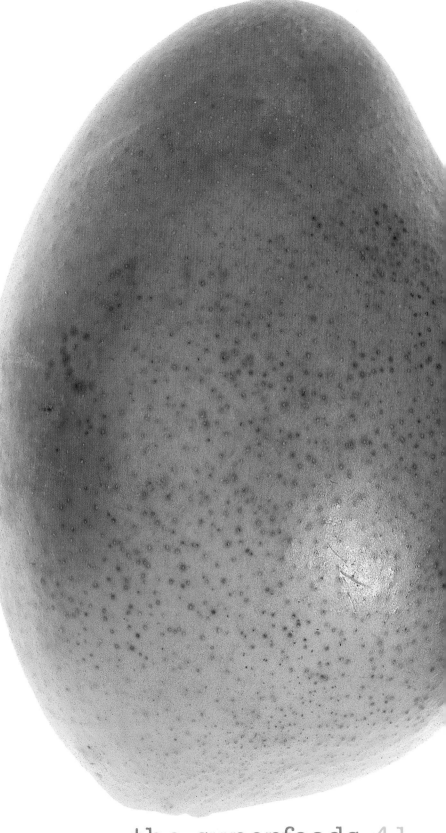

One mango provides over a day's dose of vitamin C, two-thirds the recommended amount of vitamin A, nearly half the recommended amount of vitamin E, and a quarter of your fibre, potassium, iron, and nicotinic acid for the day. It also tastes wonderful. Mangos originally grew in India, where their history goes back over 4000 years. Today, varieties are also grown in Australia, South Africa, Brazil, and Pakistan.

It's a fantastic bonus that anything tasting as good as a mango is also a source of powerful antioxidants. The mango also has medicinal properties, and in traditional Indian medicine its antiseptic twigs are chewed to protect the teeth and gums from disease. The bark is used in treating diarrhoea, while the fruit is given for high blood pressure.

Mangos actually belong to the same family as poison ivy. Wear rubber gloves to prepare them to avoid contact with their potentially irritating skin.

Recommended for:
circulatory *p.278*
fatigue *p.298*

Pineapples

★★★★

In Hawaii, people eat chunks of juicy pineapple as a delicious cure for digestive problems. We now know that the fresh fruit contains an enzyme, bromelain, which can digest many times its own weight of protein in a few minutes. Like the enzyme papain in papaya, bromelain breaks down only food and dead tissue, leaving the guts unassailed. The juice of fresh pineapples is also effective folk medicine for sore throats and was once a favourite herbal remedy for diphtheria. This reputation suggests that the pineapple contains compounds with marked antibiotic and anti-inflammatory effects.

Some of these compounds – although not bromelain – may survive the processing that produces juice or tinned fruit. But for maximum healing potential, choose the fresh, ripe fruit. When really ripe, the fruit loses the tartness that puts many people off pineapples.

When choosing a pineapple, avoid any with rotting leaves and bruised fruit. You can tug a leaf out of a ripe pineapple's crown.

• • • • • • • • • • • • • • • • • •

Recommended for:
digestive *p.284*
cancer *p.264*
circulatory *p.278*
joints *p.304*
respiratory *p.312*
skin *p.318*

Pomegranates

★★★★

Pomegranates have been grown and eaten by humans since prehistoric times. This unique fruit has been part of ancient mythology, art, and religion from the time of the ancient Egyptians to the ancient Greeks and the Old Testament. You'll even see it in the mosaic tiles in the excavations at Pompeii. It gets its name from medieval French and it means, literally, "seeded apple" – an average fruit can contain up to 800 of the tiny seeds. Although it has a long history, scientific research shows that the pomegranate is indeed a true Superfood for our modern times.

Scientists in California and Israel have shown that pomegranates are an extraordinarily powerful and natural antioxidant. One small glass of pomegranate juice provides three times the ORAC (Oxygen Radical Absorbance Capacity, a measure of a food's protective qualities) of the same quantity of red wine. What's more, the concentration of protective bioflavonoids in the fruit is even greater than that found in grapes or green tea. All the evidence supports the traditional belief that pomegranates are protective against heart disease, circulatory disorders, degenerative and inflammatory conditions, and even some types of cancer. There are even suggestions that the fruit has antiviral and antibacterial properties. Low in calories, fat, and sodium, pomegranates taste great when freshly juiced.

Recommended for:
cancer *p.264*
circulatory *p.278*

Dates

★★★★

Dates are a highly energizing and richly nourishing food that is useful for convalescents and also an excellent addition to packed lunches. They are native to North Africa and Arabia (the date palm is mentioned in the Qur'an more often than any other fruit-bearing plant), and Bedouin Arabs would travel for days across the desert with little more than a store of dates, figs, and flour with which to make unleavened bread.

Like most dried fruits, dates are a good source of the antioxidants that help boost the body's defences against some cancers. Rich in fibre, they are mildly laxative and so prevent constipation. Dates are an important source of minerals and are particularly high in potassium, helping to maintain fluid levels and the sodium/potassium balance so important in very hot climates. Most dates contain easily available iron, but some varieties provide exceptional amounts, which may explain their historical reputation as an aphrodisiac.

● ● ● ● ● ● ● ● ● ● ● ● ● ● ● ● ●

Recommended for:
digestive *p.284*
respiratory *p.312*

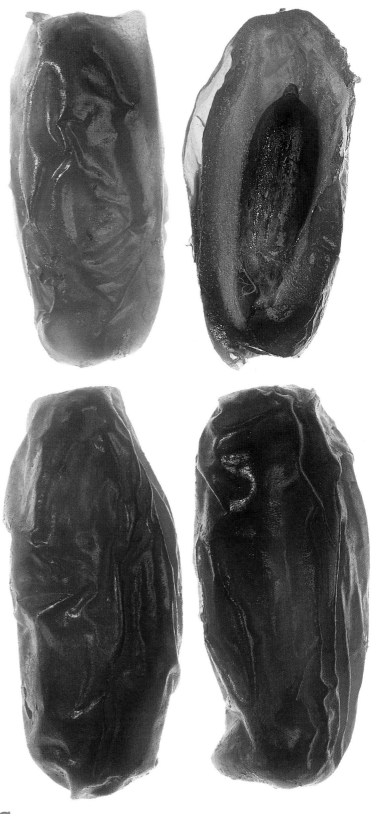

Figs

★★★★

Figs have a centuries-old reputation as a sustaining and nourishing food. In classical antiquity, athletes were often fed entirely on figs, while Pliny the Elder praised them for their ability to get rid of wrinkles. In either fresh or dried form, they are friendly to the digestion. This is because they contain an enzyme called ficin that assists the digestive process, exerting a soothing action on the gut. They are also mildly laxative. Dried figs are a rich source of fibre, iron, potassium, and calcium, making them a useful food for people with high blood pressure.

Weight for weight, figs contain more fibre than most other fruits or vegetables, so they're great for your digestive system and your cholesterol levels. They're also very high in polyphenol antioxidants, which makes them a valuable food for cancer prevention. The instant energy they provide and their ability to prevent cramps make them good for athletes too.

Recommended for:
circulatory *p.278*
digestive *p.284*
respiratory *p.312*

Raisins

★★★★

Man has been drying fruits in the sun as a means of preservation for at least 5000 years, and the Romans in particular included raisins in many of their medical prescriptions. Raisins are a perfect energy food for active people and those suffering from exhaustion. They're rich in fibre to help reduce cholesterol and improve bowel function, and also in iron, with a large handful providing more than 25 per cent of the RDA of this nutrient for women. They also contain selenium and potassium, which helps to prevent fluid retention and reduce blood pressure. Raisins contain small amounts of vitamins A and B. The combination of energy and B vitamins means they are helpful for anyone with depression, anxiety, and stress.

Raisins are treated with sulphur or mineral oil, which can both be removed by washing raisins in warm running water. Organic raisins aren't treated with these substances.

• • • • • • • • • • • • • • • • • • • •

Recommended for:
circulatory *p.278*
stress *p.292*
fatigue *p.298*

Prunes

★★★★

These wonderful dried fruits have a terrible reputation. In countries where good food is greatly appreciated, such as France, they're considered a delicacy, whereas we tend to consider them for one thing only – as a laxative – and that's the least of their value. Rich in potassium, which helps high blood pressure, and in fibre, iron, niacin, and vitamins B6 and A, prunes are also energy food. In addition, they also contain *hydroxyphenyl-isatin*, which is a gentle, non-purging laxative. Most importantly, weight for weight, prunes are the most powerful of all the protective antioxidant foods. The US Department of Agriculture has calculated the ORAC (Oxygen Radical Absorbance Capacity) of prunes at 5770 units per 100g/3½oz, compared with 2000-odd for raisins, blueberries, and blackberries. One handful of prunes provides more than the optimum protection of 5000 ORACS daily.

● ● ● ● ● ● ● ● ● ● ● ● ● ● ● ●

Recommended for:
cancer *p.264*
circulatory *p.278*
digestive *p.284*
fatigue *p.298*

47

Mushrooms

★★★★

We should all eat more mushrooms. They contain more protein than most other vegetables, they're very low in calories, and they're also a good source of phosphorus and potassium. Although most textbooks state that mushrooms are not a source of vitamin B12, the most up-to-date research reveals they are actually a valuable source of this essential nutrient. One decent-sized field mushroom, or three button mushrooms, will give you enough B12 for a day, which is vital for vegetarians and even more so for vegans, as other plant sources of B12 are very limited. The same is true for vitamin E. Again, modern research reveals that most mushrooms are a rich source of this essential nutrient, with 100g/3½oz providing more than the minimum daily requirement.

Washing spoils their delicate flesh, so just remove any grit from mushrooms and then wipe them clean with a damp cloth.

Recommended for:
stress *p.292*
fatigue *p.298*

Celery

★★★★

Celery helps calm the nerves, according to Hippocrates. Perhaps this is due to its rich calcium content. Worldwide, it has a high reputation as an anti-rheumatic, although the anti-inflammatory agent at the basis of this reputation is more concentrated in the seeds and leaves than in the edible root. In traditional medicine, it's the seeds that are specifically recommended in the form of a tea for gout, rheumatism, and other problems resulting from poor elimination of wastes. In Japan, rheumatic patients are sometimes put on a celery-only diet; celery stewed with milk and eaten with it, or with celery seed tea, is a standard Romany treatment for rheumatic ailments. If you have rheumatoid arthritis, a daily half-glass of celery juice, first thing in the morning, for 15–20 days is worth trying. More than this would be counter-productive, and the kidneys would be irritated rather than stimulated.

As well as these admirable properties, celery has a very high reputation in folk medicine as a sexual stimulant: according to Dr Vogel, it does in fact stimulate not only the thyroid and pituitary glands but also the gonads. There seems little scientific evidence in support of this claim, but folk medicine is seldom wholly misguided. And it's really true – you burn more calories chewing it than you get from eating it.

• •

Recommended for:
digestive *p.284*
stress *p.292*
joints *p.304*
urinary *p.324*

49

Radishes

★★★★

Radishes belong to the crucifer family and are valuable for those at risk from cancer. But it is for problems of the liver and gallbladder that traditional medicine has most warmly recommended them. Radish juice acts powerfully on the gallbladder, stimulating the discharge of bile, as French studies have demonstrated.

Radishes contain other nutrients, including plenty of potassium, calcium, and sulphur, as well as some vitamin A and B-complex. They should be eaten as fresh as possible, while still young and crisp. Their tops should be eaten at the same time, as this aids the digestion of the vegetable. However, beware of overindulging in radishes; too much hot, stinging radish can irritate rather than stimulate the liver, kidneys, and gallbladder.

• • • • • • • • • • • • • • • • • • •

Recommended for:
cancer *p.264*
digestive *p.284*
respiratory *p.312*

Watercress

★★★★

Watercress belongs to the powerful crucifer family, other members of which are cabbage, broccoli, Brussels sprouts, kale, turnip, and radishes. Like them, it should figure prominently in the diet of anyone at risk from cancer. Watercress is also rich in vitamin A and vitamin C, both of which play an important role in combating cancer.

Watercress is related to nasturtiums, and both contain potassium and a benzyl mustard oil, the compound that gives them "bite" and which research has shown to be powerfully antibiotic. Unlike conventional antibiotics, the substances in watercress and nasturtiums are not only harmless to our intestinal flora, they are positively beneficial to the health of our gut. Urinary and respiratory infections in particular benefit from doses of watercress. Watercress is also a good source of iodine, which is useful for those with low thyroid activity.

● ● ● ● ● ● ● ● ● ● ● ● ● ● ● ● ● ● ●

Recommended for:
cancer *p.264*
fatigue *p.298*
respiratory *p.312*
skin *p.318*
urinary *p.324*

Avocados

Every slimmer thinks that luscious avocados are a high-fat, high-calorie treat. But when ripe they are also an almost complete food, supplying lots of potassium, vitamins A and E, some B and C vitamins, and a little protein and starch, along with avocado oil, which is mainly a monounsaturated fat.

Avocado is excellent as an early weaning food when puréed with other vegetables, and for convalescents. It's good for anyone suffering from stress or sexual problems. Avocados are a particularly rich source of skin-protective antioxidants, especially vitamin E. Women, in particular, who are often warned off avocados as being extra-high in fat and calories, should eat plenty of this fruit for the sake of their skin. Together with heart-protective monounsaturated oil and the other nutrients they contain, they neutralize damaging free radicals. This makes them good for the heart, circulation, and anti-aging.

• • • • • • • • • • • • • • • • • • • •

Recommended for:
circulatory *p.278*
stress *p.292*
fatigue *p.298*
skin *p.318*

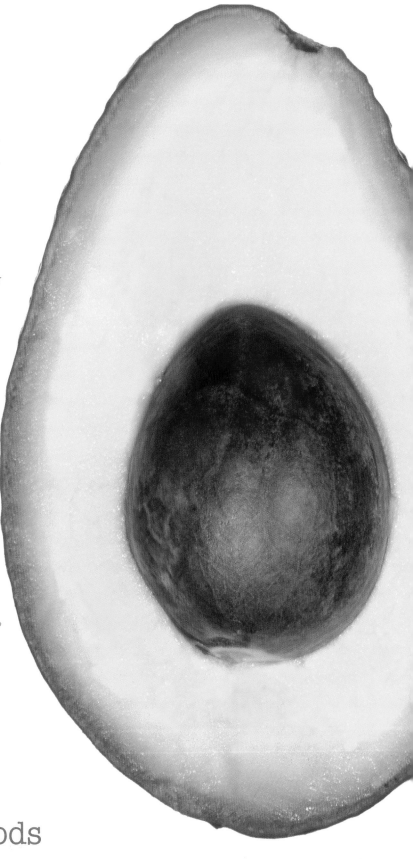

Peppers

★★★★

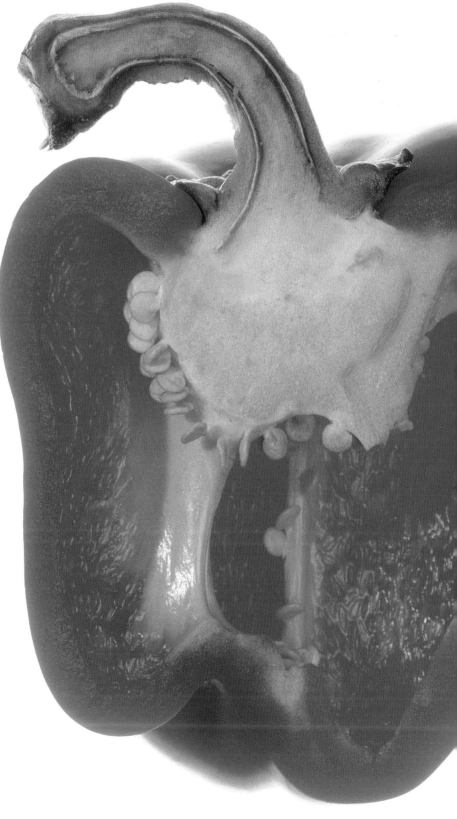

Known as sweet or bell peppers, these versatile vegetables are an excellent source of vitamin C. The red and yellow ones contain four times as much vitamin C as oranges, and a serving of green peppers will supply 100mg of vitamin C – over three times the recommended daily allowance. For this reason peppers are best eaten raw, although in the salad form popular in Spain or Italy, they conserve much of their vitamin C. Yellow and orange peppers are also a good source of beta-carotene, and of iron and potassium too. As one of the nightshade family of plants, however, peppers are perhaps best avoided by those with joint problems (*Joints, p.304*).

• • • • • • • • • • • • • • • • • • •

Recommended for:
cancer *p.264*
circulatory *p.278*
respiratory *p.312*
skin *p.318*

Tomatoes

★★★★

All of the tomatoes we eat today are descendants of the cherry tomatoes that have always grown wild along the western coast of South America. The Mexicans were probably the first to cultivate the tomato, and from Mexico, this fleshy fruit was introduced to Europe by the Spanish during the 16th century. After this, the tomato rapidly became popular across the south of Europe. Since they are members of the deadly nightshade family, tomatoes were treated with suspicion at first, but they soon became an integral component of cuisines all around the Mediterranean.

Tomatoes are very rich in antioxidants, especially beta-carotene and lycopene, and they also contain a good deal of vitamins C and E. This makes them good for the cardiovascular system. Research shows that they may also help to prevent some forms of cancer, particularly prostate cancer. Lycopene seems to protect men against this form of cancer, which is far less common in Mediterranean countries, where men may eat as many as 6–8 ripe tomatoes a day. Fortunately, in this age of processed food, processed tomatoes actually contain far more lycopene than fresh ones, so tinned tomatoes, tomato sauce, sun-dried tomatoes, and even ketchup are important sources of this antioxidant. Tomatoes are also low in sodium and rich in potassium, making them good for conditions such as high blood pressure and fluid retention.

In the largest study to date, it was evident that eating four portions of tomato sauce weekly reduced prostate cancer risk by 35 per cent. Although lycopene may be useful as a supplement, research shows that when tomato products are cooked and combined with oil, the lycopene is more biologically available – so pills aren't a substitute for the real thing. There are other plant chemicals in tomatoes that are also cancer-protective.

A ripe tomato contains more than 200 volatile compounds that make up its unique taste and smell. Green tomatoes contain a chemical called tomatine, which may trigger migraine attacks if you're a sufferer. Tomatine is destroyed by cooking but remains in quite high amounts in the pickled green tomatoes popular in the US.

There should always be a few tins of tomatoes in your cupboard, as they lose very little of their nutritional value during tinning and are a great standby for instant high-nutrient sauces.

• • • • • • • • • • • • • • • • • • • •

Recommended for:
cancer *p.264*
respiratory *p.312*
skin *p.318*

Pumpkin, squash

★★★★

Pumpkin and squash were an important part of the diet of many Native American tribes, who introduced them to the early European settlers. In North America, squash and pumpkin (especially in the form of pumpkin pie) are still served as part of the traditional Thanksgiving meal. These vegetables are not only delicious, but are also filling, inexpensive, high-energy foods.

As you might expect from their wonderful deep orange hue, pumpkins and squashes are full of beta-carotene, the vitamin A precursor that helps protect us against cancer, heart troubles, and respiratory disease. In population studies, people eating plenty of pumpkin, or other orange-yellow members of the squash family, run a lower risk of developing lung cancer.

Recommended for:
cancer *p.264*
circulatory *p.278*
respiratory *p.312*
skin *p.318*

Carrots

★ ★ ★ ★

Carrots are so rich in beta-carotene that a single "old" carrot supplies enough vitamin A for an entire day. Carrots are also near the top of the list of vegetables that protect us against cancer, and especially against lung cancer, a fact that is borne out in a number of population studies.

In traditional country wisdom favoured by many orthodox French physicians, a purée of cooked carrots is the perfect answer to infant diarrhoea, suggesting that carrots have an antibiotic as well as a nutritive action.

A two- or three-day fast, taking nothing but water and raw carrot juice, has been recommended for liver problems, and carrot juice is equally valuable for jaundice. Eating carrots increases the levels of red blood cells, and studies have also shown that carrots protect against excess ultraviolet light or radiation. Their antioxidant content is also useful for people with atherosclerosis (narrowed arteries).

● ● ● ● ● ● ● ● ● ● ● ● ● ● ● ● ● ●

Recommended for:
cancer *p.264*
circulatory *p.278*
digestive *p.284*
respiratory *p.312*

Potatoes

★★★★

Potatoes must provide a pretty good nutritional package, since the Irish peasantry thrived on almost nothing else for generations, without any obvious health problems. This Superfood, even when boiled or baked, supplies fibre, B vitamins, useful minerals, and enough vitamin C to keep scurvy at bay, even in winter. Baked potatoes are nutritionally superior, since many of the nutrients, including much valuable potassium, are found in the skins. Potato-peeling tea, which contains lots of potassium, is used in many countries for high blood pressure.

Boiled or baked, potatoes contain less than 100 calories per 100g/3½oz. Eat them with low-fat cottage cheese or Quark instead of butter, add a carrot, and that's a well-balanced, very low-calorie meal.

Raw potato juice is used in traditional medicine to treat stomach ulcers and arthritis. The taste, everyone admits, is disgusting, but can be disguised by adding honey, carrot, or lemon juice.

• • • • • • • • • • • • • • • • • •

Recommended for:
circulatory *p.278*
digestive *p.284*

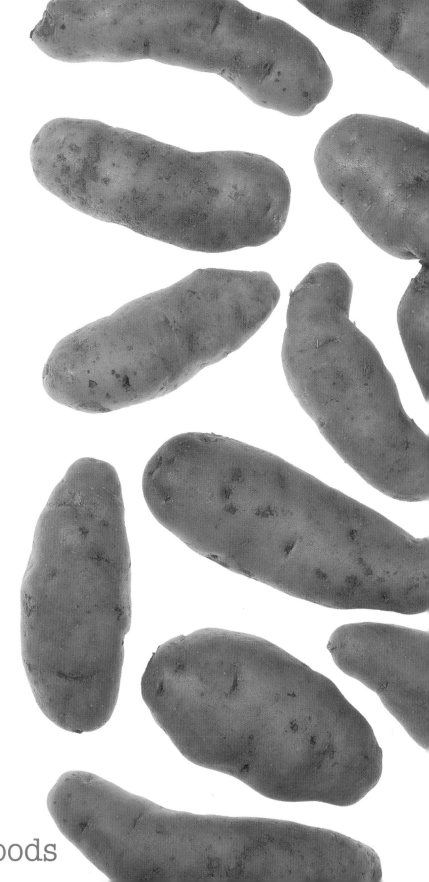

Sweet potatoes

★★★★

Sweet potatoes are an excellent source of energy, providing some protein, vitamin C and E, and lots of carotenoids, including beta-carotene. They are a powerful anti-cancer food, with one serving a day reducing the risk of lung cancer. This is even more important if you are a smoker or an ex-smoker.

Sweet potatoes are an extremely versatile vegetable and are wonderfully healthy for children and adults alike. A good way to introduce them to your family is to peel and cube a sweet potato and cook it together with ordinary potatoes, drain them, and mash with a little butter or olive oil and some grated nutmeg. They're equally delicious mashed together with parsnip or swede. They're also great roasted in a medium oven brushed with olive oil and a little black pepper. One of our favourite juices is apple, carrot, celery, and sweet potato, which tastes better than it sounds.

• • • • • • • • • • • • • • • • • •

Recommended for:
cancer *p.264*
digestive *p.284*
fatigue *p.298*
respiratory *p.312*

Swedes

★★★★

Another of the large and health-giving crucifer family, swede is often thought of as no more than cattle fodder. However, it's an excellent vegetable with a delicate flavour and all the anti-cancer properties of this family of plants. It contains protective phytochemicals and significant amounts of vitamin C, with a serving providing 75 per cent of the UK RDA, useful amounts of vitamin A, almost no sodium, a little fibre, and small amounts of trace minerals. Swede supplies only 24 calories per serving, but lots of satisfying bulk, making it a real bonus for those watching their weight.

Mashed together with potato, swedes produce a most interesting and flavoursome variation on the usual dish and are an excellent early weaning food for babies.

Note that, like other cruciferae, swedes contain goiterogens and should be eaten in moderation by anyone with thyroid problems or taking long-term thyroxin treatment.

• • • • • • • • • • • • • • • • •

Recommended for:

cancer *p.264*
skin *p.318*

Turnips

★★★★

Turnips are one of the oldest of all the cultivated vegetables, and have been a staple of the peasant diet in cold, northern European countries for many centuries. They supply plenty of energy-giving carbohydrate, along with reasonable amounts of many nutrients, including vitamins C and B6. The tops or greens are as healthy as the turnips themselves, and are best when eaten young and fresh.

Turnips are warmly recommended for gout in traditional medicine, as they are eliminators of uric acid. A thin purée of turnips, cooked in milk, is an old country remedy for bronchitis: the sulphurous compound raphanol may be responsible for this bactericidal action. It would be surprising, too, if a member of the powerful crucifer family were devoid of such healing and antibiotic powers.

Recommended for:
joints *p.304*
respiratory *p.312*

Beetroot

★★★★

In Romany medicine, beetroot juice was used as a blood-builder for patients who were pale and run-down, and in Russia and Eastern Europe it's used both to build up resistance and to treat convalescents after a serious illness. In the traditional medicine of Central Europe, beetroot has a long history of use in the treatment of cancer: it seems to contain anti-carcinogens bound to the red colouring matter, as well as possessing a striking ability to increase cellular uptake of oxygen. Many of these actions are enhanced when the beetroot is eaten raw or drunk as juice. The popular French starter crudités – which combine grated raw beetroot, raw carrot, and perhaps paper-thin slices of cucumber, all dressed with olive oil and lemon juice and garnished with chopped parsley – is a more powerful tonic for general health than a whole bottle of vitamin pills.

Recommended for:
cancer *p.264*
digestive *p.284*
fatigue *p.298*

Parsnips

★★★★

The wild parsnip has been used for centuries in Europe, where it grows around the borders of cultivated fields and in chalky soil in roadside verges. Like carrots, parsnips have long been a popular cultivated vegetable with a history of countryside use. In Germany they're often eaten with salted fish during Lent; in Holland they're used for soup; in Ireland they were boiled with water and hops for beer; and in England countrywomen made them into jam and parsnip wine.

The great herbalists, such as Culpeper, were all fans of the humble parsnip and advised giving it to humans as well as livestock. Parsnips provide calories, fibre, potassium, folic acid, vitamin E, and traces of minerals and other B vitamins. They taste best after the first hard frosts of winter. Mash them together with swede, carrot, or potato, or brush them with a little oil and roast. They're even fabulous cooked on the barbecue.

Recommended for:
circulatory *p.278*
digestive *p.284*
fatigue *p.298*

Jerusalem artichokes

★★★★

Jerusalem artichokes belong to the sunflower family and Italians call them "girasole". "Jerusalem" appears to be a corruption of the Italian word. By the 1800s they were popular in England made into "Palestine Soup".

Rich in carbohydrates, there is little sugar in them as they contain inulin, which the body deals with in the same way as fibre. Inulin isn't broken down during normal digestion but ends up in the large bowel (colon), where it provides food for billions of friendly probiotic bacteria. As with globe artichokes, the resulting fermentation can sometimes be a cause of wind, but that's a small price to pay for the fabulous taste and the low glycaemic index benefits of this much underrated vegetable. Jerusalem artichokes are ideal for diabetics and anyone who has problems keeping their blood sugar levels on an even keel, as they are filling and satisfying, and the inulin is not absorbed by the body.

Jerusalem artichokes are extremely low in calories – only 78 per 100g/3½oz – and contain hardly any salt but are a rich source of heart-friendly potassium. They also provide useful quantities of iron and some B vitamins. Dried and ground into flour, they are perfect for anyone with gluten, wheat, or other cereal allergies.

Recommended for:
circulatory *p.278*
digestion *p.284*
fatigue *p.298*

Globe artichokes

★ ★ ★ ★

Globe artichokes, as any Frenchman will tell you, are the friend of the liver. In 1975 three Frenchwomen, specialists in pharmacy, published a study of plants used in modern medicine; they listed no less than 51 different pharmaceutical preparations based on the leaves of this plant. The active compound that seems to be chiefly responsible is called cynarine, which acts powerfully on the liver to promote the flow of bile and stimulate liver cell regeneration.

These healing powers are concentrated mainly in the leaf, and when you buy artichokes in a continental market, they are sold complete with stem and leaves for those who wish to avail themselves of this excellent natural medicine. The globes, too, share some of this curative potential, making artichokes a Superfood for anyone with liver or digestive problems.

The artichoke is also a friend to the heart. In European folk medicine, it's used to treat high blood pressure and ward off heart attacks; studies have shown that artichokes have a distinct cholesterol-lowering ability, as well as a marked diuretic effect.

All of these qualities make artichokes one of the great purifying and detoxifying plants, particularly useful for those with rheumatism, arthritis, or gout.

• •

Recommended for:
circulatory *p.278*
digestive *p.284*
joints *p.304*

Onions

★★★★

Onions belong to the same botanical family as garlic, and both are the subject of intensive modern medical research, which only confirms the high reputation as a cure-all that they have always enjoyed. With garlic, onions share a protective action on the circulatory system that is fascinating cardiologists the world over. In a delightful trial carried out at Newcastle's Royal Victoria Infirmary, 22 volunteers were first asked to fast and then fed fried fatty British breakfasts, starring bacon and eggs. Half the volunteers had a little extra something on the menu: a helping of fried onions. When post-breakfast blood samples from both lots of breakfasters were analysed, they showed a startling difference. In people who ate the fry-up feasts without onions, the blood samples showed an increasing tendency to clot – a state which could eventually lead to life-threatening thrombosis. The blood of the onion-eaters, however – despite all that bacon and egg – showed a reduced tendency to clot. In a similar study in India, rich, fatty food pushed up blood cholesterol levels, and onions, whether cooked or raw, pulled it right back down. Dr Victor Gurewitch of Tufts University in the US has found that eating just half an onion daily – raw, please, not cooked – can raise blood levels of beneficial high-density lipoproteins by an average of 30 per cent.

Onions are impressive country medicine for a huge range of ailments – among them anaemia, arthritis and rheumatism, gout, and premature aging. They star in hundreds of traditional recipes, like this one for colic in babies: slice an onion, infuse it in hot water for a few minutes, let it cool, and give the baby a teaspoonful of the water. And onion soup at the end of a night on the tiles is part of Paris mythology.

Many of the onion's traditional properties are now being confirmed by modern research. In studies with rabbits, subcutaneous injections of onion extract lowered blood sugar levels more slowly than insulin, but for a longer period. It is thought this action is due to the glucokinine in onions. In other trials, onions were found to be effective against asthma. They are strongly diuretic, dissolving and eliminating urea, and they have powerful antibiotic activity.

Recommended for:
circulatory *p.278*
digestive *p.284*
fatigue *p.298*
respiratory *p.312*
urinary *p.324*

Leeks

★★★★

Leeks have been cultivated in the West for at least 4000 years, and the ancient Egyptians, the ancient Greeks, and the Romans all prized them for their medicinal value. Members of the same healing family as onions and garlic, they have the same therapeutic properties, although in a milder form. In French traditional medicine they are prescribed for respiratory problems, and being rich in potassium, they are also valued for their cleansing, diuretic powers. Their ability to eliminate uric acid means that people with gout or arthritis should eat plenty of leeks.

Recommended for:
joints *p.304*
respiratory *p.312*
urinary *p.324*

Spinach

★★★★

This vegetable is iron-rich, as every admirer of Popeye knows. Orthodox nutritionists, however, point out crushingly that the iron in cooked spinach is poorly absorbed by the body. This is because spinach has high levels of oxalic acid, which interact with magnesium and calcium to carry it out of the body in the form of insoluble salts. Spinach is also rich in uric acid, so it is best avoided by the gouty and the rheumatic.

Spinach is very rich in the dark green plant "blood" chlorophyll (*Red cabbage, p.70*), so anaemia patients or those suffering from fatigue and mental strain should eat plenty of it, raw, in the form of salads.

Cancer patients, or those at risk from cancer such as heavy smokers, should include plenty of raw spinach in their diets, too. Cancer research is increasingly focusing on the whole spectrum of carotenoids – not just beta-carotene – in dark green or brightly coloured fruits and vegetables, and spinach is more highly endowed with those potential cancer-fighters than even carrots. In population studies quoted by Jean Carper, dark green vegetables, with spinach at the top of the list, are strongly protective against cancer.

Recommended for:
cancer *p.264*
stress *p.292*
fatigue *p.298*

Red cabbage

★★★★

Cabbage has been the subject of an impressive amount of medical research. This is not surprising: its healing powers, which are long attested in traditional medicine, cover an amazing range of ailments.

Cabbage contains healing mucilaginous substances similar to those produced by the mucous membrane of the gut and stomach for their own protection. This confirms the effectiveness of the traditional raw cabbage-juice cure for ulcers. Cabbage is also loaded with sulphur compounds that, according to Dr Valnet, give it a tonic and disinfectant action in respiratory infections.

Anyone who is anaemic should eat cabbage for its iron and chlorophyll, the green "blood" of plants, which is chemically similar to the haemoglobin in human blood. Leslie Kenton quotes studies in which the red blood cells of anaemic rabbits were restored to normal after being fed crude chlorophyll for a fortnight. Centuries of use have also given the cabbage a reputation as being protective against stress, infection, and cardiac problems, while as a member of the crucifer family, it is known to contain many anti-cancer compounds. In population studies, people eating the most cabbage were the least likely to develop cancers. Perhaps even more excitingly, 50 per cent of guinea pigs fed diced raw cabbage before whole body irradiation survived, while those that were not so protected all died within 15 days. So maybe all those working with VDU screens, or facing radiation treatment or even diagnostic X-rays, should eat plenty of raw cabbage.

Most of these therapeutic effects have been observed with raw cabbage, and no doubt would also be found in sauerkraut. Traditional boiling in water not only means major nutrient losses into the water, but the disappearance or deactivation of many healing compounds. Cooked cabbage is rough on the digestion, too. So cook cabbage in its own juices, for as short a time as possible.

• • • • • • • • • • • • • • • • • • •

Recommended for:
cancer *p.264*
circulatory *p.278*
digestive *p.284*
respiratory *p.312*

71

Sauerkraut

In traditional European sauerkraut, raw cabbage is finely shredded and layered in a stone crock, with sea salt and spices. By the time the crock is full, the cabbage juices have fermented to produce a sour taste.

All over Europe, sauerkraut has been a dietary staple of the peasantry: a good way of preserving the autumn cabbages so that they could be eaten through the winter. Sauerkraut can truly be called a wonderfood: since the enzymes and vitamin C of cabbage are well preserved in it, it must have saved millions from scurvy.

Apart from being high in vitamin C, sauerkraut is also rich in calcium and a good source of potassium. Sauerkraut is traditionally a medicine too, in both preventative and curative senses. Dyspepsia, arthritis, cold, indigestion, stomach ulcers, skin problems – all were treated with sauerkraut and it was often very effective. We now know why.

Any toxins brewing in our gut may prepare the ground for a number of serious diseases. Not for sauerkraut-eaters, though, since the lactic acid that forms during fermentation does a wonderful clean-up job in the digestive tract. Benevolent bacteria multiply, killing off excess bad bacteria to produce a healthy colon once more.

Recommended for:
cancer *p.264*
digestive *p.284*
joints *p.304*

Oriental greens

★★★★

The Oriental leaves, such as pak choi, make a tasty, nutritious, and interesting contribution to healthy eating. They are superfoods in every sense, as they're extremely easy to grow, with many of them being suitable as a cut-and-come-again plant in the garden or greenhouse. Raw, stir-fried, steamed, braised, in salads, or in combination recipes, they're extremely versatile. Dark leaves contain the most beta-carotene, which is converted into vitamin A – important for the skin, immune health, and eyesight.

As members of the carotenoid family, Oriental greens protect against some cancers, particularly lung cancer. They also help to maintain vision and protect against age-related macular degeneration, which is the most common cause of visual deterioration in elderly people. These green leaves also provide valuable amounts of vitamin C, with one-third of the daily requirement delivered in an average portion, as well as some folic acid.

One of the most popular of the Oriental greens is Chinese cabbage, which is best served raw, lightly steamed, or stir-fried. Boiling it is a crime! Mizuna, with its peppery taste, is used raw, stir-fried, or in soup, and pak choi, widely available, can be eaten raw when young.

· ·

Recommended for:
skin *p.318*
cancer *p.264*

Asparagus

★ ★ ★ ★

Asparagus has somehow become infamous for the strange odour produced by your urine after you eat it: this area has not been tremendously well researched. In 1891 a scientist called Nencki asserted that the smell was due to a metabolite called methanethiol, and although other theories have arisen since, none seems to have won the day so far.

Asparagus really benefits the kidneys and the liver, and as it promotes elimination through the urine, it is warmly recommended for people who have rheumatism and arthritis. It's also a great source of folate, a B vitamin that is good for your cardiovascular system and is especially important for pregnant women, because it's known to help prevent certain birth defects, such as spina bifida. You can save the water asparagus is cooked in and drink it as a useful diuretic. Since asparagus is high in purines, people who suffer from gout should avoid it.

Recommended for:
digestive *p.284*
joints *p.304*
urinary *p.324*

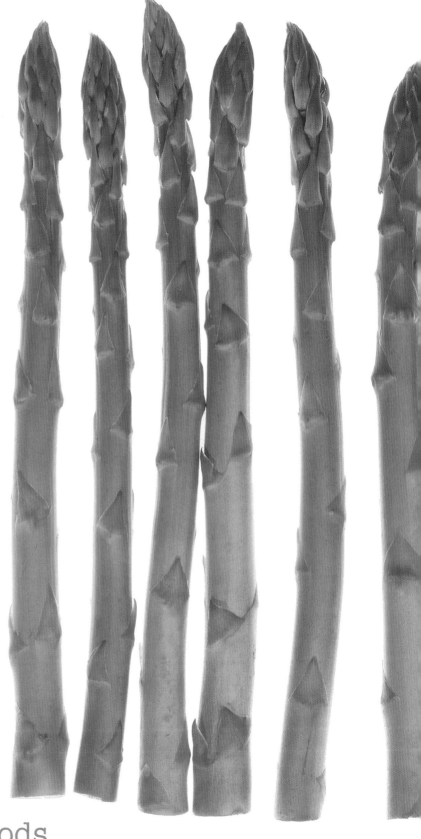

Broccoli

★★★★

Broccoli is a cruciferous plant with cancer-protective properties. Six major population studies analyzed at the US National Cancer Institute showed that the more cruciferous vegetables (including cauliflower, radishes, horseradish, cabbage, spring greens, turnips, Brussels sprouts, and kale) you eat, the lower your chances of developing bowel cancer – a finding now reinforced by the American Institute of Cancer Research.

Broccoli is an excellent source of fibre, folate, and vitamins A and C. It's a very good source of potassium, B2, and B6 and contains reasonable amounts of iron, calcium, and vitamin E. Cruciferous vegetables also suppress free-radical formation, making them good for joints and the heart.

Recent studies reveal that broccoli helps to destroy damaged cells, helps prostate cancer, prevents cataracts, and builds stronger bones.

● ● ● ● ● ● ● ● ● ● ● ● ● ● ● ● ● ●

Recommended for:
cancer *p.264*
circulatory *p.278*
joints *p.304*

Barley

★★★★

Barley has been cultivated longer than any other cereal. Bread made from barley was a staple in the Middle Ages, but was so heavy that it fell out of favour and was superseded first by oats and then by wheat. Barley has always been highly valued for its uniquely soothing qualities when used to treat inflammatory conditions of the intestines and urinary tract. Herbalists recommend plenty of barley water to help counter the painful irritation of cystitis and constipation.

Like other grains, barley is mineral-rich, with particularly high levels of calcium and potassium, and plenty of B-complex vitamins. This makes it useful for people suffering from stress or fatigue and a nourishing food for convalescence. Research on the cholesterol-lowering effect of cereals – wheat, rye, oats, and barley – have found that their coarse outer layers are rich in substances that inhibit the synthesis of cholesterol by the liver.

Nutritionally, however, pot barley – the little, beige, dehulled grains – is highly superior to cleaned or pearl barley. Use barley in soups, as stuffing for poultry, or eat it cooked on its own. You can also use it to make a delicious bread.

· ·

Recommended for:

circulatory *p.278*
digestive *p.284*
stress *p.292*
fatigue *p.298*
urinary *p.324*

Brown rice

★ ★ ★ ★

Rice is a marvellous complete food, the dietary staple of the East. Until the advent of rice-milling, it was eaten unpolished. With the new, milled white rice came a disastrous epidemic of beriberi – a disease of the brain and nervous system – that spread like wildfire around the Eastern world. Beriberi is caused by deficiency of a B vitamin, thiamine, in which the rice-polishings are rich, so white rice today is sometimes "parboiled" or "converted" by a process of steaming to drive some of the vitamins back into the grain.

Plain boiled brown rice is a universal folk remedy for diarrhoea, as is the water in which rice is boiled, which is also recommended for fevers. It seems to have a beneficial effect on the entire intestinal tract, soothing and cleansing it. A regime of plain, boiled, unsalted rice is warmly recommended by French doctors for lowering the blood pressure. To this can be added a purée of apples.

Rice should be washed in running water before cooking, but never soaked, since vital minerals and vitamins leach out with the dirt.

Recommended for:
circulatory *p.278*
digestive *p.284*
stress *p.292*
fatigue *p.298*

Buckwheat

Buckwheat, often considered a grain, is actually a seed related to rhubarb. In Russia and Poland it is a diet staple. Considering the harsh climate in these countries, this makes a lot of sense. Buckwheat is high in a flavonoid called glycoside rutin, which strengthens and tones the walls of the capillaries, the tiniest blood vessels in your body, and so protects against frostbite and chilblains. Buckwheat helps high blood pressure and atherosclerosis. Protein-rich and gluten-free, it's excellent for people with coeliac disease.

Recommended for:
circulatory *p.278*
digestive *p.284*
stress *p.292*

Lentils

This pulse is rich in protein, minerals, and fibre, is a good source of B vitamins, and is very low in fat. These complex carbohydrates are now recommended to us by cardiologists and slimming specialists alike. Lentils are a diet staple the world over, often served with grains such as barley. This pairing maximizes protein consumption, since together, they contain a better balance of the eight amino acids. Flavour lentils with herbs and spices such as cumin, fennel, and garlic, which help to counter flatulence.

Recommended for:
circulatory *p.278*
fatigue *p.298*

78 the superfoods

Beans

Dried beans (pulses) are the second largest group of foods forming man's diet. Weight for weight they contain almost as much protein as fillet steak, at a fraction of the cost and with many more health benefits.

Beans help to reduce cholesterol and protect against heart disease, circulatory problems, and bowel cancer. With a low GI, they provide slow-release energy, making them excellent for diabetics. They are also rich in plant hormones (phytoestrogens), which protect against osteoporosis and breast and prostate cancers.

Soybeans (*p.82*) are the best vegetable source of protein, with the highest phytoestrogen content and the strongest antioxidant activity. This protects against both heart disease and cancer.

Other beans have individual properties (*see below*) and a variety of flavours that make them all valuable.

Pinto potassium, fibre, folate.
Mung less starch, more folate.
Kidney fibre, potassium, zinc.
Haricot fibre, iron.
Chickpeas fibre, calcium, iron, zinc.
Butter fibre, potassium, iron.
Blackeyed fibre, selenium, folate.
Baked beans fibre, iron, selenium, iodine – but beware the salt.
Aduki fibre, magnesium, potassium, zinc.

Recommended for:
cancer *p.264*
circulatory *p.278*
fatigue *p.298*

Millet

Millet is the only grain that is a complete protein. It is also the only alkaline grain, making it particularly suitable for invalids and growing children.

It is also rich in silicon, a structural part of collagen (the tough substance that holds us together). Silicon is vital for the health of hair, skin, teeth, eyes, and nails. A lack of it can result in sagging connective tissue. Clogged arteries have much lowers levels of silicon than disease-free arteries, so it seems to benefit arterial health.

Recommended for:
circulatory *p.278*
fatigue *p.298*
skin *p.318*

Maize

Maize grows all over the world and is the staple food of millions. It is gluten-free and is used for many products – cornflakes, popcorn, cornflour, polenta, grits, and tortillas, which are all suitable for coeliacs.

Diets dependent on maize, however, can cause the deficiency disease pellagra, in which the body gets too little of the B vitamin nicotinic acid. Maize is deficient in tryptophan, which is essential for the absorption of this B vitamin.

Recommended for:
digestive *p.284*

Oats

Oats contain a lot of protein for a grain. They also contain polyunsaturated fats, vitamin E, and B vitamins. They are very high in calcium, potassium, and magnesium, which, like the B vitamins, are vital to a healthy nervous system, as well as to strong bones and teeth. Oats also supply silicon for healthy arterial walls. They also protect the digestive surfaces and soothe the stomach and intestines.

Oats have an impressive reputation in traditional medicine. Possets and caudles made from oatmeal with water, lemon juice, sugar, spices, and perhaps ale or wine were for centuries a prescription for any sickroom, along with gruel or porridge.

Herbalists turn to oats for one of their most reliable remedies for depression and general debility – a tincture of the whole plant, or just the dehusked oat. So potent is its tranquillizing effect that it is now being used by a number of health practitioners to wean people off the man-made tranquillizers to which so many thousands are addicted.

In dozens of studies, the cholesterol levels of patients fed a daily dose of oat-bran have declined an average 20 per cent. The glutinous fibre in the oat-bran appears to remove bile acids that would otherwise be converted into cholesterol. Oats should certainly figure on the diabetic's menu too, since they appear to have a very favourable effect on the metabolism of sugar.

Recommended for:

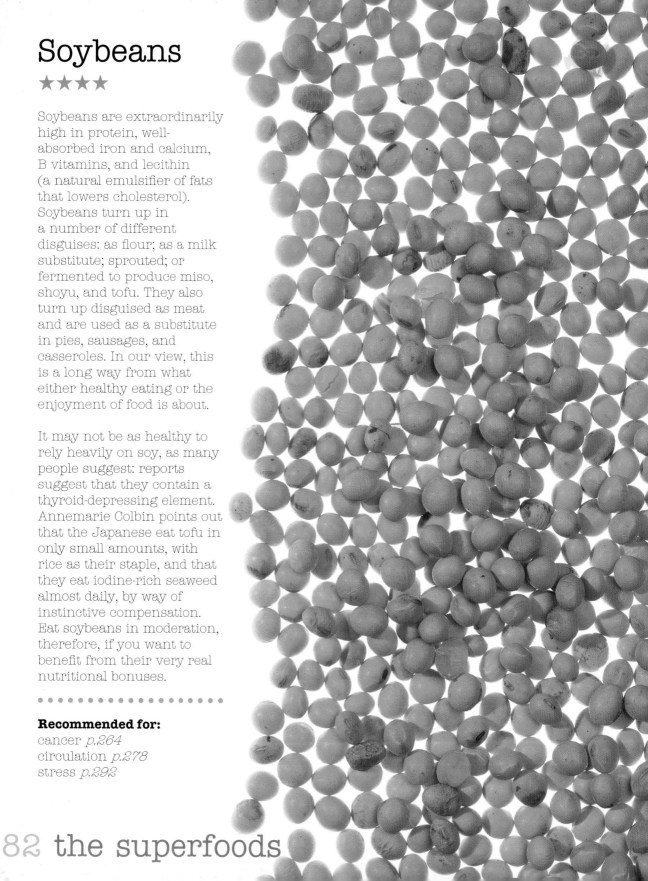

Soybeans

★★★★

Soybeans are extraordinarily high in protein, well-absorbed iron and calcium, B vitamins, and lecithin (a natural emulsifier of fats that lowers cholesterol). Soybeans turn up in a number of different disguises: as flour; as a milk substitute; sprouted; or fermented to produce miso, shoyu, and tofu. They also turn up disguised as meat and are used as a substitute in pies, sausages, and casseroles. In our view, this is a long way from what either healthy eating or the enjoyment of food is about.

It may not be as healthy to rely heavily on soy, as many people suggest: reports suggest that they contain a thyroid-depressing element. Annemarie Colbin points out that the Japanese eat tofu in only small amounts, with rice as their staple, and that they eat iodine-rich seaweed almost daily, by way of instinctive compensation. Eat soybeans in moderation, therefore, if you want to benefit from their very real nutritional bonuses.

● ● ● ● ● ● ● ● ● ● ● ● ● ● ● ● ● ● ●

Recommended for:
cancer *p.264*
circulation *p.278*
stress *p.292*

Wheat

★★★★

When most people say bread, they mean bread made from wheat flour, which is rich in zinc, magnesium, vitamin B6, pyridoxine, vitamin E, and fibre. But there is bread and there is bread. It is a long way from the loaf baked from the freshly milled wholegrain of organically grown wheat, with no additions other than salt and yeast, to the flabby white stuff made with any number of additives, from wheat produced by agrofarming, in which pesticide residues may linger, and which has had much of its goodness refined out of it.

Frumenty, made from wheat grains, is one of the most ancient of English dishes. Sprouted wheat, which is nutritionally even richer, is recommended for cancer patients.

A number of people are wheat-intolerant. For many of them, the problem lies not in the wheat itself but in pesticide residues found in it. They should experiment with bread from organically grown wheat.

· · · · · · · · · · · · · · · · · · ·

Recommended for:
circulatory *p.278*
stress *p.292*

Pasta

★★★★

Far from being a food to avoid, pasta provides complex carbohydrates for slow-release energy. Wholemeal varieties may contain more fibre, minerals, and B vitamins, but both white and wholemeal types are healthy. Pasta itself won't make you fat – it's what you put on it that makes the difference. A plate of "aglio e olio" (spaghetti with garlic and olive oil), a simple mixture of olive oil, garlic, and fresh herbs, or a dish of pasta garnished with tuna and spring onions are all filling, satisfying, delicious, and good for your waistline. Just avoid any sauces that are high in fat.

Marco Polo introduced pasta to Italy from China in 1295. Today there are palatable wholemeal varieties available, and for those who can't eat wheat, rice noodles make excellent alternatives.

A pan of boiling water, a packet of pasta, and a tin of chopped tomatoes makes a meal in 10 minutes.

Recommended for:
digestive *p.284*
fatigue *p.298*
weight control *p.330*

Bread

Good bread is indeed "the staff of life" and an important part of a healthy, balanced diet. Wholemeal bread contains five times as much fibre as white bread, and valuable amounts of vitamin E, potassium, iron, zinc, copper, magnesium, thiamin, riboflavin, pantothenic acid, folic acid, pyridoxine, and biotin. You'll also get 10 times as much manganese, twice as much chromium, and one and a half times as much selenium as you will from white bread.

The best way to avoid the high salt content in commercial bread is by making your own; it's one of the most satisfying things you can ever do in a kitchen. But if you can't be bothered with proving, kneading, and pummelling, you could buy a bread machine instead. Either way, you'll be able to control what goes into your daily bread.

Recommended for:
digestive *p.284*
stress *p.292*
fatigue *p.298*

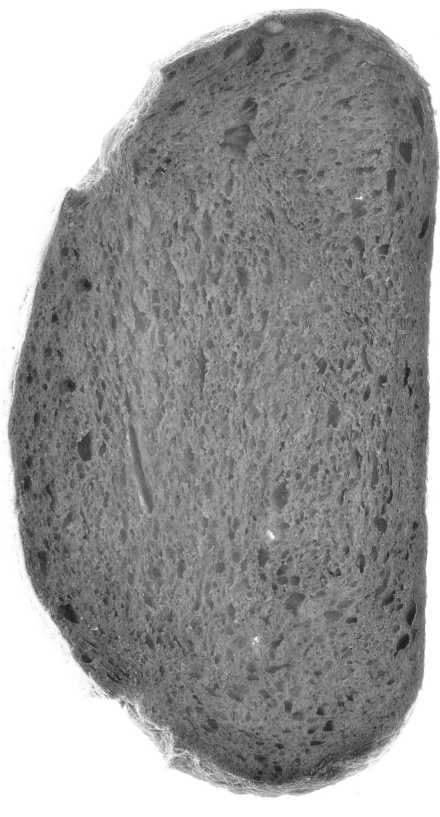

Almonds

★★★★

Almonds are not really nuts as we always imagine; they are, in fact, the seed of the fruit of the almond tree. Most importantly, almonds are a highly concentrated food that is rich in protein, fat, and vital minerals such as zinc, magnesium, potassium, and iron, as well as some B vitamins. Since they are also high in oxalic and phytic acid, which combine with these minerals to carry them out of your body, you should eat them at the same time as vitamin-C rich foods for maximum absorption.

Almonds are 20 per cent protein – weight for weight, they have one-third more protein than eggs. The oil in almonds is soothing, and almond milk is a classic sickroom drink, being both sustaining and soothing. It is recommended by herbalists for respiratory ailments as well as digestive upsets. Almond milk can be combined with barley water (*p.257*) for urinary problems. Dr Valnet has a recipe for making almond milk: soak 60g/2oz whole almonds in tepid water, then skin them. Measure out 900ml/1½pt of water, and pound the almonds with a few tablespoons of the water (you can do this easily in a food processor), adding the rest of the water once you've produced a paste. Add a tablespoon of honey, and strain through muslin.

Recommended for:
digestive *p.284*
respiratory *p.312*
urinary *p.324*

Cashews

★★★★

This delicious nut is always sold shelled. Avoid the salted ones and choose the plain roasted variety instead. Cashews, like olive oil, are high in healthy heart-protecting monounsaturated fats. Whizzed in a processor with a little walnut oil, they make wonderful cashew nut butter. They're also a very good source of copper and a good source of magnesium, tryptophan, and protein. Cashews also contain some folic acid, potassium, and fibre.

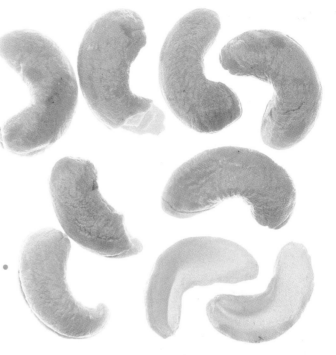

Recommended for:
circulatory *p.278*
digestive *p.284*
stress *p.292*
fatigue *p.298*

Hazelnuts

★★★★

Deliciously crunchy hazelnuts can be bought ready-shelled to eat as a nourishing snack. They contain the B vitamin thiamine (deficiency of which can make you feel low and lethargic) and they also supply the omega-3 fats needed to balance omega-6 fats in our diets. Dry roast hazelnuts in a hot frying pan, chop them, and sprinkle on fruit or green salads. They're a good source of protein and also contain fibre, magnesium, and vitamin E.

Recommended for:
fatigue *p.298*
stress *p.292*
joints *p.304*

Pumpkin seeds

★★★★

Pumpkin seeds contain measurable amounts of zinc, iron, and calcium, and they're an excellent snack food, supplying protein and B-complex vitamins. In traditional medicine in many parts of the world, particularly in Eastern Europe, they also have a high reputation as a male sexual tonic and protector of the prostate gland.

For prostate disorders, Russians simmer 100g/3½oz of the unshelled seeds in 750ml/1¼pt of water for 20 minutes and take a wineglassful three times a day. The protective action of pumpkin seeds has been ascribed to a plant hormone that is found in them, but more research in this area is needed.

Recommended for:
stress *p.292*
fatigue *p.298*
skin *p.318*

Sesame seeds

★★★★

These little seeds are the vegetarian's friend. A large handful will supply about 26 grams of protein, or about two-thirds of a day's needs for a reasonably active man. Unusually for vegetable sources, they are also rich in the amino acids methionine and tryptophan, which are important for good liver and kidney health. They are also well endowed with minerals, containing over 7mg iron and 10.3mg zinc per 100g/3½oz. Eat a vitamin C-rich fruit or vegetable at the same meal, though, to help your body absorb the minerals. Sesame seeds are also a good source of polyunsaturated fatty acids and vitamin E.

In ancient Babylon – as today all over the Arab world – halvah was made from pounded sesame seeds and honey and eaten to enhance sexual vitality. Paavo Airla, one of the US's most highly respected naturopaths, listed sesame seeds among ten foods for maintaining and enhancing sexual vigour.

· · · · · · · · · · · · · · · · · ·

Recommended for:
circulatory *p.278*
fatigue *p.298*

Sprouted seeds

★★★★

Sprouted seeds are a wonderful source of vitamins and minerals. They have been described as "the most live, pure, nutritious food imaginable". They are cheap and easy to grow even if you don't own so much as a window box, and if you sprout them yourself, you can be sure that they are organic, produced without fertilizers or pesticides.

When you sprout beans or seeds, what you produce is an enormously enhanced package of the nutrients already present in the original seeds. This can include the full range of vitamins and minerals, plus a powerhouse of plant enzymes, which are at their most abundant in the early sprouting stage. Plant enzymes are thought to activate the body's own enzyme systems and boost the ability to metabolize fats and oils.

One researcher found that levels of vitamin B2 in oats rose by 1300 per cent almost as soon as they began sprouting, and by the time green leaves formed, the increase was 2000 per cent. B6 (pyridoxine) was up 500 per cent, and folic acid 600 per cent. In one study, only small amounts of vitamin C were found in unsprouted wheat grains, and this increased by 600 per cent while sprouting over the next few days.

Their wealth of 100 per cent natural nutrition, free of chemical pollution, makes sprouts an obvious choice for cancer patients. They are used extensively at many clinics practising the natural approach to treating cancer. They are also valuable for anyone anxious to boost their immune defences, and for all conditions needing first-class nutrition.

More and more supermarkets are now selling sprouted seeds. If your local one doesn't, or only stocks one or two kinds, write to the manager suggesting that they extend their range.

• •

Recommended for:
cancer *p.264*
stress *p.292*
fatigue *p.298*
skin *p.318*

Sunflower seeds

★★★★

These seeds are concentrated nourishment, containing protein, B-complex vitamins, and useful levels of minerals. They are also rich in polyunsaturated oils, which is why you should examine hulled nuts carefully before you eat them: they easily turn rancid, when they become a most unhealthy food. Fresh hulled nuts are a pale, uniform grey – rancid ones are yellowy brown. Buy unshelled sunflower seeds, and enjoy cracking them open to find the fresh nuts the way children do all around the Mediterranean.

Eaten regularly, sunflower seeds will help to counter fatigue, depression, irritability, and lack of energy. Smokers trying to give up the habit find chewing them particularly helpful. They're also an excellent addition to the school lunchbox.

Recommended for:
stress *p.292*
fatigue *p.298*

Walnuts

★★★★

Walnuts are protein-rich, containing as much protein, weight for weight, as eggs. They are also high in potassium and other minerals, such as zinc and iron. Eat them in salads, where vitamin C-rich foods will help your body absorb these minerals.

Recommended for:
circulatory *p.278*
fatigue *p.298*

Chestnuts

★★★★

Chestnuts must be cooked and can then be added to sweet and savoury dishes, soups, stuffings, or vegetables. Try them with Brussels sprouts or broccoli and Stilton soup. Unlike other nuts, they contain virtually no fat and only 170 calories per 100g/3½oz. Because they're high in starch, they can be dried and ground into excellent gluten-free flour. They don't supply much protein, but they do contain the B vitamins thiamin (B1), riboflavin (B2), and pyridoxine (B6), and potassium.

Recommended for:
circulatory *p.278*
fatigue *p.298*

Peanuts

★★★★

A large-scale experiment has shown that a teaspoon of peanut butter five days a week produces an average pound a week weight loss. The monounsaturated fats reduce cholesterol and prevent heart disease. With a very low glycaemic index rating, peanuts may also help to prevent adult-onset diabetes, as they hardly raise blood-sugar levels. They also provide vitamin B3, folate, and protein. Peanuts and organic peanut butter should be part of a healthy diet.

Recommended for:
circulatory *p.278*
fatigue *p.298*

Milk

★★★★

Cow's milk is extremely nutritious, a first-class protein, and a rich source of calcium. It also provides some B vitamins and a little iron and zinc. As a fast-food, and as a regular part of a child's diet, it can be warmly recommended.

Milk, however, is a fatty food. If you order skimmed milk to avoid the fat, you also lose the vitamins A, D, and E present in whole milk. Moreover, the mineral calcium needs to be in balance with another important mineral, magnesium, deficiency of which is very common in modern Western diets; and milk is a poor source of magnesium.

A number of adults – and whole populations in the eastern and southern hemispheres – lack the digestive enzyme lactase, which is needed in order to absorb all the goodies in milk. Many more people may be intolerant to milk, and to other dairy products such as butter and cheese. So milk is not a Superfood for everyone.

• • • • • • • • • • • • • • • • • •

Recommended for:
stress *p.292*
joints *p.304*

Yoghurt

★★★★

Yoghurt is a valuable food for your digestive system. When the natural balance between beneficial and harmful bacteria in the gut is upset, it can lead to fermentation, wind, putrefaction, constipation, and poor absorption. If ignored, this may give rise to even more severe health problems. Live yoghurt contains *Lactobacillus bulgaricus*, a microbe which helps restore equilibrium in the gut.

Yoghurt's lactic acids aid digestion by synthesizing B vitamins and increasing the uptake of nutrients, particularly of calcium (which yoghurt also supplies). They regulate bowel function, and have properties that can stop a budding infection, such as E. coli. Antibiotics destroy both good and bad bacteria in the gut so, when taking them, eat plenty of yoghurt of counter this.

Recommended for:
digestive *p.284*
stress *p.292*
joints *p.304*

Eggs

★★★★

Free-range eggs are free from unwanted chemicals and lower in cholesterol than battery-farmed eggs. For all but a tiny minority of people, the cholesterol in eggs does not affect blood cholesterol. Eggs are easily digested and supply protein, zinc, B vitamins, and other nutrients.

Recommended for:

stress *p.292*
skin *p.318*

Butter

★★★★

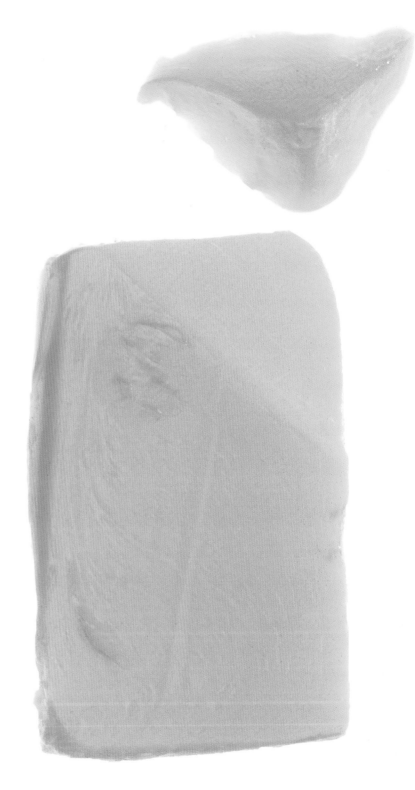

After many years of being told that margarine is better for you than butter, the tide has turned. Used modestly, butter is healthier than most margarines, which often contain artery-damaging trans-fats, and it's delicious too. Butter is virtually all fat, and 60 per cent of that is saturated fat. One hundred grams of butter provides 740 calories, but it also supplies vitamins A, D, and E. Salted butter may contain up to 1300mg of salt per 100g/3½oz; you can avoid this by simply choosing an unsalted variety. Under UK regulation, butter can be coloured but it may not contain antioxidants, unless the finished product is used exclusively for catering or manufacturing. It's best to choose uncoloured brands.

Be sparing with the butter and your food will taste better for it.

Recommended for:
fatigue *p.298*
joints *p.304*
skin *p.318*

Cheese

For thousands of years, cheese has been important for human nutrition. The ancient Greeks and Romans made cheese, and it was so much a part of the Roman diet that every Roman legionnaire was entitled to a daily portion.

We worry that so many young women avoid this vital source of bone-building calcium, protein, and vitamins A, B, and D. They do it in the pursuit of thinness, just because cheese contains some fat. Apart from calcium and vitamins, cheese also supplies some zinc in a form the body can easily use – 100g/3½oz of cheese supplies one-quarter of the daily zinc requirement for adults. Cheese can benefit men, too – zinc is vital for normal male sexual function. Cheese is also good for children and adolescents, as they need the calcium for their developing bones. Worryingly, statistics indicate that around half of British youngsters aren't getting enough calcium in their diets.

People who get migraines may react badly to a chemical known as tyramine, which cheese contains and which can trigger migraine attacks. There are also people with an allergy to cow's milk. Goat's and sheep's cheeses make wonderful alternatives to cow's milk cheese and for both of these groups, they usually present no problems. Most goat's cheese is soft and mild. If you like hard cheese, Spanish Manchego is an exceptional one (made from sheep's milk) with a full but mild flavour. French Roquefort, Italian Pecorino, and Greek Feta are stronger sheep's cheeses.

Recommended for:
fatigue *p.298*
stress *p.292*

Beef, lamb

★★★★

These meats contain protein, iron, zinc, and B vitamins. Free-range cattle produce CLA, a unique fat that helps to control cholesterol and aids weight management. Beef and lamb from biologically reared livestock is much lower in saturated fat than intensively reared meat. This meat is also free of the chemical cocktail found in intensively reared meat, which includes hormones, antibiotics, pesticides, and insecticides. Excessive consumption of red meat is linked to bowel cancer, but three portions a week is fine.

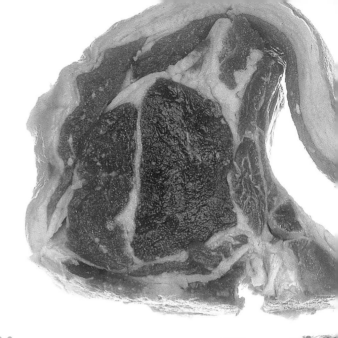

Recommended for:
fatigue *p.298*

Liver

★★★★

Liver is lovely and an amazing source of essential nutrients, but we don't eat enough of it these days. It supplies iron and zinc that can be easily absorbed, and is the richest dietary source of vitamins A and B12. It also contains other B vitamins. Don't eat liver, however, if you are, or are trying to become, pregnant as excessive vitamin A may cause birth defects; an average portion of liver provides five times your daily requirement of this nutrient.

Recommended for:
stress *p.292*
fatigue *p.298*

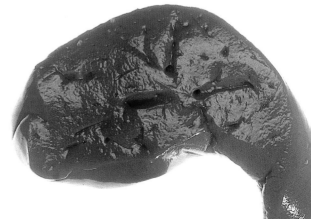

Chicken

★★★★

Free-range or organic chicken, like beef and lamb from biologically reared livestock, not only tastes better than the factory-farmed birds, but is also a great deal healthier. A properly reared chicken, without the antibiotics, growth hormones, and other unwanted chemicals poured down its throat from hatching to dispatching, will have a lower fat content than red meat or commercially produced chicken. Most of the fat will be in the skin and is easily removed. Because they are feeding on natural grasses, free-range chickens have more of the healthy omega-3 fatty acids and much less of the worst saturated fats than their commercially reared counterparts.

Free-range birds also build more muscle, and more muscle means more protein. In addition, they are an excellent source of B vitamins and of easily absorbed iron and zinc. And chicken soup is comforting as well as anti-viral.

• • • • • • • • • • • • • • • • • • •

Recommended for:
circulatory *p.278*
stress *p.292*

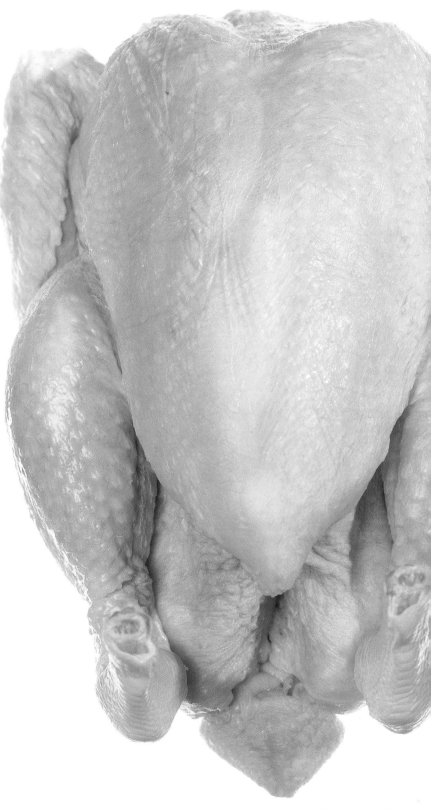

Oily fish

★★★★

Over the last hundred years, our consumption of fish has slowly declined, even as we've made more and more exciting discoveries about its nutritional role in our diets. Oily fish, in particular, is one of the richest known sources of a vital ingredient in human health – the essential fatty acid omega-3.

Professor Hugh Sinclair was the first person to recognise the importance of essential fatty acids, or EFAs. He wanted to know why the Inuit, who ate primarily whale blubber and fish (a diet which, according to the wisdom at that time, was high in saturated fats and therefore very heart-unfriendly), should have low levels of cardiovascular disease. There was one clue: the Inuit were known to bleed very easily. So Sinclair put himself on a diet of whale blubber for 100 days and at the end of the study, his platelet and cholesterol levels had gone down, and he too bled easily. An ingredient was thinning his blood. The secret ingredients, he eventually worked out, were the EFAs, and one in particular, called omega-3.

Historically, we have consumed a diet with equal levels of omega-3 and omega-6 fatty acids, but in the last century, as our diet has contained more vegetable oils and refined grains and less oily fish, the balance has been upset. The deficiency in omega-3 fatty acids may be partly responsible for soaring levels of depression, heart disease, and behavioural problems in the young, as well as a spectrum of illnesses. So remember to eat that oily fish!

There are two problems that complicate the issue further. The survival of some species is currently threatened, and certain fish should be eaten only rarely because they may be contaminated with pollution. Fortunately, the healthiest fish are less threatened: you can eat herring, mackerel, pilchards, sardines, sprats, trout (not farmed), whitebait, anchovies, and carp (farmed) without anxiety or guilt. Non-oily fish, Pacific cod, Dover sole, white bass, and Alaskan and Pacific halibut are all sustainably caught and good sources of protein.

• •

Recommended for:
circulatory *p.278*
fatigue *p.298*
joints *p.304*

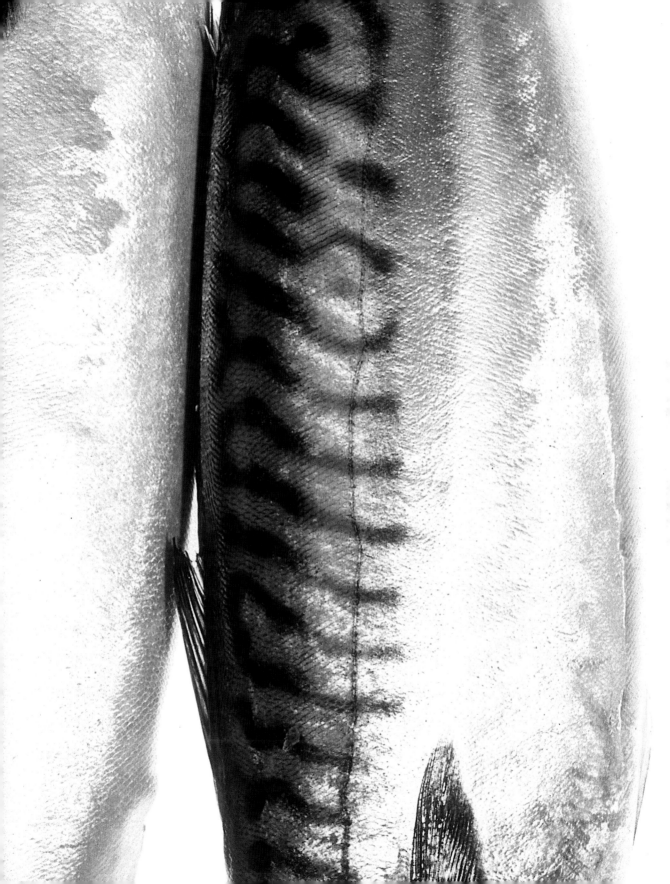

Molluscs

★★★★

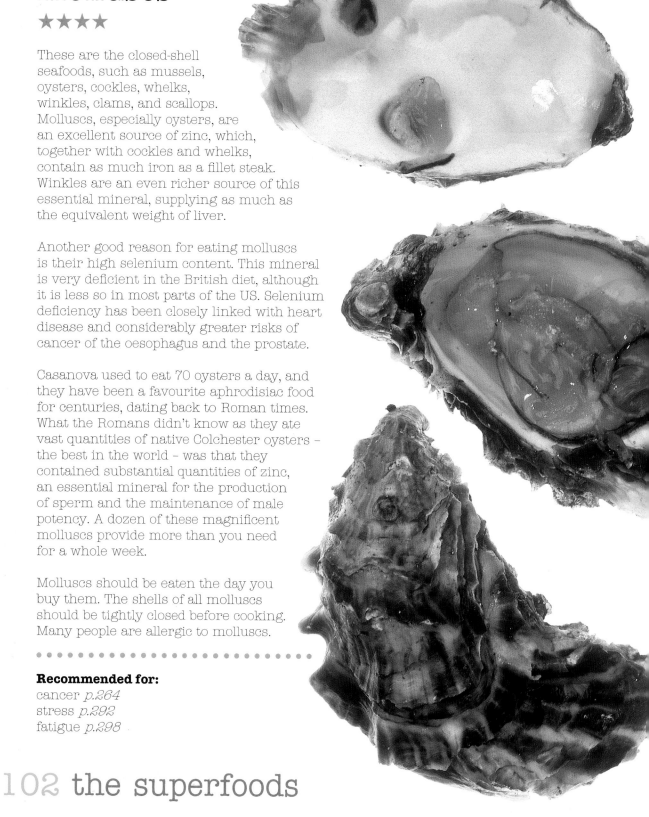

These are the closed-shell seafoods, such as mussels, oysters, cockles, whelks, winkles, clams, and scallops. Molluscs, especially oysters, are an excellent source of zinc, which, together with cockles and whelks, contain as much iron as a fillet steak. Winkles are an even richer source of this essential mineral, supplying as much as the equivalent weight of liver.

Another good reason for eating molluscs is their high selenium content. This mineral is very deficient in the British diet, although it is less so in most parts of the US. Selenium deficiency has been closely linked with heart disease and considerably greater risks of cancer of the oesophagus and the prostate.

Casanova used to eat 70 oysters a day, and they have been a favourite aphrodisiac food for centuries, dating back to Roman times. What the Romans didn't know as they ate vast quantities of native Colchester oysters – the best in the world – was that they contained substantial quantities of zinc, an essential mineral for the production of sperm and the maintenance of male potency. A dozen of these magnificent molluscs provide more than you need for a whole week.

Molluscs should be eaten the day you buy them. The shells of all molluscs should be tightly closed before cooking. Many people are allergic to molluscs.

• •

Recommended for:
cancer *p.264*
stress *p.292*
fatigue *p.298*

Crustaceans

★★★★

Crabs, lobsters, prawns, shrimps, crayfish, and langoustines are the most popular edible crustaceans. They provide the same amount of protein and other nutrients as white fish, although they are much saltier.

There has been controversy about the cholesterol content of crustaceans, but most experts believe that this is only a hazard if you have an inherited tendency to high cholesterol levels. Far from increasing the risk of heart disease, a regular intake of shellfish reduces levels of LDL (bad) fat, which are most dangerous. Crustaceans also contain valuable amounts of essential omega-3 fatty acids.

All crustaceans are highly nutritious alternatives to meat. They are excellent sources of protein, selenium, and tryptophan, and are very good sources of vitamins B12 and D. They also provide good amounts of minerals, including iron and zinc. Unfortunately, many people have an allergy to crustaceans. They also contain purines, which can aggravate gout.

Recommended for:
circulatory *p.278*
stress *p.292*
fatigue *p.298*

Basil

★★★★

Basil is the traditional accompaniment to tomatoes in Mediterranean cookery and an ingredient of the green Italian pasta sauce pesto (pistou in Provence). Basil is both tonic and calming to the nervous system, making it a natural tranquillizer for the kind of frazzled nerves that lead to insomnia. If this is your problem, have a good "soupe au pistou" in the evening.

· ·

Recommended for:
digestive *p.284*
stress *p.292*

Mint

★★★★

This popular herb comes in many varieties, and is often used for flavouring light summer dishes. Mint sauce with lamb was for a long time regarded by the French as culinary barbarism, but now they have acknowledged mint's beneficial effect on the digestion and have devised their own sauce paloise. Fragrant peppermint tea is a popular digestive throughout the Middle East. Mint also stimulates the heart and nerves. Drink this delicious tea instead of coffee for its mild lift.

· ·

Recommended for:
circulatory *p.278*
digestive *p.284*

Oregano

★★★★

Oregano is the distinctive note in the smell of pizza. An obliging herb, it is almost as delicious dried as fresh. It is an effective antiseptic for the respiratory tract, so enjoy plenty of it in winter. It's also good for colic.

Recommended for:
digestive *p.284*
respiratory *p.312*

Chives

★★★★

Chives share many of the healing properties of garlic and onions, which belong to the same family. They impart a milder flavour, however, so are good for flavouring delicate sauces. The pretty mauve flowers of chives can also be eaten, and look good when scattered on a summer salad.

Recommended for:
cancer *p.264*
circulatory *p.278*

Sage

★★★★

Sage and onion stuffing for roast goose or turkey is true kitchen medicine, since sage aids the digestion of rich, heavy food. Italian cooks always add a leaf of sage to the pan when they fry sausages or pork.

Sage also acts as a stimulant to the central nervous system, making it a valuable tonic for convalescents or for those suffering from stress or nervous exhaustion. It is good for respiratory complaints, and the French make a tonic wine with it, which is admirable for those who are run down or are getting over a nasty viral infection.

Sage is powerful stuff, however – it can dry up mother's milk – so don't use it medicinally for more than a week at a time.

● ●

Recommended for:
digestive *p.284*
stress *p.292*
respiratory *p.312*

Marjoram

★★★★

Sweet or pot marjoram is the gentler garden variety of wild marjoram or oregano (*p.105*), which grows on the hillsides of Greece. In medieval times, sweet marjoram was an important household herb and was used to scent rooms and as a furniture polish.

Unsurprisingly, perhaps, marjoram and oregano have similar properties. Sweet marjoram is particularly valued for its calming qualities, and the essential oil is strongly sedative. The leaves can be used to make a soothing tea, or they can be chopped finely and added as a flavouring to salads and sauces, and other dishes.

Recommended for:
digestive *p.284*
stress *p.292*

Parsley

★★★★

Parsley is rich in vitamins A and C and in iron, calcium, and potassium, as well as in life-giving chlorophyll. Use it fresh and use it lavishly.

Herbalists value parsley for its diuretic action, and parsley tea was used in the trenches in World War I for soldiers suffering from kidney complications following dysentery. It also helps to eliminate uric acid, making it useful in the treatment of rheumatism and gout. Parsley tea was an old country aid to digestion: Maurice Messegué recalls the monster pot brewed by his grandmother Sophie after a Lucullan feast of foie gras, roast chicken, sautéed mushrooms, crêpes, custards, and apple tart.

Add a bunch of fresh parsley whenever you make a freshly pressed vegetable juice to enjoy the full benefits of this important herb.

Recommended for:
digestive *p.284*
joints *p.304*
urinary *p.324*

Rosemary

★★★★

Rosemary originated in the hot, dry climate of the Mediterranean countries, where it has long been an important medicinal and household herb. We know it mainly as the inseparable companion of roast lamb and chicken in Mediterranean cookery. It is once more a powerful friend to the digestive system, prompting the production of extra bile for fat digestion.

"Rosemary for remembrance" is an old adage, and it's true that rosemary also stimulates the adrenal cortex. Rosemary wine, in small doses, is valuable in states of general debility, including loss of memory, strain, and nervous tension.

● ● ● ● ● ● ● ● ● ● ● ● ● ● ● ● ●

Recommended for:
digestive *p.284*
stress *p.292*

Savory
★★★★

Savory is one of the oldest herbs used for flavouring, and the ancient Romans often used it in sauces. The German name of this peppery little plant means "bean-herb", since it eases the digestion of this challenging food. Try it with split peas, broad beans, and lentils too. It benefits the entire digestive tract and has an antiseptic action on the gut.

· ·

Recommended for:
digestive *p.284*

Fennel
★★★★

The dark green fronds of fennel are a classic ingredient of the court-bouillon for fish dishes and soups. You can also add them to mayonnaise to serve with cold fish in summer. Fennel goes particularly well with rich fish such as mackerel. An excellent aid to digestion, it prevents wind or colic.

· ·

Recommended for:
digestive *p.284*

Tarragon

★★★★

The delicate, distinctive flavour of this herb seems particularly French. Tarragon is often used with roast chicken, in sauces, in omelettes, or to flavour a wine vinegar. The dried herb, however, is a pale shadow of the fresh. Tarragon can help relieve wind, flatulence, and acidity.

Recommended for:
digestive *p.284*

Thyme

★★★★

Thyme contributes to the deepest aromatic note in a bouquet garni, and it would be hard to imagine a robust peasant daube of beef, or a springtime lamb stew, without this herb. Its medicinal qualities are just as impressive. Thyme is a powerful antiseptic as well as a general stimulant to the body's natural resistance, with marked antiviral and antibacterial activity. It is also a tonic to the nervous system.

Recommended for:
stress *p.292*
respiratory *p.312*

Dill

Both the ancient Egyptians and the Greeks valued dill for its medicinal properties and used it to treat indigestion and other stomach complaints. The leaves, flowers, and seeds of this pretty, feathery herb are all useful in cooking, and the seeds are still sometimes served as a digestive following a rich meal. Dill is a favourite accompaniment to fish in Scandinavia, and it is particularly good with salmon, whether fresh or smoked. Dried dill is a piquant addition to bland cheeses or to salad dressings.

Babies may first taste dill in the form of gripe water, where it is highly effective; in fact its name comes from an Anglo-Saxon word meaning "to lull".

Recommended for:
digestive *p.284*
stress *p.292*

Dandelion

★★★★

The bitter taste of dandelion leaves is a clue to their usefulness: they have a long-standing reputation in the treatment of liver problems. Juice from the roots could be found at every apothecary for centuries. A digestive and urinary system tonic, dandelion is also a gentle, effective diuretic, helping to eliminate uric acid, excess cholesterol, and urea. The plant supplies enough potassium to compensate for the amount lost in the urine. It is also known as a blood-cleanser and is helpful for toxic or inflammatory conditions of the skin or joints.

The leaves are nearly as useful as the root. They are rich in vitamins A and C, beta-carotene, and chlorophyll, and the iron that they supply is more readily taken up by the body than the iron in spinach. Add the young leaves – the older leaves are too bitter – to any mixed green salad and enjoy an all-round tonic.

• • • • • • • • • • • • • • • • • • •

Recommended for:
circulatory *p.278*
digestive *p.284*
fatigue *p.298*
joints *p.304*
urinary *p.324*

Bay leaves

★★★★

The distinctive flavour of bay leaves is an intrinsic part of the classic French bouquet garni (a bunch of herbs used to flavour slowly cooked dishes). Bay leaves are prized for their antiseptic properties and for their assistance to the digestion, helping to ward off wind and cramps.

Recommended for:
digestive *p.284*
respiratory *p.312*

Juniper

★★★★

These tiny berries are responsible for giving gin its unique flavour. They impart a powerful tang when used in cooking. Herbalists use them as a diuretic and to help clear excess uric acid from the body. Like so many culinary herbs, they are also a tonic to the digestive system.

Recommended for:
digestive *p.284*
urinary *p.324*

Nutmeg

This spice, familiar from so many favourite winter sweet treats, can have a mildly uplifting effect in small doses and is also good for the digestion. Don't overdo it, though, because it can be hallucinogenic in large quantities.

Recommended for:
digestive *p.284*
stress *p.292*

Cinnamon

This excellent spice lends its delicate but distinctive flavour to dozens of minced meat and other dishes in Middle Eastern cookery. In Northern Europe it's one of the warming winter favourites used in festive puddings or mulled wine. Cinnamon is a potent antiseptic. It is also a tonic and a stimulant, warming the whole system and helping to combat the fatigue and listlessness that so often attend bouts of flu or other viral infections. Add a stick to the hot, sweet toddy you take to bed at the start of a cold.

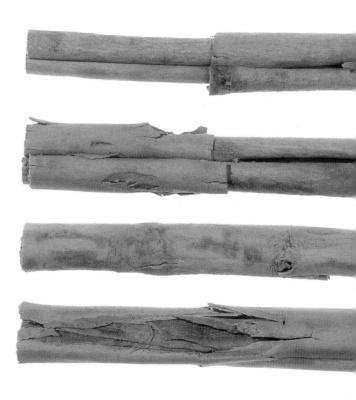

Recommended for:
digestive *p.284*
respiratory *p.312*

Chilli peppers

★ ★ ★ ★

These small, hot peppers are used fresh, or dried in the form of chilli powder or cayenne pepper. Chillis are popular wherever people like their food with a real kick to it. Nineteenth-century herbalists had boundless faith in the life-saving and restorative powers of chilli or cayenne pepper. They used teaspoon doses for typhoid and cholera patients in extremis. Research has confirmed the chilli pepper's beneficent effect on the heart and circulatory system. A shot of chilli or cayenne added to a hot drink is a sure boost to a sluggish digestion. Scientists have found that certain pungent foods, such as mustard, horseradish, chilli, and garlic, contain constituents called mucokinetic agents that help shift excess mucus from the lungs, so that it can be coughed up. Thus chillis and their derivatives also have a tonic effect on the respiratory system.

• •

Recommended for:
circulatory *p.278*
digestive *p.284*
respiratory *p.312*

Caraway

★★★★

A spice whose use dates from ancient times, caraway has been found in ancient Egyptian tombs and is mentioned in the Bible. Although it has long been popular in the cold northern European countries, caraway is also used in Indian cuisine, where the seeds are served as a digestive after the meal. Similarly, in Central Europe, caraway seeds are a well known aid to digestion – people often chew a few of them before sitting down to a rich meal. They are particularly effective for coping with wind or flatulence (as is dill, which contains the same compound, carvone). Add caraway seeds to potentially "windy" dishes, such as cabbage or beans.

• • • • • • • • • • • • • • • • • • •

Recommended for:
digestive *p.284*

Cloves

★★★★

Cloves come from a tropical evergreen tree and have been important in European culture ever since the spice routes opened up in the Middle Ages. The spiky whole cloves are actually dried, unopened flower buds. They have been used for centuries for purposes as diverse as flavouring foods, treating toothache, and freshening the breath.

Like cinnamon, cloves are both powerfully antiseptic and a warming boost to the circulation. They are used in much the same way as cinnamon, and like that spice, they can be added to dishes whole or can be ground into a powder first. Try adding a bruised clove or two to any herbal tea to provide an extra lift.

Recommended for:
digestive *p.284*
stress *p.292*
respiratory *p.312*

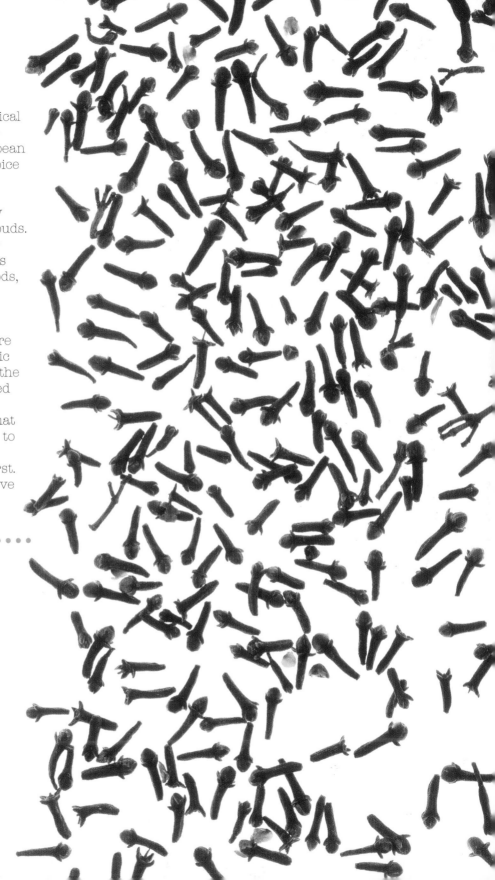

Cumin

★★★★

People often associate cumin with Indian curries, but the incomparable smell given off by the warmed, crushed seeds evokes Middle Eastern cookery, too. Cumin is also an important flavouring in Mexican cuisine and is an essential ingredient in many Mexican dishes. Like so many herbs and spices, cumin has a soothing effect on the digestive system, which is probably why it is mixed with yoghurt to make the cooling lassi drinks of Indian cuisine.

Use cumin in rich fried dishes or with beans to counter flatulence and dyspepsia. It has a special affinity with lamb dishes.

· · · · · · · · · · · · · · · · · · · ·

Recommended for:
digestive *p.284*

Coriander

Coriander is mentioned in Sanskrit writings and in the Bible. It was introduced into Europe by the ancient Romans, who found it useful as a preservative for meat. Today, we know coriander seed as an essential ingredient of curry powders. It is also added to cold starters cooked *à la grecque*. Powdered coriander seed adds a distinctive North African flavour to meat and fish dishes. In hot, stimulating food, this mild spice is valued for its cooling quality and its assistance to the digestion.

The chopped leaves also have a delicious, piquant flavour and are good added to a plain green salad. The fresh leaves also go well with cold cooked chicken.

Recommended for:
digestive *p.284*

Garlic

★★★★

The word garlic comes from two Anglo-Saxon words that together mean "spear leek". This name probably derived from the shape of the garlic plant's leaves, which are sharp and pointed.

Garlic is yet another food that was introduced to Britain by the Romans. The Roman soldiers used to put cloves of garlic between their toes in order to prevent fungal infections of the feet. In Britain, the plant was established in the wild from the cloves that dropped to the ground.

Garlic is not only a delicious flavouring for food, but it also has many health-giving properties. From ancient times right up to the end of the nineteenth century, garlic was the most frequently used medicinal plant throughout the world. All sorts of diseases and conditions, including bronchitis, asthma, indigestion, gout, and even (as the Romans apparently knew) athlete's foot, can be helped by garlic. It has antiviral, antibacterial, and antifungal properties, with virtually no side effects apart from irritation of the gut in some sensitive people.

The most exciting discovery about garlic so far, however, has been its effect on the heart and circulation. Like its close relative the onion (*p.66*), garlic has the ability to thin the blood. It contains the sulphur compound allicin, which helps the body eliminate cholesterol and also reduces the amount of unhealthy fats produced by the liver.

When, in studies, garlic was given to healthy volunteers who were fed diets rich in fatty foods, garlic reduced blood cholesterol by up to 15 per cent. In another study, people with high cholesterol levels who took garlic supplements – but did not otherwise change their diets – reduced their cholesterol levels by an average of 12 per cent over a four-month period.

· ·

Recommended for:
circulatory *p.278*
digestive *p.284*
joints *p.304*

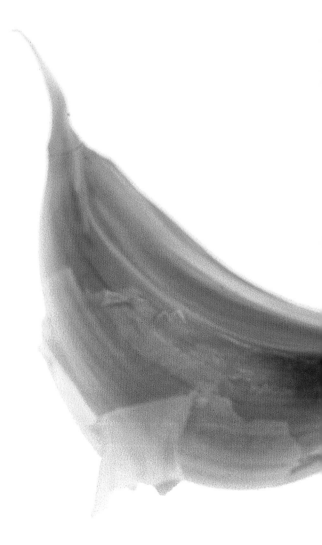

Ginger

★★★★

Ginger is another warming, antiseptic spice. It is widely used in the cookery of meat and fish in the East, where it helps counter putrefaction. It is equally popular as a sweet spice in the West. It is the tuberous root of a perennial plant found in tropical regions and should be peeled before slicing or grating.

It's far better to use the fresh root wherever possible, since dried ginger is poor stuff by comparison. Ginger aids digestion and is unexpectedly useful against nausea. In fact, clinical trials have shown it to be more effective than the standard drugs against motion sickness. Another benefit is that it has none of the side effects of conventional anti-nausea drugs, and pregnant women and children can use it safely. Fresh ginger grated into hot lemon and honey as a bedtime drink can stop a cold or chill in its tracks.

• • • • • • • • • • • • • • • • • • •

Recommended for:
digestive *p.284*
joints *p.304*

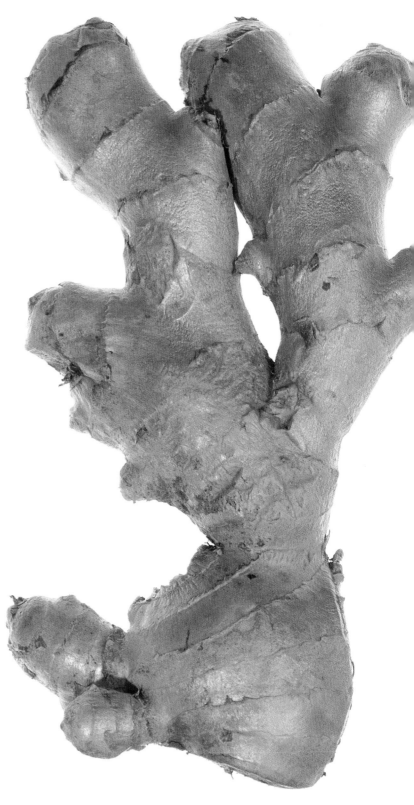

Horseradish

★★★★

Horseradish was originally a medicinal herb, but these days most of us know it only as a condiment made up in jars and eaten as a flavouring with roast beef. It deserves to be used more adventurously: try the fresh root grated into salad dressing, mayonnaise, or cottage cheese, or try adding a little horseradish to some natural yoghurt as a tangy accompaniment to smoked fish.

Horseradish is an invigorating herb and is powerfully stimulant to the digestion, which is a reason for eating it with rich foods, such as roast beef or oily fish. It also clears excess catarrh and counters infection. Since the volatile oil that gives horseradish its flavour is destroyed by heat, the herb should only be added fresh to food after cooking.

● ● ● ● ● ● ● ● ● ● ● ● ● ● ● ● ●

Recommended for:
digestive *p.284*

Brewer's yeast

★★★★

Although it is no longer quite the healthfood shop star of former days, brewer's yeast is still an unrivalled source of the B-complex vitamins, which serves many purposes: it helps to break down carbohydrates, proteins, and fats and supports the nervous system, among other functions. With particularly high levels of iron, zinc, manganese, magnesium, and potassium, brewer's yeast supplies protein, and is also high in chromium, which has been shown to help lower cholesterol and reduce blood sugar levels. It is rich in the nucleic acid RNA, which is vital to the immune system.

On its own, brewer's yeast does not taste agreeable, but spooned into your morning smoothie and blended with milk, yoghurt, and fruit juices, with a little honey, it registers as a pleasant, nutty flavour.

Since brewer's yeast is high in purines, it should be avoided by people with gout.

• • • • • • • • • • • • • • • • •

Recommended for:
circulatory *p.278*
stress *p.292*
fatigue *p.298*

Oils

Olive oil Like all cold-pressed vegetable oils, extra-virgin olive oil is extracted from the olives without the use of heat or chemicals, resulting in the purest possible finished product. Olive oil is the best digested of vegetable oils and provides the strongest stimulation of the gallbladder, an aid to all fat digestion.

Just two tablespoons of extra-virgin olive oil provides almost 90 per cent of monounsaturated fat and nearly 20 per cent of the vitamin E that you need for a whole day. The monounsaturated fats in olive oil help reduce cholesterol levels, and the oil acts as a strong antioxidant as well due to its high vitamin E content, protecting cells from damage. Some of the natural chemicals in olive oil prevent the absorption of cholesterol and increase the level of HDL (good) fat in the bloodstream. One study showed that adding two tablespoons of olive oil to the daily diet with no other dietary changes produced a significant fall in cholesterol levels.

Flaxseed oil Cold-pressed flaxseed oil is extremely rich in omega-3 fatty acids, especially alphalinolenic acid (ALA). Some people believe that flaxseed oil is as healthy as fish oils, as the ALA can be converted in the body into EPA – eicosapentaenoic acid. Not all people produce the enzyme necessary for this to happen, however. ALA is important as a balance to omega-6 fatty acids in the diet. Flaxseed oil turns rancid if exposed to heat, light, or air. Keep it in the refrigerator and use it well before its sell-by date. It's not suitable for frying or cooking, but it's perfect added to dressings, sauces, and marinades.

Recommended for:
cancer *p.264*
circulatory *p.278*

Honey

★★★★

Ancient societies used honey for energy and sweetening and as a preservative. To this day, milk and honey is a popular bedtime remedy for insomnia.

Traditionally, honey has been valued for both internal and external medicine, relieving coughs, stomachache, indigestion, and injuries. New Zealand Manuka honey is now widely used in hospitals as a sterile dressing for plastic surgery wounds and severe ulceration. It kills most bacteria, including the dreaded MRSA.

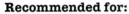

Recommended for:
digestive *p.284*
fatigue *p.298*
respiratory *p.312*

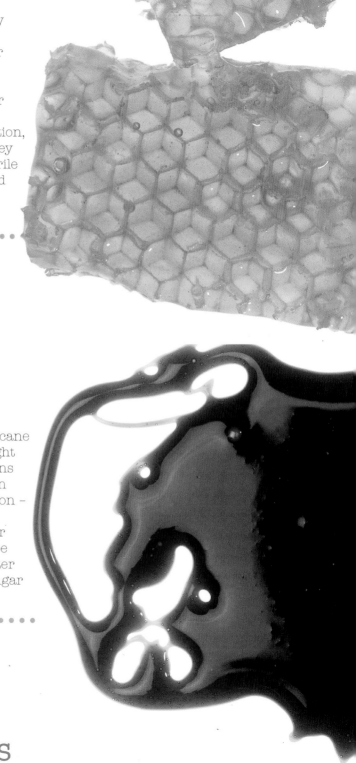

Molasses

★★★★

Molasses is the last extract from sugar cane when the sugar is refined out of it. Weight for weight, crude black molasses contains more calcium than milk, more iron than eggs – three milligrams in one tablespoon – and a very high level of potassium. It is also rich in many B vitamins. Its flavour is quite powerful. Molasses should not be eaten straight from the spoon as a matter of habit, however, because of its high sugar content – a risk to teeth and gums.

Recommended for:
stress *p.292*
fatigue *p.298*
joints *p.304*

Chocolate

★★★★

When the famous botanist Linnaeus came to name the cocoa tree, he called it *theobroma*, which means "food of the gods". He had good reason for this – a major constituent of the bean is a chemical called theobromine, which acts in the brain to trigger the release of natural feel-good chemicals called endorphins. These chemicals kindle feelings of romance, love, and arousal, and combat depression. Chocolate also contains caffeine, which is a stimulant that makes chocolate a mild diuretic.

Dark chocolate contains fat and provides 500 calories per 100g/3½oz serving. However, it also supplies iron, magnesium, useful amounts of protein, and traces of some other minerals, as well as some B vitamins. You'll need to do two hours of brisk walking, ride your bike for an hour and a half, or swim non-stop for a full hour to burn off a large chocolate bar.

• • • • • • • • • • • • • • • •

Recommended for:
stress *p.292*

Beer

★★★★

Beer is one of the best nutritional sources of silicon, which is essential for bones. As little as half a pint a day could help prevent osteoporosis, which causes more than 200,000 fractures every year, most of them in women.

There's more good news about beer, as recent research reveals that the hops used in traditional brewing are a good source of phytoestrogens, which are natural plant hormones that protect against osteoporosis. If you really want strong bones, next time you have a pub lunch order a ploughman's and a glass of beer. The calcium in the cheese and the phytoestrogens in the beer are perfect bone-builders.

Beer is also rich in vitamins B6 and B12 and folic acid, which many women lack in their diets. As a bonus, hops have a natural antibiotic action that kills the *Helicobacter pylori* bacterium, which is the cause of most gastric ulcers. With lots of potassium but little sodium, sensible quantities of beer can be good for blood pressure.

● ●

Recommended for:
circulatory *p.278*
digestive *p.284*

Red wine

★★★★

In most parts of the world, the drinker's toast is to their companion's good health – "à votre santé","salud", "skoal", "prost", "l'chayim" – and there are indeed some health benefits in drinking red wine. It's one of the factors in the Mediterranean diet that is known to protect against heart disease. Research done in France shows that men who drink moderate amounts of red wine regularly have a 30 per cent lower risk of death from all causes than either men who drink heavily or those who abstain from alcohol completely. This may be due at least in part to the natural antioxidants, known as phenolic compounds, that red grapes contain. These phenolic compounds are known to protect against heart and circulatory disease.

People who drink white wine in moderation may also be improving their health, as studies done in the US show that white wine drinkers have the healthiest lungs.

· · · · · · · · · · · · · · · · · ·

Recommended for:
circulatory *p.278*
respiratory *p.312*

Tea

★★★★

Nutritionally, tea contains very little in terms of vitamins and minerals. The leaves do contain tannins, which are good for eye problems – a used teabag dipped in cold water and placed over closed eyes for 10 minutes gives instant relief for sticky, itchy, and tired eyes.

By far the most exciting benefits of tea come from the bioflavonoids it contains. These natural plant chemicals, which act as antioxidants, neutralize the damaging free radicals that cause heart and circulatory problems. Two to four cups of tea a day are necessary for this extra protection, and although green tea is richer in protective substances, British brew also contains significant amounts. Green tea is the most cancer-protective of all teas.

Tea can even help concentration, and it's not the caffeine. There's another ingredient that helps concentration and speeds up the learning process, but we don't yet know what it is.

• • • • • • • • • • • • • • • • • •

Recommended for:
cancer *p.264*
circulatory *p.278*

Coffee

Coffee is known for containing caffeine, but there's also caffeine in tea, chocolate, and cola drinks. On the positive side, caffeine stimulates the brain, aids concentration, and fights fatigue. Surprisingly, coffee may also help some people with asthma, it increases the potency of painkillers, and may even improve migraine.

On the other hand, coffee can increase blood pressure in non-regular users by 10 per cent for three hours after consumption. Too much coffee is addictive. It is also linked to PMS, cyclical breast lumps, poor fertility, and low birth weight in babies.

Caffeine adversely affects the body's absorption of the minerals iron and zinc, so pregnant women and vegetarians should reduce the amount of coffee they drink. Coffee also stimulates the production of stomach acid, which can lead to heartburn and indigestion.

It's fine to enjoy a cup of good coffee, a pot of fragrant tea, or a mug of soothing cocoa, but limit the amount you drink to avoid caffeine addiction.

Recommended for:
fatigue *p.298*
respiratory *p.312*

134

Recipes

- ★ Soups and starters
- ★ Eggs and pasta
- ★ Seafood
- ★ Meat, chicken, and game
- ★ Grains and pulses
- ★ Vegetables
- ★ Snacks
- ★ Salads
- ★ Puddings
- ★ Drinks
- ★ Basic recipes

★ ★ ★ **Soup was probably** the very first recipe that followed the discovery of fire. From light broths to "stand the spoon up", they're comforting and nourishing as snacks, starters, or a one-pot meal.

Soups and starters

- ★ Pumpkin soup
- ★ Onion soup
- ★ Spanish white garlic soup
- ★ Borscht
- ★ Carrot soup
- ★ Jerusalem artichoke soup
- ★ Brown rice and celery soup
- ★ Verdant broth
- ★ Sweetcorn and haddock chowder
- ★ Oats and broccoli pottage
- ★ Watercress soup
- ★ Leek and cheese soup
- ★ White bean soup
- ★ Stilton soup
- ★ Fresh tomato soup

- ★ Cold cucumber and yoghurt soup
- ★ Vegetable and barley soup
- ★ Carrot, leek, and ginger soup
- ★ Florida cocktail
- ★ Artichoke vinaigrette
- ★ Avocado, walnut, and pear salad
- ★ Green and white pâté
- ★ Asparagus citronette
- ★ Classic crudités
- ★ Beetroots in white sauce
- ★ Pear and celery almondaise
- ★ Marinated mushrooms
- ★ Hummus plus

Pumpkin soup serves 4

DIGESTIVE *P.284* RESPIRATORY *P.312* SKIN *P.318*

750g/1½lb piece of pumpkin
1tsp olive oil
1 large onion, sliced
1 clove garlic, chopped
1 bay leaf
750ml/1¼pt vegetable stock
   (*p.261*)
2 carrots, finely grated
2tbs parsley, chopped
wholemeal garlic
   croutons (*p.254*)

Cut the pumpkin into wedges, skin and all, remove seeds and save them, put the pumpkin in an ovenproof dish, and bake for half an hour at 140°C/270°F/gas 1. Drain off the surplus water, which you save, and remove the skin. Heat the oil in a heavy-bottomed pan and sweat the onion, the garlic, and the bay leaf for a few minutes over a gentle heat. Add the stock, pumpkin and its water, and simmer for 30 minutes. Stir in the grated carrots, add the chopped parsley, check the seasoning, and serve with the croutons.

Onion soup serves 4

CIRCULATORY *P.278* RESPIRATORY *P.312* URINARY *P.324*

2 large onions
1tbs oil
900ml/1½pt vegetable stock
   (*p.261*)
fresh thyme
black pepper
½tsp salt-free yeast extract
4 slices wholemeal bread
125g/4oz grated Cheddar
   cheese

Peel and slice the onions, heat the oil in a heavy-bottomed pan, and sweat the onions until slightly golden. Add the stock, thyme, pepper, and yeast extract, bring to the boil, and simmer gently for 15–20 minutes. Pour the soup into flameproof bowls, if you have them, float the bread on top, sprinkle grated cheese on top of the bread, and put under a hot grill until melted.

Spanish white garlic soup serves 4

CANCER *P.264* CIRCULATORY *P.278* JOINTS *P.304* RESPIRATORY *P.312*

175g/6oz almonds, blanched
or ground
4 big cloves garlic, crushed
1 thick slice white bread,
    soaked in water and
    squeezed dry
100ml/3fl oz olive oil
100ml/3fl oz iced water
a little lemon juice
salt
a few peeled Muscat grapes,
    if in season

If you have fresh almonds, soak them in tepid water for 10 minutes, then the skins will slip off easily. Whole almonds should be ground in a food processor or coffee mill. Add the garlic and the bread to the ground almonds, and process thoroughly until smooth. Then add the olive oil drop by drop, as for a mayonnaise. Add the iced water until the soup is a thick cream. Add lemon juice, and salt to taste.

Traditionally this soup is served with a few peeled white Muscat grapes floating in it.

Borscht serves 4

CANCER *P.264* FATIGUE *P.298*

500g/1lb raw beetroot
30g/1oz butter
1tbs olive oil
1 medium-sized onion, sliced
2 carrots, peeled and sliced
2 sticks celery, chopped
1 small bulb fennel, chopped
1.2litre/2pt vegetable
    stock (*p.261*)
1tsp fresh thyme, chopped
1tbs fresh parsley, chopped
1 bay leaf
salt and pepper
juice of 1 lemon
1–2tbs natural yoghurt
wholemeal croutons (*p.254*)

Peel the beetroot and slice into thin strips. Heat the butter and oil in a heavy-bottomed pan, sweat the onion, then add the beetroot and the carrot, celery, and fennel. Sauté over a very low heat for a few minutes, and then add the stock and the herbs. Bring to the boil, turn the heat down, and simmer until the vegetables are soft – about 30 minutes.

Strain into another pan, purée the vegetables in a blender or food processor, return them to the soup, add the lemon juice, and seasoning to taste. Serve with a swirl of natural yoghurt in each bowl, and wholemeal croutons.

Carrot soup serves 4 ▶

CIRCULATORY *P.278* RESPIRATORY *P.312* SKIN *P.318*

375g/12oz old carrots
1 small onion
1 tbs olive oil
600ml/1pt vegetable stock
    (*p.261*)
juice of 3 oranges, and grated
    rind of 1 orange
a sprig of fresh mint
150g/5oz natural yoghurt

Clean and coarsely grate the carrots; clean and finely chop the onion. Heat the oil in a heavy-bottomed saucepan, add the carrots and onion, and cook very gently until the carrots are soft and mushy. Pour on the stock, add the mint, and leave to simmer for 20 minutes. Blend or liquidize, add the orange juice, and season to taste. Serve hot or cold with yoghurt and sprinkled with the grated orange rind.

Jerusalem artichoke soup serves 4

JOINTS *P.304* SKIN *P.318* CIRCULATORY *P.278* FATIGUE *P.298*

1 tbs vegetable oil
500g/1lb Jerusalem
    artichokes, thoroughly
    washed and sliced
1 medium-sized onion, finely
    chopped
900ml/1½pt vegetable stock
    (*p.261*)
1 small bunch watercress,
    washed and trimmed
wholemeal garlic croutons
    (*p.254*)
2 tbs fresh parsley, finely
    chopped
a little cream, if desired

Heat the oil, add the artichokes and onion, and sauté until the onion is just transparent, but not browned. Add the vegetable stock and simmer until the artichoke pieces are soft and tender. Put in a liquidizer or blender, together with the watercress, return to the pan, and reheat. Serve piping hot with wholemeal garlic croutons and sprinkled with chopped parsley. Add a swirl of cream for luxury.

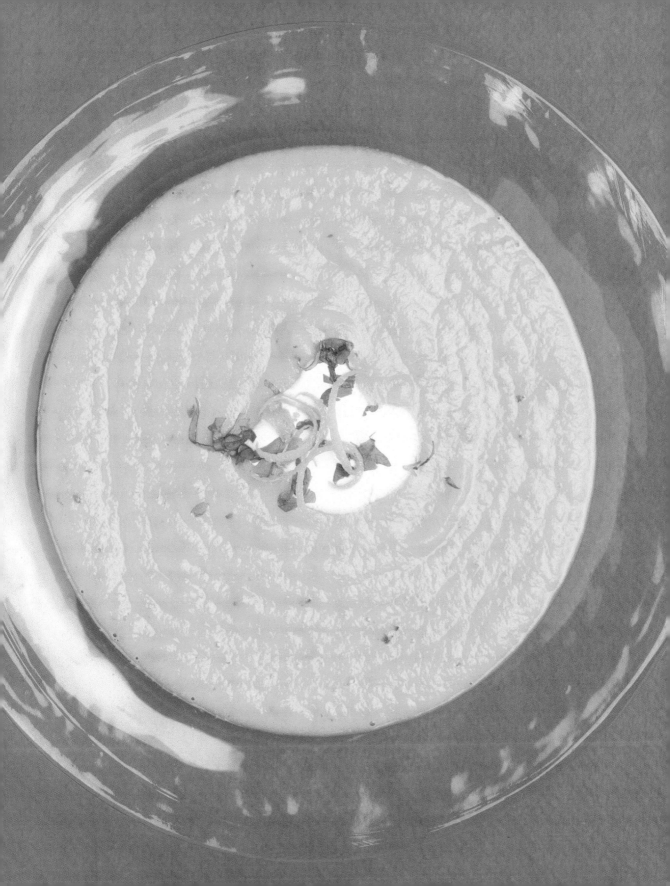

Brown rice and celery soup serves 4

CANCER *P.264* DIGESTIVE *P.284* FATIGUE *P.298* JOINTS *P.304* URINARY *P.324*

1litre/1¾pt vegetable stock
(*p.261*)
4 sticks celery, cleaned and
diced
2tbs olive oil
1 medium-sized onion,
finely chopped
30g/2oz brown rice, washed
and drained
salt and pepper
1tbs fresh parsley, chopped

Put the stock in a pan, add the diced celery, bring to the boil and simmer until the celery is soft. Strain off the stock and reserve. Purée the softened celery in a food processor or blender. In a clean pan, heat the oil, melt the onion; when it is transparent, add the rice, stir it around; add the celery purée, the vegetable stock, and season with salt and pepper to taste. Bring to the boil, and simmer until the rice is cooked through – about 35 minutes. Sprinkle with the parsley.

Verdant broth serves 4

CANCER *P.264* CIRCULATORY *P.278* JOINTS *P.304* SKIN *P.318* RESPIRATORY *P.312*

1 fat leek, washed, trimmed,
and sliced
1 head celery, washed,
trimmed, and sliced
1litre/1¾pt water
1tbs olive oil
1 large onion, sliced
1 bunch watercress
1 bunch parsley
1tbs olive oil
salt and pepper
wholemeal garlic
croutons (*p.254*)

Boil the water in a large pan. Put the cleaned green top of the leek and the top and tough outer leaves of the celery into the boiling water to make a stock. Simmer for 30 minutes, then discard the vegetables. Heat the oil, sauté the finely sliced white part of the leek and the sliced onion until translucent, but don't let them brown. Add the sliced celery and the stock, season with salt and pepper to taste, and simmer for half an hour. Then put in the food processor together with the watercress and parsley, both carefully cleaned. Serve this fresh-tasting broth with garlic croutons.

Sweetcorn and haddock chowder serves 4

CIRCULATORY *P.278* DIGESTIVE *P.284*

2tbs sunflower oil
90g/3oz streaky bacon, cut
   into strips
1 onion, chopped
1 bay leaf
a sprig of fresh thyme
2 medium-sized potatoes,
   peeled and diced
375g/12oz tin of sweetcorn,
   drained
300ml/½pt milk
300ml/½pt buttermilk
150ml/¼pt water
250g/8oz undyed smoked
   haddock, cut into 2.5cm/1in
   cubes, skinned and boned
1tbs fresh chives, chopped
salt and pepper

This is a one-pot meal. Keep the cooking time short by cutting the potatoes small so that they cook through in 10 minutes. Ideally they should crumble and thicken the soup.

Heat the oil, and fry the bacon until crisp. Remove and reserve. Fry the onion until softened but not brown, add the bay leaf, thyme, potato, sweetcorn, milk, buttermilk, and water. Simmer for 10 minutes, add the fish and chives, and simmer gently for a further 5 minutes. Season to taste with salt and pepper, and serve with the strips of bacon arranged over the top.

Oats and broccoli pottage serves 4

CANCER *P.264* CIRCULATORY *P.278*

1tbs olive oil
6 spring onions, chopped
500g/1lb broccoli florets
60g/2oz porridge oats
1litre/1¾pt half and half milk
   and vegetable stock (*p.261*)
freshly ground pepper
freshly ground nutmeg
1tbs single cream
1tbs fresh chives, chopped

Heat the oil and sweat the onions until they are soft. Add the broccoli and stir for a couple of minutes. Add the oats, and stir for another minute or two. Slowly add the milk and stock, stirring. Cover and simmer very gently for 10 minutes. Season with a little freshly ground pepper and nutmeg. Just before serving the soup, stir in the cream and sprinkle with the chopped chives.

Watercress soup serves 4

CANCER *P.264* FATIGUE *P.298* RESPIRATORY *P.312* URINARY *P.324*

1tbs olive oil
1 medium-sized onion,
   finely chopped
2 cloves garlic, finely chopped
1tsp curry powder
3 bunches watercress,
   thoroughly washed, with
   stalks remaining
900ml/1½pt vegetable stock
   (*p.261*)
salt and freshly ground
   black pepper
small carton of fromage frais

Heat the oil, sweat the onion until soft, add the garlic, and cook for 1 minute. Add the curry powder and cook for another minute, stirring vigorously. Turn down the heat, add the watercress, and stir for 2 minutes until it wilts. Add the stock, season with salt and pepper to taste, and simmer for 10 minutes. Liquidize and serve hot with a swirl of fromage frais in each dish. Alternatively, this soup is delicious served chilled as a summer starter.

Leek and cheese soup serves 4

CIRCULATORY *P.278* DIGESTIVE *P.284* RESPIRATORY *P.312* URINARY *P.324*

500g/1lb leeks
30g/1oz butter
30g/1oz wholemeal flour
400ml/scant ¾pt chicken
   stock
300ml/½pt milk
90g/3oz soft cheese –
   perhaps Boursin with herbs
   – cut into small pieces
1tbs fresh dill, finely chopped
salt and pepper

Wash, trim, and finely slice the leeks. Heat the butter and sauté the leeks until they are soft. Stir in the flour and cook for a couple of minutes. Add the chicken stock and milk. Cover, and simmer for about 15 minutes, then put in a blender or food processor, and blend until smooth. Transfer back to the pan, add the cheese, and heat until it has melted. Stir in the dill, season with salt and pepper to taste, and serve immediately.

White bean soup serves 4

CIRCULATORY *P.278* FATIGUE *P.298*

8tbs extra-virgin olive oil
1-2 cloves garlic, chopped
1.2kg/2½lbs tinned
   cannellini beans, drained
   and rinsed
salt
freshly ground black pepper
125ml/4fl oz tinned
   concentrated beef
   consommé, diluted in water
   to make 250ml/8fl oz
   stock
2tbs fresh parsley,
   finely chopped

This recipe comes from Marcella Hazan's beautiful book, *The Essentials of Classic Italian Cooking*. This soup is almost solid enough to serve as a side dish, but if you'd like it thinner, just add a little more stock or water.

Put the oil and garlic in a soup pot on a medium heat. Sauté until the garlic is a very pale gold. Add the beans, and salt and pepper to taste. Cover and then simmer gently for 5-6 minutes.

Take a teacupful of beans from the pot and purée them through a mouli or food processor. Return to the pot, add the stock, and simmer for another 5-6 minutes. Taste, correct for salt and pepper, swirl in the parsley, and turn off the heat.

Stilton soup serves 4

FATIGUE *P.298*

1tbs olive oil
1 large onion, finely chopped
2 sticks celery, finely
   chopped
1 large potato or 3-4 small
   ones, peeled and diced
900ml/1½pt water
150ml/¼pt white wine
250g/8oz Stilton
150ml/¼pt single cream
1tbs fresh parsley, finely
   chopped

Heat the oil in a big pan, add the onion and celery, and sauté until they are just beginning to soften. Add the potato, water, and wine, and cook until the vegetables are done - about 15 minutes. Crumble in the Stilton, and heat through until it has melted into the soup. Then stir in the cream, reheat, and serve sprinkled with the parsley. Don't add salt - the Stilton will make the dish salty enough.

Fresh tomato soup serves 4

CANCER *P.264* CIRCULATORY *P.278* RESPIRATORY *P.312* SKIN *P.318*

1 medium-sized onion,
   finely chopped
2-3 cloves garlic, chopped
3tbs olive oil
750g/1½lb tomatoes, peeled
   and quartered
900ml/1½pt vegetable
   stock (*p.261*)
2-3 thick slices stale
   wholemeal bread with
   crusts removed
salt and pepper
1tbs ready-made pesto

Make this in summer when you can find beautifully ripe, red tomatoes that are full of flavour.

Sauté the onion and garlic in the olive oil. When they are translucent, add the tomatoes, and cook over a moderate heat until they melt. Add the vegetable stock, cook for 4-5 minutes, add the bread, coarsely crumbled, and cook for another 2-3 minutes. Season with salt and pepper to taste, and serve tepid, with the pesto.

Cold cucumber and yoghurt soup serves 4

DIGESTIVE *P.284* FATIGUE *P.298* SKIN *P.318* URINARY *P.324*

1 medium-sized cucumber
salt
300ml/½pt natural yoghurt
1 clove garlic, finely chopped
1tsp white wine vinegar
1tbs fresh dill, chopped
salt and pepper
2tsp olive oil
1tsp lemon juice

Peel the cucumber, slice it paper-thin, and put to drain in a colander with a little salt sprinkled over it. After 10 minutes, rinse it and put it in a blender or food processor with the yoghurt, garlic, vinegar, and dill. Blend thoroughly. Season to taste with salt and pepper, and chill. Serve with the oil and lemon juice dribbled over the surface.

Vegetable and barley soup serves 4

CANCER *P.264* CIRCULATORY *P.278* DIGESTIVE *P.284* JOINTS *P.304* RESPIRATORY *P.312* SKIN *P.318* STRESS *P.292* URINARY *P.324*

3 sticks celery
2 large carrots
3–4 green cabbage leaves,
    finely shredded
1 large leek
1 small turnip
2 large onions
1tbs olive oil
1 bay leaf
2tbs pot barley, well washed
1litre/1¾pt vegetable stock
    (*p.261*)
black pepper
1tbs fresh parsley, chopped

Clean and chop the vegetables, using the celery leaves as well as the sticks. Chop one onion and a little of the celery and leek very finely and soften in the oil in a large pan. Add the remaining vegetables to the pan along with the bay leaf and the barley. Add the vegetable stock, season with the black pepper, and bring to the boil, stirring well. Allow to simmer covered until the vegetables are soft – about 45 minutes. Serve sprinkled with fresh parsley.

Carrot, leek, and ginger soup serves 4

CANCER *P.264* STRESS *P.292* CIRCULATORY *P.278* SKIN *P.318* RESPIRATORY *P.312*

2 large leeks
2 large carrots
1tbs olive oil
2.5cm/1in piece fresh
    ginger, peeled
900ml/1½pt vegetable stock
    (*p.261*)
1 bay leaf
2tbs single cream
1tbs fresh coriander, chopped

Clean and finely slice the leeks, including some of the green part; scrub and thinly slice the carrots. Heat the oil and melt the leeks, but on no account let them change colour. Add the carrots, stir, grate in the peeled ginger, add the stock and the bay leaf. Bring to the boil and simmer for 30 minutes. Remove the bay leaf and purée the soup in a blender or food processor. Reheat and serve in individual bowls with a swirl of cream and a sprinkling of chopped fresh coriander.

Florida cocktail serves 4

CIRCULATORY *P.278* DIGESTIVE *P.284* FATIGUE *P.298* RESPIRATORY *P.312*

1 orange
1 pink grapefruit
2 kiwifruit
1 small bunch white grapes
juice of a big juicy orange
juice of half a lemon
a sprig of mint

Peel the orange, the grapefruit, and the kiwifruit. Wash, halve, and de-pip the grapes. Split the oranges and grapefruit into segments, divide between four serving glasses, cut the kiwifruit into wedges, and add them to the glasses, with the grapes. Add the orange and lemon juice and then decorate with mint leaves.

Artichoke vinaigrette serves 4

CIRCULATORY *P.278* DIGESTIVE *P.284* JOINTS *P.304* SKIN *P.318*

4 medium-sized globe
    artichokes
juice of half a lemon
4tbs olive oil
1tbs tarragon vinegar
black pepper
4 spring onions, finely
    chopped
a pinch of dried mixed herbs
1 clove garlic, finely chopped

Clean the artichokes by soaking them pointed end downwards in cold water for 30 minutes and then shaking the water off. Trim off the stalks to just below the base (if they're small, young artichokes, you can leave a bit more of the stalk), and cook them in a big pan of boiling water – to which you have added the juice of half a lemon – until you can easily slide a sharp knife into them. Drain pointed end downwards. Beat together the oil, vinegar, and the other ingredients to make the vinaigrette. Serve the artichokes cold, with the vinaigrette as a dip.

NOTE: This vegetable is eaten with the fingers. Starting at the outside, pull off a leaf, dip the thick end into the vinaigrette, chew the goodness out of it, and discard it. Smaller leaves near the middle may be eaten whole. In the very middle is the hairy choke, which should be removed with a knife. You can now enjoy the grey-green heart beneath. Provide napkins, fingerbowls, and side dishes to dispose of the leaves.

Avocado, walnut, and pear salad serves 4

FATIGUE *P.298* STRESS *P.292* SKIN *P.318*

1 bunch watercress
2 avocados, peeled and stoned
2 firm, ripe pears, washed,
    cored, and sliced
juice of half a lemon
60g/2oz walnuts
2tbs walnut oil
salt and pepper

Wash, dry, and trim the watercress; arrange it on four plates. On top, put alternate slices of the avocados and pears. Sprinkle a little of the lemon juice over them to keep their colour fresh. Divide the walnuts between the plates, and scatter them over the top. Mix together the oil, the rest of the lemon juice, the salt and pepper, and pour over.

Green and white pâté serves 4

JOINTS *P.304*

1tbs vegetable oil
250g/8oz leeks, cleaned
    and sliced
juice of 1 lemon
250g/8oz celeriac, peeled
    and diced
250g/8oz fresh spinach – or
    use frozen spinach
salt and pepper, freshly
    ground
2tbs fresh chives, chopped
½tsp ground nutmeg
250g/8oz low-fat soft cheese
1tbs powdered gelatine
lamb's lettuce and red
    radicchio garnish

Grease and line a 600ml/1pt loaf tin. Heat the oil and soften the leeks for 5 minutes. Drain on kitchen paper, purée in a food processor, and set aside to cool. Boil a big pan of water, add the lemon juice to it, and cook the celeriac for 5 minutes, until soft. Drain, purée, and cool. If using fresh spinach, squeeze out all the moisture; if using frozen, heat gently in a pan until it defrosts. Drain and squeeze out excess water. Cool. Season the purées with salt and freshly ground black pepper. Stir chives into the leek purée, and nutmeg into the spinach. Divide the cheese into three and beat one-third into each purée. Dissolve the gelatine in 3 tablespoons of hot water. Cool slightly. Stir 1 tablespoon of the liquid into each purée. Spread the leek purée in the base and top with the celeriac, then the spinach. Chill for at least half an hour, then turn out onto a serving plate and garnish with the salad leaves. Serve with hot toast.h

Asparagus citronette serves 4 ▶

DIGESTIVE *P.284* URINARY *P.324*

500g/1lb asparagus
3tbs extra-virgin olive oil
juice of a big lemon
black pepper

Wash the asparagus thoroughly and trim off the tough bottoms of the stalks: do not discard these, as you can use them for soup together with the asparagus cooking water. An asparagus steamer gives the best results, but failing that, cook them lying flat in boiling water in a deep, wide frying pan – or even a wok. They are done when you can easily pierce the fleshiest part of the stems with a knife. Drain – saving the water – and set aside to cool. To make the dressing, combine the oil, lemon juice, and pepper in a jug.

NOTE: To make asparagus soup from the stock and trimmings, put the cut-off ends – all but the really dirty ones – into the cooking water. Add 2-3 small, peeled potatoes and 1 whole spear of asparagus. Bring to the boil, simmer until the potatoes are done, liquidize, and serve with a swirl of low-fat natural yoghurt.

Classic crudités serves 4

CANCER *P.264* DIGESTIVE *P.284* FATIGUE *P.298* RESPIRATORY *P.312* SKIN *P.318*

6-10 radishes, washed
2 carrots, peeled
4-6 young beetroots,
   washed
2-3 sticks celery, washed
juice of half a lemon
1tbs olive oil
1tbs fresh parsley, chopped

In French restaurants, crudités can run to a dozen different dishes. The classics are fresh radishes with their green tops; raw carrots, peeled and grated; grated raw young beetroot; and chunks of crisp celery. All of these may be served with a lemon and olive oil dressing, with a sprinkling of fresh parsley on top.

Beetroots in white sauce serves 4

CANCER *P.264* CIRCULATORY *P.278* FATIGUE *P.298*

12 raw baby beetroots
  – allow 3 per person
2tbs cider vinegar
30g/1oz butter
1 heaped tbs plain white flour
a pinch of white pepper
a pinch of nutmeg
600ml/1pt skimmed milk

Rinse the beetroots clean – don't scrub too hard or they will bleed – then top and tail, leaving a little of the leaf-top and the stem. Put in a pan, cover with water, add the cider vinegar, bring to the boil, and simmer for about 30 minutes. Meanwhile, prepare the sauce. Melt the butter in a heavy-bottomed saucepan until froth subsides; do not allow to brown. Add the flour and stir briskly into a thick paste with a wooden spoon; continue stirring for another couple of minutes. Add a pinch of white pepper and nutmeg. Heat the milk and add it, a little at a time over a gentle heat, to the paste. Stir continuously, until there are no lumps. When the sauce comes to the boil, continue stirring until it thickens. Remove from the heat and cover. Drain the beetroots, and very carefully, holding them in a thick bunch of kitchen paper, remove the skins. Arrange in a white china dish, and pour the sauce over. Serve immediately.

Pear and celery almondaise serves 4

FATIGUE *P.298* JOINTS *P.304* SKIN *P.318*

4 sticks celery
500g/1lb pears
1tbs lemon juice
90g/3oz cucumber, peeled
  and chopped
60g/2oz ground almonds
1tbs olive oil
a few walnuts
lettuce leaves

Trim the celery – save the leaves – and cut into chunks. Chop up the leaves and set aside. Peel, core, and chop up the pears. Put lemon juice, cucumber, and ground almonds into a food processor and blend until well mixed. Beat in the oil a little at a time, mix the celery and pear together, and toss in the dressing. Line a salad bowl with lettuce leaves, put in the mixture, and garnish with walnuts and chopped celery leaves.

Marinated mushrooms serves 4

CANCER *P.264* STRESS *P.292*

2tbs olive oil
1 medium-sized onion, sliced
3 cloves garlic, crushed
300ml/½pt red wine
2tbs lemon juice
1tsp runny honey
¼tsp ground black pepper
½tsp ground coriander
2 large tomatoes, skinned
   and chopped
375g/12oz button mushrooms
1tbs fresh parsley, chopped

In a large, heavy-bottomed saucepan, heat the olive oil and sweat the onion until transparent. Add the garlic and cook for 2 minutes. Add the red wine, lemon juice, honey, black pepper, coriander, and tomatoes. Bring to the boil and simmer for 5 minutes. Add the mushrooms and continue to simmer until soft. Put in a bowl, marinate in the fridge for 4 hours or overnight. Serve with a sprinkling of fresh chopped parsley.

Hummus plus serves 4

CANCER *P.264* DIGESTIVE *P.284* FATIGUE *P.298* SKIN *P.318*

125g/4oz soaked chickpeas
juice of 2 lemons
3tbs tahini (sesame
   seed paste)
2 garlic cloves, crushed
sea salt
2tbs extra-virgin olive oil
¼tsp paprika

Serve this famous Middle Eastern chickpea dip with wholemeal pitta bread and olives. At a pinch, it can be made with chickpeas out of a tin, but dried chickpeas taste much better. Wash the chickpeas and soak in a big bowl of water the night before, or 6–8 hours before you need them. Drain and put in a big pan of fresh water, bring to the boil and simmer for about an hour, or until soft. Drain, saving the cooking water. Put in a blender or food processor with a little of their cooking liquid, gradually adding enough to make a thick paste. Add the lemon juice, tahini, and the garlic. Season with sea salt to taste. Serve with a swirl of olive oil over the surface and a sprinkling of paprika. Cover and chill. Accompany with hot pitta bread, a bowl of mixed black and green olives, and radishes complete with their leaves.

★ ★ ★ **For speed, variety, nutrition, and value,** nothing compares with eggs and pasta.

Eggs and pasta

- ★ Tomato and herb omelette

- ★ Eggs with smoked haddock

- ★ Tuna and fennel pasta

- ★ Red and yellow eggs

- ★ Eggs Mornay

- ★ Tuna and black olive sauce

- ★ Eggs tonnato

- ★ Pasta pesto with vegetables

- ★ Tagliatelle with artichokes

- ★ Green pasta salad

- ★ Pasta shells with broccoli

- ★ Meatball and tomato sauce

Tomato and herb omelette serves 1 ▶

DIGESTIVE *P.284* FATIGUE *P.298* RESPIRATORY *P.312*

1 medium-sized tomato
1tbs olive oil
3 free-range eggs
2tbs fresh herbs, chopped –
    parsley, chives, chervil
salt and pepper

Omelettes are best made one at a time, although two people can share a big one. These quantities make one good-sized omelette, for 2 people, you can double the quantities, but use 5 rather than 6 eggs.

Skin the tomato – dip it in boiling water for a couple of minutes, then the skin slides off easily. Chop it. Beat the eggs in a bowl, then add the chopped tomatoes, the herbs – save a sprinkle for garnishing – and seasoning. Have a hot plate ready. Heat the oil. When it is sizzling hot, tip in the egg mixture. With a fork, keep lifting the edges so that the uncooked egg on top can run underneath. The whole operation should take less than a minute, and the egg should still be slightly runny on top when you roll the omelette out onto the plate. Sprinkle with the remaining herbs and serve at once.

Eggs with smoked haddock serves 2

CIRCULATORY *P.278* FATIGUE *P.298*

175g/6oz smoked haddock –
    avoid the lurid yellow kind
150ml/¼pt milk
4 free-range eggs
freshly ground black pepper
1tbs butter

Cook the haddock in the milk for 2–3 minutes, then strain and save the milk. Flake the haddock, discarding skin and bones, and keep it hot. Beat the eggs with 2 tablespoons of the fishy milk, and season with a little pepper, but don't add salt. Melt the butter in a non-stick pan. Add the eggs, and stir briskly off the heat. Just before the eggs set, add the flaked haddock and stir it in. Serve with hot wholewheat toast. If you wish to serve 4 peoplé, simply double the quantities.

Tuna and fennel pasta serves 4

CIRCULATORY *P.278* FATIGUE *P.298* JOINTS *P.304* SKIN *P.318* URINARY *P.324*

200g/7oz tuna, tinned in oil
1 large fennel bulb
1 tbs olive oil
2 cloves garlic, chopped
125ml/4fl oz vegetable stock
   (p.261)
375g/12oz spaghettini

Drain the oil from the tuna. Clean the fennel, chop up, including most of the feathery fronds, and mince in a food processor. Heat the oil in a saucepan, add the garlic and minced fennel, and fry gently until soft. Flake in the tuna, add the vegetable stock, and heat through. Meanwhile, cook the spaghettini in lots of boiling water until *al dente* (just tender). Drain, and quickly toss in the hot fennel and tuna sauce.

Red and yellow eggs serves 2

FATIGUE *P.298* URINARY *P.324*

1 large red pepper
1 large yellow pepper
1 medium-sized onion
3–4 ripe red tomatoes
60g/2oz butter
6 free-range eggs
salt and freshly ground
   black pepper
1 tbs fresh parsley, chopped

Halve the peppers, remove the ribs and seeds, and slice into fat strips. Finely chop the onion. Skin and roughly chop the tomatoes. Heat the butter in a non-stick pan. Add the peppers and onion and stew gently, covered, until they are softened, or for about 10 minutes. Stir in the tomatoes, and cook for about another 5 minutes. Beat the eggs, season with salt and pepper, and add the parsley. Add to the vegetable mixture, and stir until the eggs are just set.

Eggs Mornay serves 4

FATIGUE *P.298* URINARY *P.324*

Sauce Mornay (*p.260*)
1tbs butter
4 free-range eggs
1tbs grated Cheddar or other
   sharp cheese

Prepare the Sauce Mornay in advance. Heat the oven to 190°C/375°F/gas 5. Butter a heatproof casserole, break the 4 eggs carefully into it, and top with the Sauce Mornay. Sprinkle the cheese on top and bake in the oven for 5 minutes.

Tuna and black olive sauce serves 4

CIRCULATORY *P.278* JOINTS *P.304*

Tomato sauce (*p.255*)
200g/7oz tuna, tinned in oil
8–10 pitted black olives
salt and pepper
250g/8oz pasta, any shape

Make the tomato sauce. Add the tuna, drained of its oil, and the olives. Season to taste with salt and pepper, and heat through. Meanwhile, cook the pasta in a large pot of boiling water until *al dente* (just tender). Drain the pasta, stir in the sauce, and serve.

Eggs tonnato serves 4

CIRCULATORY *P.278* FATIGUE *P.298*

4 free-range eggs
200g/7oz tuna, tinned in oil
6tbs mayonnaise
1 small onion, finely chopped
2tbs fresh parsley, chopped
salt and pepper

This can be either a substantial starter or a light meal in itself. In the latter case, you may wish to use a few more eggs.

Hard-boil the eggs for 10 minutes. Peel the eggs, halve them, and arrange them face-down in a flat salad bowl. Drain the tuna, flake it, and add to the mayonnaise. Stir in the onion and 1 tablespoon of the parsley – save a little to garnish. Season to taste with salt and pepper. Spoon the mayonnaise over the eggs, and sprinkle with the rest of the parsley.

Pasta pesto with vegetables serves 4 ▶

CIRCULATORY *P.278* DIGESTIVE *P.284* STRESS *P.292* FATIGUE *P.298*

1 tsp salt
300g/10oz spaghetti
60g/2oz French beans,
    cleaned and finely chopped
60g/2oz new potatoes, peeled
    and finely diced
60g/2oz courgettes, cleaned
    and diced
2–3tbs pesto sauce
a few fresh basil leaves
Parmesan cheese, grated

To prepare the sauce, you can use ready-made pesto, available in jars.

Heat a large pan of water. When it boils, add the salt, and plunge in the spaghetti and the vegetables. By the time the pasta is cooked *al dente* (just tender), the vegetables should also be just tender. Just before you drain the spaghetti, take a tablespoon of the cooking water and stir it into the pesto. Drain the pasta and vegetables, and quickly transfer them to a hot dish. Stir in the pesto and toss. Garnish with the basil leaves and serve. Have a little grated Parmesan cheese ready for those who want it.

Tagliatelle with artichokes serves 4

CANCER *P.264* DIGESTIVE *P.284* FATIGUE *P.298* SKIN *P.318* URINARY *P.324*

2tbs butter
1 medium-sized onion,
    finely chopped
1tbs plain flour
glass of dry white wine
1 425g/14oz tin or jar of
    artichoke hearts, quartered
2tbs fresh parsley, chopped
2 heaped tbs of grated
    Parmesan
500g/1lb tagliatelle or
    other pasta

Traditionally, this recipe is made with fresh baby artichokes, but it can also be made with artichoke hearts packed in oil and sold in jars.

Heat the butter in a large saucepan and melt the onion without browning it. Add the flour and stir vigorously for 1–2 minutes. Drizzle in the wine and carry on stirring. Add the artichoke hearts and parsley, simmer, covered, until heated through – about 5 minutes. Add half the cheese, mix thoroughly, and keep warm. Boil a large pan of water and cook the pasta until *al dente* (just tender). Drain the pasta and put it in a large heated dish. Add the sauce, stir through quickly, and serve with the rest of the Parmesan.

Spaghetti con aglio e olio serves 4

CIRCULATORY *P.278* JOINTS *P.304* URINARY *P.324* FATIGUE *P.298*

4tbs extra-virgin olive oil
3 cloves garlic, chopped
½tsp dried red chilli pepper,
  finely chopped
pinch of salt
500g/1lb spaghetti or
  spaghettini
2 heaped tbs parsley, chopped

Heat the olive oil in a small pan and sauté the garlic and the chilli pepper until the garlic is just beginning to change colour. Turn off the heat and add a little salt. Put a big serving dish to warm. Cook the pasta in plenty of well-salted, boiling water. Stir occasionally and cook until the pasta is *al dente* (just tender). Drain, turn into the warmed serving dish, and add the sauce. Sprinkle the parsley over, toss, and serve immediately.

Green pasta salad serves 4

CANCER *P.264* CIRCULATORY *P.278* JOINTS *P.304* RESPIRATORY *P.312* SKIN *P.318*

2 very young, tender
  courgettes
4 spring onions
250g/8oz green fusilli or any
  other green pasta
handful of mangetout peas
3-5 baby sweetcorns
2tbs fresh parsley, chopped
3tbs extra-virgin olive oil
juice of a large lemon
seasoning to taste
oakleaf lettuce

Wash and grate the courgettes without peeling them. Wash and coarsely chop the spring onions. Boil a saucepan of water and cook the pasta until it is *al dente* (just tender). Drain and return to the pan. Add the olive oil and lemon juice, the courgettes, chopped spring onions, mangetout peas, and baby sweetcorn. Toss, turn into a dish lined with oakleaf lettuce leaves, sprinkle with the chopped parsley, and serve at once.

Pasta shells with broccoli serves 4

CANCER *P.264* CIRCULATORY *P.278* RESPIRATORY *P.312* SKIN *P.318*

375g/12oz fresh broccoli
4tbs olive oil
squeeze of anchovy paste
generous pinch of chilli
    powder – or a deseeded,
    chopped-up, small chilli,
    according to preference
black pepper, freshly milled
375g/12oz pasta shells or
    other pasta
a big nut of butter
3tbs Parmesan cheese, grated

Put plenty of water on to boil for the pasta. Wash the broccoli and break into small florets. Cook in boiling water until tender – 5–6 minutes. Drain. Heat the oil in a large frying pan, and add the anchovy paste and the chilli or chilli powder. Add the broccoli, sprinkle with pepper, and sauté for 5 minutes. Keep the sauce warm while you cook the pasta. When it's ready, drain, return to the saucepan, add the butter and cheese, and toss. Turn into a warmed dish, add the sauce, and fold in quickly.

Meatball and tomato sauce serves 4

CANCER *P.264* FATIGUE *P.298*

500g/1lb minced beef
3 cloves garlic, chopped
1tbs chopped fresh mint
1tbs chopped fresh parsley
salt and black pepper
1 egg
2tbs olive oil
Tomato sauce (*p.255*)

This is an American-style recipe that turns spaghetti into a substantial meal.

Mix together the minced beef, garlic, fresh herbs, and salt and pepper. Break the egg into the mixture and mix it up with your hands. Form the mixture into meatballs the size of table-tennis balls. Heat the oil in a frying pan and fry the meatballs gently for 7–10 minutes. When they are cooked through, add them to the tomato sauce, and serve with spaghetti, cooked until it is just tender.

★ ★ ★ **Eat fish for your brains,** said the old wives, and how right they were. White fish, oily fish, pink fish, yellow fish, little fish, big fish, and even shellfish – the more you eat, the healthier you'll be.

Seafood

- ★ Big Macks
- ★ Haddock and broccoli au gratin
- ★ Grilled garlicky gambas
- ★ Salmon with green sauce
- ★ Sardines with mustard sauce
- ★ Herrings in oatmeal
- ★ Herb-coated sea bass
- ★ Prawn, broccoli, and leek stir-fry

- ★ Peppered fish with vinaigrette
- ★ Baked fish provençal
- ★ Salmon en papillote
- ★ Far-Eastern fish
- ★ Grilled red mullet
- ★ Marinated fish
- ★ Prawn and tomato curry
- ★ Cod with sesame and spinach

Big Macks serves 4

CIRCULATORY *P.278* FATIGUE *P.298* JOINTS *P.304* URINARY *P.324*

250g/8oz cooked mackerel or
  mackerel tinned in brine
175g/6oz mashed potato
30g/1oz butter
2-3 spring onions, cleaned
  and chopped
1tbs fresh parsley, chopped
1tbs milk or vegetable
  stock (*p.261*)
1tbs fine oatmeal
2tbs vegetable oil
watercress and tomatoes
  to garnish

Skin and bone the mackerel. Flake, and mix with the mashed potatoes and melted butter. Add the spring onions. If the mixture is very stiff, moisten with a little milk or stock. Shape into burgers and chill for at least half an hour.

When you are ready to eat, dust the burgers with oatmeal and fry until golden brown on both sides. Drain on kitchen paper. Serve with watercress and slices of tomato. Big Macks can also be eaten cold, in a wholemeal bun or bap, with cress and slices of cucumber.

Haddock and broccoli au gratin serves 4

CIRCULATORY *P.278* DIGESTIVE *P.284* JOINTS *P.304* FATIGUE *P.298*

500g/1lb broccoli
30g/1oz butter
30g/1oz plain white flour
450ml/¾pt milk
125g/4oz grated Cheddar
salt and pepper
750g/1½lb haddock fillets,
  skinned

Steam the broccoli until barely tender. Melt the butter and stir in the flour. Add the milk, heated to near boiling point, stir, and bring to the boil. Add half the cheese, and a little salt and pepper. Butter an ovenproof casserole dish, put in the broccoli, lay the haddock fillets on top, and pour over the cheese sauce. Sprinkle with the rest of the cheese. Heat the oven to 180°C/350°F/gas 4, for 30-40 minutes, when the top should be golden and bubbling.

Grilled garlicky gambas serves 4

CANCER *P.264* CIRCULATORY *P.278* STRESS *P.292* RESPIRATORY *P.312* SKIN *P.318*

16–20 big Pacific prawns in
   their shells (fresh are best,
   but if you do use frozen,
   thaw them thoroughly and
   blot completely dry)
3–4 large cloves garlic
2tbs olive oil
lettuce leaves for garnish
chunks of lemon for serving

Wash and dry the prawns if fresh. Chop the garlic up very small, put in a small bowl, and add the olive oil. Marinate for a couple of hours. Turn the grill on high, use a pastry brush to paint the prawns with the garlicky oil, and grill until the shells are almost burned. Serve on a bed of lettuce, with chunks of lemon to squeeze over them.

Salmon with green sauce serves 2

CANCER *P.264* CIRCULATORY *P.278* RESPIRATORY *P.312*

2 150g/5oz fresh salmon
   steaks
½ thick slice of wholewheat
   bread with crusts removed
2tbs lemon juice
1 clove garlic, finely chopped
2tbs pine nuts
2tbs fresh parsley, finely
   chopped
2tbs fresh basil, finely
   chopped (if no basil, use
   all parsley)
yolk of 1 hard-boiled
   egg, mashed
175ml/6fl oz extra-virgin
   olive oil
a sprig of fresh parsley
   to garnish

To make the sauce: soak the bread in the lemon juice for 10 minutes. Mash it up in a mixing bowl. Add the garlic, pine nuts, parsley, basil, and mashed egg yolk. Combine and mash with a fork. Dribble in the oil a little at a time, beating as you do so. Leave to stand for at least an hour before you need it, so that the flavours can mingle. (You can also make the sauce in a blender or food processor: put in the ingredients except the oil, blend them together very lightly, then add the oil first in a trickle and then in a steady stream with the blades running.) When you're ready to eat, brush the steaks with a little olive oil on each side and heat under a red-hot grill until just forming a crust on each side and turning brown at the edges. Serve on hot plates and spoon the sauce around, but not over, the steaks. Garnish with parsley, and serve with boiled new potatoes.

Sardines with mustard sauce serves 4

CANCER *P.264* CIRCULATORY *P.278* STRESS *P.292* JOINTS *P.304* SKIN *P.318*

12–16 sardines
1 tbs olive oil
150g/5oz low-fat natural
  yoghurt
1 tbs fresh parsley, finely
chopped
1 tbs Dijon mustard
1 lemon, quartered

Split and clean the sardines, brush with the oil, and grill under a red-hot grill for a minute or so on either side. Combine the yoghurt, parsley, and mustard to make the sauce. Serve the sardines with this sauce, and a quarter of the lemon for each serving.

Herb-coated sea bass serves 4

CANCER *P.264* FATIGUE *P.298* RESPIRATORY *P.312* SKIN *P.318* URINARY *P.324*

2 medium-sized onions,
  finely chopped
1 tbs mixed fennel, parsley,
  and tarragon, chopped
150ml/¼pt water and dry
  white wine (mixed half
  and half)
1 1kg/2lb sea-bass, washed
  and dried
1 tbs olive oil
1 lemon
30g/1oz butter
salt and pepper

Combine the onion and herbs with the water and wine. Slice the lemon thinly and remove the seeds. Lay the cleaned and dried fish in an oval, ovenproof baking dish and moisten with the olive oil. Pour the wine-and-herb mixture over it, cover with the slices of lemon, dot with the butter and season to taste. Bake in the oven at 230°C/450°F/gas 8 for 25–30 minutes. Baste while cooking.

Herrings in oatmeal serves 4

CIRCULATORY *P.278* STRESS *P.292* JOINTS *P.304* SKIN *P.318*

4 fresh herrings (ask your
fishmonger to split and
trim them)
60g/2oz coarse oatmeal
freshly ground black pepper
2tbs sunflower or
grapeseed oil
1 lemon, quartered
2tbs fresh parsley, chopped

Wash and pat dry the herrings and put the oatmeal on a plate with a generous sprinkling of freshly ground black pepper. Dip the herrings in the oatmeal and turn them over until completely coated. Heat the oil to smoking point in a large frying pan and fry the herrings until golden brown – 3–4 minutes each side. Serve them immediately with a wedge of lemon and a sprinkle of parsley.

Prawn, broccoli, and leek stir-fry serves 2

CANCER *P.264* CIRCULATORY *P.278*

2tbs sunflower oil
1 clove garlic, crushed
125g/4oz broccoli florets
1 leek, finely sliced
1tbs dark soy sauce
4tbs vegetable stock (*p.261*)
1 tomato, chopped
1tbs plain flour
125g/4oz cooked prawns
1 carrot, peeled and cut into
thin matchsticks
2.5cm/1in piece fresh ginger,
cut into thin matchsticks
90g/3oz fresh watercress
Any green vegetable, such as
beans or spinach, can be
used in this recipe

Heat the oil in a large frying pan or wok and quickly fry, but do not brown, the garlic. Add the broccoli, and cook for 2 minutes, then add the leek, and cook for another minute, stirring constantly. Stir in the soy sauce, stock, and tomato. Mix the flour with 2 tablespoons of water to make a smooth paste, and stir into the sauce. Cook until thickened. Add the prawns, carrot, and ginger, and cook over a rapid heat for 1 minute. Stir in the watercress, and serve immediately.

Peppered fish with vinaigrette serves 4 ▶

CIRCULATORY *P.278* DIGESTIVE *P.284* RESPIRATORY *P.312*

1 heaped tbs mixed
   peppercorns
1 heaped tbs plain flour,
   seasoned with a little salt
2 fresh or frozen white fish
   fillets, each weighing
   approx. 200g/7oz
1 tbs olive oil

For the vinaigrette:
1 clove garlic, crushed
2 tsp coarse-grain mustard
grated rind and juice of
   2 limes
4 tbs olive oil
salt and freshly ground black
   pepper
fresh coriander, chopped

This delicious recipe was presented in a leaflet by a British supermarket to their customers.

Coarsely crush the peppercorns and mix them together with the seasoned flour. Skin the fish fillets, wipe with kitchen paper, and coat them with the peppercorn mixture, pressing it well onto both sides. Set aside. Meanwhile, prepare the vinaigrette. Combine in a bowl the garlic, mustard, lime rind and juice, 4 tablespoons of oil, salt, pepper, and coriander.

Heat a tablespoon of olive oil in a large frying pan. When hot, add the fish and fry for 3 minutes on each side, until crisp and golden. Keeping the heat high, pour the vinaigrette around the fish, and maintain heat for a couple of minutes to reduce the liquid.

Baked fish provençal serves 2

DIGESTIVE *P.284* FATIGUE *P.298* RESPIRATORY *P.312*

750g/1½lb skinned white fish
2 tbs dry white wine
juice of 1 lemon
1 tbs oil
1 medium-sized onion
2 cloves garlic
1 425g/14oz tin of tomatoes,
   roughly chopped
mixed herbs, salt, and pepper
1 tbs fresh parsley, chopped

Put the fish into a shallow casserole dish, and pour over the white wine and lemon juice. Leave to marinate. Chop the onion and garlic finely, heat the oil, and cook them until soft. Remove the fish from its marinade, drain, and add the marinade to the onion and garlic. Let it reduce a little, then add the tomatoes and herbs and season. Wipe and lightly oil the casserole, put in the fish fillets, pour over the sauce, and bake at 200°C/400°F/gas 6 for 20 minutes. Sprinkle with parsley and serve.

Salmon en papillote serves 4

CIRCULATORY *P.278* STRESS *P.292* JOINTS *P.304* SKIN *P.318*

4 salmon steaks or fillets
2tbs olive oil
3tbs fresh tarragon, chopped
2tbs fresh flat-leaf parsley,
    chopped
1tbs capers, chopped
1 small tin of anchovies,
    drained and chopped
salt and freshly ground black
    pepper
juice of 1 lemon or to taste

This is an impressive, but incredibly simple, recipe to prepare – an ideal choice for dinner parties. You could use foil instead of paper, but then you wouldn't want to present the fish wrapped at the table, which is part of the impact.

Heat the oven to 200°C/400°F/gas 6. Cut 4 pieces of greaseproof paper large enough to wrap around the fish. Brush lightly with oil and place the fish in the centre. Scatter the herbs, capers, and anchovies over the fish, season with salt and pepper, a squeeze of lemon juice, and a drizzle of olive oil. Fold the paper around the fish to form a secure parcel – you can staple it together – place on a baking tray, and cook it for 15–20 minutes, depending on the thickness of the fish.

Far-Eastern fish serves 4

CIRCULATORY *P.278* STRESS *P.292* SKIN *P.318*

750g/1½lb firm white fish
5tbs groundnut oil
1 small onion, finely chopped
4–6 spring onions, finely
    chopped
1tbs fresh ginger, grated
2tbs each light and dark
    soy sauce
2tsp white sugar
a pinch of salt
125ml/4fl oz chicken or
    vegetable stock (*p.261*)

This classic Chinese recipe is best made in a non-stick frying pan. Wash and blot dry the fish, then cut it into big pieces. Heat the oil in a pan. Add the fish and brown it. Remove it and put it to drain on kitchen paper. Pour off most of the remaining oil, add the onion and the spring onions, and fry for a minute. Add the ginger, soy sauces, sugar, salt, and stock, and heat to boiling point. Turn the heat down, put the fish back in the pan, cover, and simmer for about 5 minutes. Put the fish in a serving dish and pour the sauce over. Serve with plain boiled rice.

Grilled red mullet serves 2

CIRCULATORY *P.278* STRESS *P.292* JOINTS *P.304* SKIN *P.318*

1 head red radicchio
2 red mullet, cleaned
100ml/3fl oz olive oil
2 cloves garlic, chopped
1tsp chopped fresh thyme or
   oregano, or a pinch of dried
   herbes de Provence

Quarter the radicchio and cut out the thick stem. Heat the grill and grill the mullet for just 3 minutes on each side. Mix together the oil, garlic, and herbs, and place the grilled mullet in the mixture to cool. Brush the radicchio with a little of the marinade oil, and grill until it begins to wilt and turn brown. Serve the mullet on top of the radicchio.

Marinated fish serves 4

CANCER *P.264* CIRCULATORY *P.278* STRESS *P.292*

2-3 ripe tomatoes, chopped
   fairly small
a handful of fresh dill, or
   parsley, or fennel fronds,
   finely chopped
1 small onion, finely chopped
salt and freshly ground black
   pepper
3tbs olive oil
4 fish fillets (you can use
   frozen fish, but defrost first)

Heat the oven to 200°C/400°F/gas 6. Put the chopped tomatoes in a wide, shallow dish with the herbs, onion, salt and pepper, and oil. Put the fillets in this marinade, and leave for 15 minutes. Then take them out, and put aside.

Cut 4 sheets of foil big enough to enclose each fillet. Put a small spoonful of the mixture in the middle of each piece of foil. Lay the fillets on top, and divide the rest of the mixture between them. Seal up by folding the foil and twisting the edges together. Bake in the hot oven for 15 minutes.

Prawn and tomato curry serves 4 ▶

CANCER *P.264* CIRCULATORY *P.278*

1 medium-sized onion, chopped
425g/14oz tin of tomatoes
1 clove garlic, chopped
2tbs fresh coriander, chopped
3tbs frozen peas
½ vegetable stock cube
1tsp ground cumin
1tsp ground coriander
a good squeeze of tomato
  paste from a tube
salt
1tsp Garam Masala
2tbs curry powder
1 red chilli, deseeded and
  chopped
375g/12oz prawns, shelled
  and cooked (if using frozen,
  defrost in the fridge all day)
150ml/¼pt single cream

Put the onion, tomatoes with their juice, garlic, half of the fresh coriander, frozen peas, and crumbled stock cube in a pan. Let them simmer for about 5 minutes.

Make a paste with the cumin, ground coriander, tomato paste, salt, and a little water. Add the Garam Masala, curry powder, and chilli. Add this mixture to the tomato sauce, and simmer for about 5 minutes.

Add the prawns, and let them simmer in the sauce for a further 3 minutes – no longer or they will go leathery. Then turn off the heat, stir in the cream, sprinkle with the rest of the fresh coriander, and serve at once with plain boiled rice. To make this a more substantial dish, add a tin of sweetcorn in unsweetened water to the tomato sauce.

Cod with sesame and spinach serves 2

CANCER *P.264* CIRCULATORY *P.278* DIGESTIVE *P.284* FATIGUE *P.298* URINARY *P.324*

2 white fish steaks
salt and pepper
1 egg, beaten
60g/2oz sesame seeds
a knob of butter
250g/8oz young spinach
¼tsp nutmeg, freshly grated
2tbs crème fraîche

Heat the oven to 175°C/350°F/gas 4. Season the fish with salt and pepper, brush with beaten egg, and coat the fish with sesame seeds. Place the fish on a baking sheet and cook in the oven for 20 minutes. Just before serving, melt the butter in a large frying pan and wilt the spinach leaves in it. Add the nutmeg, salt and pepper to taste, and the crème fraîche. Divide between two plates, resting the cod on top. Serve with lemon wedges.

★ ★ ★ **The most expensive** but, if you're a carnivore, the most delicious of the protein foods. Men don't need as much as they think, but always buy the best you can afford, and organic if you can.

Meat, chicken, and game

★ Hearty beef stew

★ Carpaccio

★ Italian pan-fried liver

★ Lamb and pine nut koftas

★ Lamb burgers

★ Ginger lamb stir-fry

★ Devilled chicken

★ Spicy chicken wings

★ Chicken with garlic

★ Chicken jalfrezi

★ Tandoori chicken

★ Citrus chicken

★ Chicken livers with warm salad

★ Bedouin chicken

★ Rosemary chicken

★ Guinea fowl casserole

★ Duck breasts with orange juice

★ Duck breasts in green pepper sauce

Hearty beef stew serves 4

STRESS *P.292* FATIGUE *P.298* RESPIRATORY *P.312*

1 large onion

1 tbs olive oil

2 cloves garlic

500g/1lb lean rump steak,
    cubed

2 heaped tbs wholewheat
    flour, well seasoned

150ml/¼pt red wine

600ml/1pt vegetable stock
    (*p.261*)

2 large carrots, sliced

1 large leek, cut into chunks

1 stick celery, thickly sliced

1 parsnip, thickly sliced

1 bay leaf

6 peppercorns

a sprig of fresh thyme

Cut the onion in half, finely chop one half, and slice the other. Heat the oil in a heavy-bottomed pan and soften the chopped onion and the garlic. Then toss the cubes of meat in the flour so that each cube is liberally covered. Add the floured meat to the pan and stir briskly over a high heat to sear all the surfaces. Reduce the heat, add the wine, bring to the boil, and let it bubble for a couple of minutes. Then add the stock and all the vegetables and seasonings. Cover the pan tightly, turn the heat down, and simmer, stirring occasionally, for about an hour and a half. Add more stock or boiling water if it looks dry.

Carpaccio serves 4

FATIGUE *P.298* RESPIRATORY *P.312*

300g/10oz best fillet steak
    (get your butcher to slice it
    paper-thin for you, or
    sharpen your best knife
    and do it yourself!)

1 small bunch rocket or
    watercress

1 bunch celery leaves

4tbs Parmesan cheese,
    freshly grated

4tsp extra-virgin olive oil

freshly ground black pepper

Pound the slices of steak between 2 sheets of waxed paper until they are as thin as possible. Arrange on individual plates and decorate with the rocket or watercress and celery leaves. Sprinkle over the Parmesan, drizzle over 1 teaspoon of oil per steak, and add a generous amount of freshly ground black pepper. Serve with coarse wholemeal bread.

NOTE: The recipe requires the very finest and freshest of ingredients. Tough steak, stale Parmesan, or poor-quality oil could ruin it.

Italian pan-fried liver serves 2

STRESS *P.292* FATIGUE *P.298*

5tbs sunflower oil
30g/1oz butter
1 onion, coarsely chopped
2 rashers bacon, stretched
　　with the back of a knife,
　　and cut in two
375g/12oz calf's liver, thinly
　　sliced
salt and pepper
3tbs fino, or other dry sherry
a handful of chopped parsley

The last-minute addition of dry sherry makes a delicious sauce, but if no sherry is to be found, use vermouth, or failing that, just water.

Heat the oil and butter together until foaming, and then add the onion. Cook until softened and beginning to brown. Remove the onion, and add the bacon. Cook until just beginning to brown, then remove. Season the liver with salt and pepper, and sauté it over a high heat for 1 minute on either side, or until it is just turning brown. Return the onions and bacon to the pan, and pour in the sherry. Heat until bubbling, and a sauce has formed. Stir in the parsley, and serve immediately.

Lamb and pine nut koftas serves 4

FATIGUE *P.298*

1 onion
60g/2oz pine nuts
500g/1lb minced lamb
1tbs fresh mint, chopped
1 egg, beaten

Heat the grill to maximum. Place the onion and pine nuts in a food processor and chop finely. Add the lamb, mint, and egg, and blend to a smooth paste. Shape into walnut-sized balls or small sausage shapes and press tightly onto kebab sticks. Grill for 2 minutes on each side. Serve with wholewheat pitta bread, lemon wedges, and a green salad of rocket, watercress, and cos.

Lamb burgers serves 4 ▶

STRESS *P.292* FATIGUE *P.298* RESPIRATORY *P.312*

1 slice wholemeal bread
   with crusts removed
500g/1lb minced lamb
1 large onion, finely chopped
1 egg
a good pinch of dried oregano
a good pinch of dried thyme
1tbs fresh parsley, chopped
1tbs fresh mint, chopped
salt and freshly ground black
   pepper

Soak the bread in water, then squeeze out the excess. If you have a food processor you can put in all the other ingredients and process them briefly – chop the onion finely first. However, it's quite easy to mix them by hand. Crumble the bread into a bowl with the minced lamb. Some supermarkets sell low-fat, ready-minced lamb, or you can buy fillets, and mince them in a food processor. Add the onion. Beat the egg, and add it. Add the herbs, salt and pepper, and mix. This mixture can be left to gather flavour for 2–3 hours, or you can leave it all day in the refrigerator in a bowl covered with cling film.

When you're ready to cook, heat the grill to maximum, shape the lamb mixture into burgers, oil the grill rack, and grill for 3–4 minutes on each side. Serve with Tomato sauce (*p.255*).

Ginger lamb stir-fry serves 4

STRESS *P.292* FATIGUE *P.298* RESPIRATORY *P.312*

375g/12oz lean lamb
2tsp dry sherry
4tsp soy sauce
½tsp sesame oil
2tsp olive oil
white part of 1 leek, sliced
1 spring onion, chopped
2 cloves garlic, thinly sliced
2.5cm/1in piece of fresh
   ginger, peeled and grated

Remove all fat from the lamb and cut it into thick strips. Put it in a flat dish with the sherry, soy sauce, and sesame oil, and leave to marinate for 30 minutes. Drain, reserving the marinade. Heat a wok or frying pan and add the olive oil, then the lamb with some marinade. Stir for 3 minutes over a high heat. Add the leeks and stir for 2 minutes, then add the spring onions, garlic, and ginger, and stir for another 3 minutes.

Devilled chicken serves 4

CIRCULATORY *P.278* DIGESTIVE *P.284* FATIGUE *P.298* RESPIRATORY *P.312*

8 chicken drumsticks – allow
  2 per person
2 cloves garlic, crushed
5tbs Dijon mustard
2tbs olive oil
2tsp cayenne pepper
5cm/2in fresh ginger,
  peeled and grated
1tsp soft brown sugar
a dash or two of
  Worcestershire sauce
salt and pepper

Tangy spices, such as mustard and chilli, are often assumed to be deadly to the disordered digestive system. In fact, unless you consume them in heroic quantities, they can actually be beneficial to the gut, toning and stimulating the digestive action. Mustard is one such spice. We found this recipe (originally for Devilled Turkey) in a splendid book devoted to a herb that has been cultivated since at least 4000BC, and is the second most common condiment in the world. *The Compleat Mustard* is by Rosemary Man and Robin Weir.

Score the drumsticks deeply in several places, then mix the garlic with the mustard, oil, cayenne, grated ginger, sugar, and Worcestershire sauce. Season lightly with salt and pepper and paint each drumstick, liberally and evenly, with the paste. Chill for a minimum of 12 hours, bringing to room temperature before cooking.

Heat the grill to very hot, then turn it low and cook the drumsticks for 30–40 minutes. Turn frequently and baste with any juices that have poured off them until they are very dark and the meat is cooked through. Then turn the grill to high and cook for 3–4 minutes, turning them round to warm thoroughly and crisp up the skin. Serve hot or cold, with a sharp green salad.

If you use turkey drumsticks, allow one for each person, and extend the cooking time to around 1½ hours.

Spicy chicken wings serves 4

CIRCULATORY *P.278* DIGESTIVE *P.284* RESPIRATORY *P.312*

750g/1½lb chicken wings,
  with the tips removed
8tbs tomato ketchup
3tbs Worcestershire sauce
1tbs runny honey
3tsp paprika
3tsp English dried mustard
  powder
1tsp turmeric
salt and freshly ground
  black pepper

Put the chicken in a flat dish. Combine the other ingredients and pour over the chicken, reserving a few tablespoons. Leave to marinate for 15 minutes, turning the chicken a few times.

Heat the grill and line the grill pan with foil. Cook the chicken for 10-12 minutes, turning them 2-3 times and basting them with the remaining marinade. Serve with a large salad – and plenty of paper napkins, as the only way to eat these is with your fingers – and a cold beer.

Chicken with garlic serves 4

CIRCULATORY *P.278* STRESS *P.292* RESPIRATORY *P.312*

3tbs extra-virgin olive oil
15g/½oz butter
4 leg quarters of chicken
salt and plenty of freshly
  ground black pepper
at least 10 large cloves garlic
  – up to 30 if you're brave!
300ml/½pt dry white wine
1tbs fresh parsley, chopped

This recipe is good for the heart, but is not for the faint-hearted! Heat the oil and butter in a large, deep frying pan. Season the chicken with salt and pepper, add it to the pan, and cook until it is evenly browned on both sides for 8-10 minutes. Reduce the heat, and place the unpeeled cloves of garlic under the chicken on the bottom of the pan. Cook for a further 10 minutes, shaking the pan regularly, then add the wine, and scrape all the cooking bits from around the pan with a wooden spoon. Continue cooking for another 8-10 minutes until the chicken is thoroughly cooked.

Arrange the golden garlic around the pieces of chicken, and sprinkle with the parsley. Serve with bread and the rest of the dry white wine.

Chicken jalfrezi serves 4

CIRCULATORY *P.278* STRESS *P.292* RESPIRATORY *P.312*

3tbs sunflower seed oil

1tsp cumin seeds

3 cloves garlic, chopped

2.5cm/1in piece fresh
    ginger, peeled and
    finely grated

1tsp turmeric

4tsp bottled mild curry paste

750g/1½lb chicken breast,
    skinned and cubed

2 fresh green chillis, deseeded
    and thinly sliced

1 medium-sized red pepper,
    deseeded and cut into
    2.5cm/1in cubes

10 cherry tomatoes, halved

100ml/3fl oz tinned
    coconut milk

1 level tbs Garam Masala

1tbs fresh parsley or
    coriander, chopped

375g/12oz easy-cook rice

This recipe, from the Lal Quila Restaurant in Surrey, England, is quoted in *Favourite Restaurant Curries* by Pat Chapman.

Heat the oil in a large frying pan, or better still, a wok. Add the cumin seeds, stir, add the garlic, and stir for half a minute. Add the ginger, stir for another half a minute, add the turmeric, a tablespoon of water, and then the curry paste.

Add the chicken pieces and stir continuously for another 2 minutes. Add the chillis, red pepper, and tomatoes, and cook for about 10 minutes, adding the coconut milk little by little. Add the Garam Masala and the coriander or parsley, and stir for 5 minutes. Make sure the chicken is cooked right through, and serve with the rice, which can be cooked while you are preparing the rest of the meal.

Tandoori chicken serves 4

CIRCULATORY *P.278* DIGESTIVE *P.284* RESPIRATORY *P.312* SKIN *P.318*

4 chicken quarters, skinned
2tbs lemon juice
2 cloves garlic, crushed
1 green chilli, deseeded
   and thinly sliced
2.5cm/1in piece fresh
   ginger, peeled and chopped
4tbs low-fat natural yoghurt
1tbs ground cumin
1tbs Garam Masala
1tbs paprika
2tbs sunflower or
   grapeseed oil
1 red pepper, sliced
iceberg lettuce leaves,
   shredded
1 lemon, quartered

Prick the chicken all over with a sharp fork. Put into an ovenproof dish, coat with the lemon juice, cover, and leave for half an hour. Put the garlic, green chilli, ginger, and a tablespoon of water in a blender and mix to a smooth paste. Stir into the yoghurt, adding the cumin, Garam Masala, paprika, and oil. Mix and pour over the chicken. Cover and leave to marinate in a cool place for at least 4 hours, preferably overnight. Turn occasionally.

Heat the oven to 170°C/325°F/gas 3, put in the dish, and cook uncovered for about an hour. Spoon the juices over the chicken from time to time, and turn at half-time. Serve surrounded by slices of red pepper, shredded lettuce, with lemon quarters.

Citrus chicken serves 4

CIRCULATORY *P.278* FATIGUE *P.298* RESPIRATORY *P.312* SKIN *P.318*

4 chicken breasts
2 courgettes, thinly sliced
   lengthways
1 red pepper, deseeded and
   cut into strips
2 cloves garlic, crushed
a sprig of fresh rosemary
150ml/¼pt dry white wine
300ml/½pt vegetable stock
   (*p.261*)
juice of 2 lemons
black pepper

Skin the chicken breasts, wipe with a damp cloth, and place in an ovenproof casserole. Lay the sliced courgettes and strips of red pepper on top of the chicken, sprinkle over the garlic, and put a piece of fresh rosemary on each breast. Add the white wine, stock, and lemon juice, cover, and cook at 175°C/350°F/gas 4 for 30 minutes. Season with black pepper to taste.

Chicken livers with warm salad serves 4

CIRCULATORY *P.278* RESPIRATORY *P.312* SKIN *P.318*

750g/1½lb chicken livers –
   preferably free-range
4tbs walnut oil
1½tbs red wine vinegar
4 cloves garlic, finely chopped
pepper and salt
1 small head radicchio
1 bunch watercress
1 head chicory
50g/2oz butter

Wash the livers and pat dry. Put 4 plates to warm in the oven until very hot. Make the salad dressing with the oil, vinegar, finely-chopped garlic, pepper, and salt. Wash and dry the salad leaves, pulling the radicchio apart and separating the watercress into sprigs and the chicory into its long leaves. Melt the butter in a heavy non-stick frying pan, toss the livers for about 5 minutes, then remove the pan from the heat. Quickly arrange the radicchio, watercress, and chicory leaves on the 4 hot plates. Remove the livers from the pan with a slotted spoon and distribute among the plates. Pour the dressing over and serve at once. (Have an oven-cloth handy and warn diners that the plates are hot!)

Bedouin chicken serves 4 ▶

CIRCULATORY *P.278* FATIGUE *P.298* RESPIRATORY *P.312* URINARY *P.324*

1tsp oil
1 small onion, finely chopped
60g/2oz cooked barley (*p.257*)
1 small apple, diced
4 fresh dates, stoned and
   chopped
30g/1oz raisins, well washed
1tsp chopped almonds
½tsp allspice
½tsp cinnamon
1 1.4kg/3lb chicken
salt and pepper
juice of half a lemon
1 lemon, quartered to garnish

Heat the oil and fry the onion until just transparent. Put it, together with all the other stuffing ingredients and spices, in a mixing bowl, and combine. Stuff the chicken with the mixture, tie it up, put it in a roasting pan, and season liberally with pepper, salt, and a squeeze of lemon juice. Heat the oven to 220°C/425°F/gas 7. Put in the chicken and cook for 10 minutes, then turn the oven down to 190°C/375°F/gas 5, and roast for 1¼ hours or until the juices run clear from the thigh when you pierce it with a skewer

Eat with a plain lettuce salad and a lemon and oil dressing.

Rosemary chicken serves 4

CANCER *P.264* CIRCULATORY *P.278* DIGESTIVE *P.284* STRESS *P.292* JOINTS *P.304*

1 1.4kg/3lb chicken –
  preferably free-range
several sprigs of fresh
  rosemary
1tbs butter
1tbs olive oil
2tbs white wine or vegetable
  stock (*p.261*)
salt and freshly ground black
  pepper

Clean the chicken inside and out and pat dry. Put the sprigs of rosemary inside it, saving one of them. Close it up with a piece of string and tuck the extra sprig into the knot. If possible, do this as soon as you get the chicken home, or at least some hours before cooking.

Heat the oven to 200°C/400°F/gas 6. Melt the butter and oil in a cocotte that will go into the oven (or you can use a frying pan, and transfer it and its juices to the ovenproof dish). Brown the chicken on all sides, then transfer to the oven. Pour the stock or wine over it and baste with its juices from time to time during the cooking.If the liquid dries up, add more. Towards the end of cooking, season with a little salt and freshly ground black pepper. Roast for about an hour, or until the juices run clear when you push a skewer into the fattest part of the thigh.

Guinea fowl casserole serves 4

CIRCULATORY *P.278* FATIGUE *P.298* RESPIRATORY *P.312*

1 whole head garlic, peeled
1 1–1½kg/2½–3lb guinea fowl
half a lemon
a sprig of thyme
1tbs olive oil
2 large carrots, cleaned and
  sliced
1 medium-sized onion, sliced
pepper

Take two cloves of garlic, cut into slivers, and slide under the guinea fowl skin. Rub it with lemon, put the sprig of thyme inside, wrap loosely in foil, and refrigerate. Heat the oven to 180°C/350°F/gas 4. Heat the oil in a heavy casserole and brown the guinea fowl on all sides. Turn on its back and add the carrots, onions, and remaining garlic cloves. Add a little pepper. Cover and bake in the preheated oven for about 40 minutes. Serve with Braised red cabbage (*p.200*).

Duck breasts with orange juice serves 2

FATIGUE *P.298*

2 duck breasts with skin
juice of 2 oranges and rind of
   half an orange
1–2tbs clear honey
salt and freshly ground
   black pepper

Heat a large frying pan until hot. Prick the duck skin all over with a fork and place skin-side down into the ungreased, but hot, pan. Cover and cook for 6 minutes. The fat will run out of the skin and can be poured away, and the skin will become crisp. Turn the duck breasts over and cook for a further 2 minutes on the second side for pink flesh. (If you like your duck well done, or the duck breasts are large, you will need to cook them for longer.) Pour the freshly squeezed orange juice, add the orange rind, cut into very thin julienne strips, and the honey into the pan, and increase the heat. Season with salt and pepper, and as the liquid forms a thickish sauce, spoon it over the duck. Serve with crisp vegetables, such as mangetout, or French beans.

Duck breasts in green pepper sauce serves 4

FATIGUE *P.298*

1tbs butter
4 duck breasts
1 medium-sized onion, very
   finely chopped
1tbs green peppercorns
salt
4tbs dry sherry
100ml/3fl oz single cream

Heat the butter in a pan and fry the duck breasts for 3–5 minutes on each side until they are a rich brown colour. Remove the breasts and keep them warm. Fry the onion in the butter over a moderate heat until it is just beginning to colour. Add the green peppercorns, a pinch of salt, and the sherry. Stir together and simmer for 10 minutes. Add the cream and simmer for another 2–3 minutes. Meanwhile, cut the duck breasts into short strips, put them in a dish, and keep them warm. When the sauce is ready, pour it over the duck, and serve at once.

★ ★ ★ **These Cinderellas of the food world** deserve to be glorified. Versatile, digestible, full of fibre, and the best nutritional value for money throughout the world.

Grains and pulses

- ★ Sun-dried tomato risotto
- ★ Red hot rice
- ★ Bean casserole
- ★ Quick bean ragout
- ★ Vegetable risotto
- ★ Warm bulgur with aubergines
- ★ Rainbow peppers

Sun-dried tomato risotto *serves 4*

CANCER *P.264* CIRCULATORY *P.278* FATIGUE *P.298*

2tbs vegetable oil
1 medium-sized onion,
    chopped
2 cloves garlic, chopped
250g/8oz brown rice
175g/6oz sun-dried tomatoes,
    chopped
750ml/1¼pt vegetable stock
    (p.261)
4 ripe red tomatoes, peeled
    and chopped
salt and freshly ground black
    pepper
1tbs fresh basil, chopped
2tbs grated Cheddar,
    Parmesan, or other
    hard cheese

Heat the oil, and fry the onion and garlic for 2–3 minutes. Add the rice, sun-dried tomatoes – drain them first if they are in oil – stock, and fresh tomatoes. Bring to the boil, season with salt and pepper to taste, and simmer for approximately 40 minutes. Add the basil, and stir in the cheese before serving.

NOTE: For a quicker version of this recipe, you can use boil-in-the-bag or easy-cook brown rice. While it's cooking according to the packet's instructions, heat the oil, and fry the onion and garlic until they are just changing colour. Add the sun-dried and fresh tomatoes, and sauté for another 5 minutes. When the rice is ready, stir it into the tomato mixture, season to taste, add the basil, stir in the cheese, and serve.

Red hot rice *serves 4*

CIRCULATORY *P.278* DIGESTIVE *P.284* FATIGUE *P.298* RESPIRATORY *P.312*

125g/4oz boil-in-the-bag
    brown rice
1 small red pepper
1 small, fresh red chilli
3tbs vegetable oil
1 medium-sized onion,
    finely sliced
2 cloves garlic, finely sliced

Boil a pan of water, and cook the rice – it will take 20–25 minutes. Meanwhile, wash the pepper, remove the ribs and seeds, and slice it into strips. Wash, slit open, and deseed the chilli – rinse your hands carefully afterwards. Heat the oil, and gently sauté the chilli in it for 5 minutes, then fish it out with a fork, and discard it. Add the onion, garlic, and red pepper, and sauté them over a low heat until they are soft. When the rice is cooked, put it in a salad bowl, pour in the contents of the frying pan, and stir through.

Bean casserole serves 4

CANCER *P.264* CIRCULATORY *P.278* JOINTS *P.304* RESPIRATORY *P.312* URINARY *P.324*

60g/2oz dried butter beans, soaked overnight
60g/2oz dried red kidney beans, soaked overnight
1 tbs vegetable oil
1 large onion, finely chopped
2 cloves garlic, finely chopped
2 large carrots, sliced
2 courgettes, sliced
2 sticks celery, sliced
200g/7oz tinned tomatoes
a small sprig of fresh thyme or a pinch of dried thyme
salt and pepper

Drain the beans, put in separate pans, and cover with cold water. Bring to the boil and boil rapidly for 10 minutes, then turn the heat down, cover, and simmer for about an hour, or until the beans are tender. Drain, reserving the liquid. Heat the oil in a heavy pan, add the onion and garlic, and let them soften. Add the carrots, courgettes, celery, tomatoes, thyme, and salt and pepper to taste. Add enough of the bean cooking water to moisten. Cover and simmer for about 15 minutes, adding more of the bean water if necessary, until all the vegetables are soft. Add the beans – and more liquid as needed – cover, heat through gently, and serve.

Quick bean ragout serves 4

CANCER *P.264* CIRCULATORY *P.278* DIGESTIVE *P.284* SKIN *P.318*

1 tbs olive oil
1 tsp dill seeds
4 cloves garlic, finely chopped
1 small onion, finely chopped
1 Savoy cabbage, shredded
600ml/1pt vegetable stock (*p.261*)
60g/2oz each tinned flageolet beans, kidney beans, black beans, and soybeans
250g/8oz each tinned borlotti beans, fresh runner beans, and shelled broad beans
1 tbs fresh parsley, chopped

A seven-bean sampling for real bean addicts – using tinned beans, without all that pre-soaking.

Heat the oil in a big casserole. Sweat the dill seeds, garlic, and onion until soft. Add the shredded cabbage and stir briskly. Add the stock. Open all the tins of beans and rinse them under running cold water (you can use up the surplus in a salad). Add them, bring to the boil and simmer for 20 minutes. Then add the broad beans and the runner beans. Cook for another 10 minutes. Serve sprinkled with the parsley.

Vegetable risotto serves 4 ▶

CANCER *P.264* CIRCULATORY *P.278* STRESS *P.292* JOINTS *P.304* RESPIRATORY *P.312*

3tbs olive oil
2 cloves garlic, chopped
2 large onions, sliced
125g/4oz whole unsalted peanuts
2 sticks celery, sliced
2 large carrots, sliced
1 large leek, sliced
375g/12oz brown rice, washed
900ml/1½pt vegetable stock (*p.261*)
125g/4oz button mushrooms
salt and pepper
125g/4oz cucumber, peeled and diced

Heat the oil in a large frying pan or skillet, and sauté the garlic, onions, and peanuts. Add the celery, carrot, and leek, and sauté for another 5 minutes, stirring frequently. Add the rice and continue to stir for another 5 minutes. Add the stock, mushrooms, and salt and pepper to taste, and bring to the boil. After 6–7 minutes, add the cucumber. Cover and simmer until the rice is tender and all the liquid is absorbed. Add more stock to the mixture if necessary.

Warm bulgur with aubergines serves 4

CIRCULATORY *P.278* STRESS *P.292* FATIGUE *P.298*

125g/4oz bulgur or cracked wheat
4–6tbs olive oil
1 large onion, thinly sliced
1 large aubergine, cut into cubes
2tsp ground coriander
2tsp ground cumin
90g/3oz flaked almonds
60g/2oz raisins
salt and freshly ground black pepper

Simmer the bulgur wheat in twice its volume of water for 10 minutes, or until the grains are soft. Drain if necessary. Meanwhile, heat a little oil and fry the onion until it turns brown. Add the aubergine and, stirring frequently, sauté until it is brown – you might need to add a little extra oil. Add the coriander and cumin to the pan and cook for 1 minute, stirring constantly. Lower the heat, add the almonds and raisins, and brown lightly. Stir the cooked bulgur wheat into the vegetables, season with salt and pepper, add extra oil, and sauté for 1 minute to heat through.

Rainbow peppers *serves 4*

CANCER *P.264* CIRCULATORY *P.278* DIGESTIVE *P.284* FATIGUE *P.298* JOINTS *P.304*

90g/3oz brown rice
150ml/¼pt vegetable stock
(*p.261*)
1tsp salt, plus extra to taste
   for seasoning
2tbs olive oil
1 large onion, chopped
2 cloves garlic, chopped
1tbs currants
1tbs pine nuts
juice of 1 lemon
1 tbs oregano
freshly ground black pepper
4 peppers: 1 red,
   1 yellow, 1 green, and
   1 orange
1tbs tomato purée
150ml/¼pt water

An hour before you want to start preparing the dish, cook the rice. Wash it thoroughly and put it in a small ovenproof casserole. Add 1 teaspoon of salt and enough stock to come up to the depth of a thumbnail over the surface of the rice. Cover tightly, and cook in an oven pre-heated to 175°C/350°F/gas 4. After 35–40 minutes, the rice should have absorbed all the stock and be cooked through but still slightly moist.

Heat 1 tablespoon of the oil, and soften the onions in it. Add the chopped garlic, and cook for a moment longer. Add the onion and garlic to the cooked rice, together with the currants, pine nuts, lemon juice, oregano, a little freshly ground pepper, and a touch of salt to taste.

Wash the peppers, then slice the tops off and reserve them. Scrape out the seeds and fibrous ribs, pack with the rice mixture, and replace the tops. Stand the peppers in an oven-dish just big enough to hold them, so that they don't collapse sideways; if necessary, slice off a sliver from the bottoms to steady them. Brush with oil and stir the tomato purée into the water and pour it in. Place in an oven pre-heated to 200°C/400°F/gas 6. Bake for about 45 minutes, checking periodically to ensure the liquid hasn't dried out, adding a little more water or stock if necessary.

Serve with Tomato sauce (*p.255*) and a green vegetable or a salad.

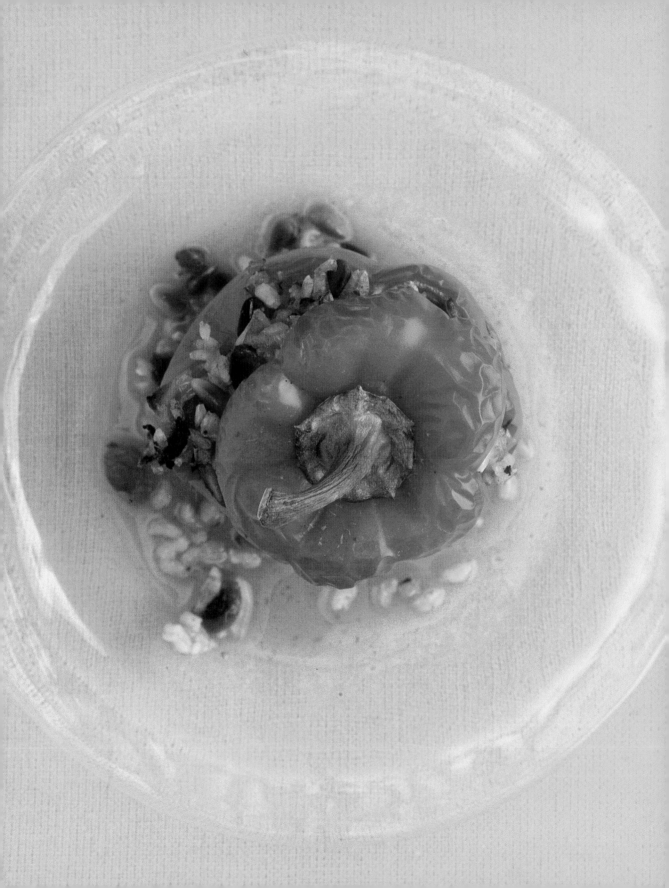

★ ★ ★ Vegetables: the natural health service – no other foods provide so much protection against heart disease, skin disorders, cancer, and high blood pressure, and give the body all-round vitality.

Vegetables

★ Braised red cabbage

★ Tofu and vegetable stir-fry

★ Cabbage with onion and bacon

★ Spiced red cabbage

★ Potato galette

★ Ratatouille

★ Grilled red radicchio

★ Cauliflower and broccoli cheese

★ Vegetable couscous

★ Roasted vegetables

★ Aromatic mushrooms

★ Quick mashed potatoes

★ Turnip and potato cream

★ Turnip purée

★ Braised fennel

★ Spinach Italian-style

★ Vegetable samosas

★ Sweet potato and nutmeg mash

★ New potato and beer salad

Braised red cabbage serves 4

CIRCULATORY *P.278* FATIGUE *P.298*

1 medium-sized red cabbage
3tbs olive oil
1 large onion, chopped
3 garlic cloves, chopped
4–5tbs apple cider vinegar
1tsp brown sugar
salt and pepper

Rinse the cabbage, shred and drain. Heat the oil, sauté the onion gently, add the garlic and cabbage, and stir until well mixed. Add the vinegar and sugar, and salt and pepper to taste. Lower the heat and cook covered, stirring occasionally, until tender – about half an hour – or cook covered in a moderate oven. If you like, add a dash of lemon before serving.

Tofu and vegetable stir-fry serves 4

CIRCULATORY *P.278* FATIGUE *P.298* JOINTS *P.304* SKIN *P.318* URINARY *P.324*

3tbs vegetable oil
250g/8oz tofu
1 medium-sized onion, finely
    chopped
1 green pepper, chopped
1tsp grated fresh ginger
1 stick celery, chopped
2 medium-sized carrots, sliced
a chunk of cabbage, cut into
    thin wedges
4–5 mushrooms, sliced
125g/4oz cashews
250ml/8fl oz vegetable stock
    (*p.261*)
a dash of soy sauce

Heat the oil in the wok, add the tofu, and fry lightly until golden brown. Remove with a slotted spoon and leave on one side. Sauté the onion, green pepper, ginger, and celery over medium heat until soft but not brown. Add the carrots and the cabbage and sauté for 3–4 minutes; then add the mushrooms and cashews and sauté for 1 minute more. Add a cup of stock, return the tofu, cover, and steam until the vegetables are soft. Stir in a dash of soy sauce.

Cabbage with onion and bacon serves 4

CIRCULATORY *P.278* FATIGUE *P.298*

1 medium-sized cabbage
1 tbs vegetable oil
1 medium-sized onion,
   coarsely chopped
3–4 rashers streaky bacon,
   cut in pieces
salt and pepper

Wash and shred the cabbage, but don't dry it. Heat the oil in a big saucepan, and gently fry the onion and bacon together until the onion is just changing colour, and the bacon is nearly crisp. Add the cabbage, salt and pepper, and stir. Put the lid on, turn down the heat, and simmer. Shake the pan, and give the contents a stir a couple of times – the cabbage will steam cook – until the cabbage is cooked *al dente* (just tender).

Spiced red cabbage serves 4

CIRCULATORY *P.278* FATIGUE *P.298*

1 small red cabbage
1 large cooking apple, peeled
   and sliced in segments
3 tbs red wine vinegar
10 cloves
salt and pepper
1–2 tsp brown sugar

Wash and shred the cabbage and put it in a pan with the apple, red wine vinegar, cloves, and salt and pepper. Sprinkle over 2–3 tablespoons of water, add the brown sugar, cover, and simmer for 20 minutes.

Potato galette serves 4

CIRCULATORY *P.278* DIGESTIVE *P.284* FATIGUE *P.298*

4 medium-sized potatoes
2 egg yolks
1 medium-sized onion, grated
3 tbs fresh parsley, chopped
2 cloves garlic, finely chopped
1 tsp plain flour
1 tsp ground nutmeg
sunflower or corn oil

Peel the potatoes and grate in a food processor. Turn into a bowl and mix with the egg yolks, onion, parsley, and garlic. Form into a cake and dust with flour. Heat enough oil in a frying pan to come about half way up the side of the cake. Add the cake and fry on both sides until golden. Drain on kitchen paper and dust with nutmeg.

Ratatouille serves 4

CANCER *P.264* CIRCULATORY *P.278* DIGESTIVE *P.284* URINARY *P.324*

2 courgettes
1 large aubergine
salt
2 large red peppers
1 large onion
2 cloves garlic
4tbs extra-virgin olive oil
1 small tin of tomatoes
a few coriander seeds or ½tsp
    ground coriander
1tbs fresh basil or parsley,
    chopped

Wash the courgettes and aubergine and cut into small slices. Place in a colander, sprinkle with salt, and leave for an hour.

Deseed the peppers and cut into thin strips. Peel and finely slice the onion and garlic. Heat the oil in a heavy-bottomed saucepan. Add the onion and sweat until transparent. Rinse and pat dry the aubergines and courgettes, and add them, together with the peppers and garlic. Cover and simmer gently for about 40 minutes. Add the tomatoes and coriander, and cook for another 30 minutes – but don't let it get too mushy. Stir in the basil or parsley, and serve hot.

Grilled red radicchio serves 4

CANCER *P.264* CIRCULATORY *P.278* DIGESTIVE *P.284* JOINTS *P.304*

2-3 radicchio heads
3-4tbs extra-virgin olive oil
salt and freshly ground
    pepper
lemon slices

Clean the radicchio, stripping off wilted outer leaves. Slice thickly, rinse, and pat completely dry with kitchen paper. Lay the slices in a shallow, ovenproof dish. Mix 3-4 tablespoons of oil with a little salt and freshly ground pepper, and pour over the radicchio. Leave it to soften for 5 minutes, while you heat the grill. Grill for no longer than it takes for the leaves to change colour a little. Lift out and serve with slices of lemon, and bread to mop up the tangy juices.

Cauliflower and broccoli cheese serves 4

CANCER *P.264* STRESS *P.292* FATIGUE *P.298*

1 small cauliflower
1 small head of broccoli
500ml/16fl oz milk
60g/2oz butter
1tbs wholemeal flour
60g/2oz Cheddar, grated
1tsp Dijon mustard
salt and pepper

Preheat the oven to 180°C/350°F/gas 4. Break the vegetables into florets and cook them in the milk until just tender. Drain, reserving the milk, and put the vegetables in a buttered gratin dish. Melt the butter in a saucepan. Stir in the flour, 1 tablespoon of the cheese, the mustard, and seasoning. Stir in the hot milk to make a smooth sauce. Pour over the vegetables, scatter the rest of the cheese on top, and bake for 15–20 minutes.

Vegetable couscous serves 4

CANCER *P.264* DIGESTIVE *P.284* FATIGUE *P.298*

olive oil, for frying
1 small onion, finely chopped
2 carrots, halved lengthways
    and sliced
1 courgette, halved
    lengthways and sliced
half red pepper, deseeded
    and chopped
1tsp (or more to taste)
    ground cumin
2 tomatoes, skinned and diced
salt
1–2tbs fresh coriander
    leaves
400g/13oz tinned chickpeas,
    drained
150g/5oz couscous

Heat a little olive oil in a frying pan. Add the onion and fry until golden. Add the carrots, courgette, red pepper, and ground cumin and continue to fry for a few minutes. Add the tomatoes, a little salt, and the coriander leaves. Simmer for about 10 minutes, or until the vegetables are cooked and nicely tender. Add the chickpeas and heat through. While the vegetables are cooking, steam the couscous, according to packet instructions. Serve the vegetables and steamed couscous together. If a child insists on having meat with this, you can fry a few small pieces of chicken with the onion.

Roasted vegetables serves 4 ▶

CANCER *P.264* CIRCULATORY *P.278* RESPIRATORY *P.312*

1 red pepper, cored, deseeded, and cut into chunks
1 yellow pepper, cored, deseeded, and cut into chunks
2 onions, quartered
2 medium-sized or 4 small courgettes, thickly sliced
8 cherry tomatoes
4 cloves garlic, crushed
4tbs olive oil
salt and black pepper
1 bunch fresh coriander, basil, or parsley, chopped

Preheat the oven to 200°C/400°F/gas 6. Arrange all the vegetables and the garlic in a shallow roasting tin. Add the olive oil, and push the vegetables around until they are well coated with the oil. Sprinkle with a little salt and pepper, and roast in the oven for about 40 minutes, stirring once or twice. The vegetables should be tender and just starting to turn golden-brown. Sprinkle with the chopped fresh herbs.

Serve these vegetables with plain brown rice (*p.257*), couscous, or bulgur for an appetizing and colourful supper. The vegetables are also a delicious accompaniment to the Sunday roast, grilled fish or meat, or to a simple omelette.

Aromatic mushrooms serves 4

CIRCULATORY *P.278* DIGESTION *P.284* SKIN *P.318*

500g/1lb small white or flat field mushrooms
3tbs olive oil
2 cloves garlic, sliced in half
1 bay leaf
6–8 coriander seeds
salt and freshly ground black pepper

Clean the mushrooms, and slice them thinly. Warm the olive oil in a pan. Add the garlic slices, bay leaf, coriander seeds, and salt and pepper. Add the mushrooms, and cover the pan. Shake gently, and cook over a very low heat for 20 minutes. Remove the bay leaf before serving the mushrooms. Serve with Michael's millet and buckwheat (*p.261*) and a green salad.

Quick mashed potatoes serves 4

CIRCULATORY *P.278* DIGESTIVE *P.284*

500g/1lb potatoes, peeled
   and diced
150ml/¼pt milk
a little sea salt
60g/2oz butter
a pinch pepper
1tbs fresh parsley, finely
   chopped

Put the potatoes in a pan with the milk and a touch of salt. Bring to the boil, lower the heat, cover, and simmer for 10–15 minutes until the potatoes are tender.

Mash with a potato masher – add a little more milk, if needed – and stir in the butter and pepper. Sprinkle with the parsley and serve.

Turnip and potato cream serves 4

JOINTS *P.304* RESPIRATORY *P.312*

500g/1lb small turnips
1 medium-sized potato
3tbs single cream
salt and pepper
1tbs fresh parsley, finely
   chopped

If the turnips are young and tender, they won't need peeling – just scrub them and cut into small dice. Scrub and dice the potato. Put the vegetables in a pan with enough water to cover. Bring to the boil and simmer until they are tender – about 15 minutes. Drain off all but 1 tablespoon of cooking water, and mash the potatoes and turnips into this – it should be quite a rough consistency. Stir in the cream, season to taste with salt and pepper, and sprinkle with the parsley.

Turnip purée serves 4

JOINTS *P.304* RESPIRATORY *P.312*

500g/1lb young turnips
150ml/¼pt milk
60g/2oz butter
a pinch of nutmeg

Clean and quarter the turnips. Cook in the milk, over a low heat, until tender. Purée, stir in the butter, and sprinkle with the nutmeg.

Braised fennel serves 4

DIGESTIVE *P.284* STRESS *P.292*

2 large or 4 small heads of
   fresh fennel
1 tbs olive oil
1 tbs fresh parsley, chopped
a sprig of fresh thyme
6 peppercorns
150ml/¼pt dry white wine

Clean the fennel and cut it into halves or quarters. Heat the oil in a shallow casserole dish and fry the pieces of fennel until they are lightly browned. Add the parsley, thyme, and peppercorns, then pour in the wine and let it bubble for a minute. Cover the dish and cook over a very low heat for about 25 minutes.

Spinach Italian style serves 4

CANCER *P.264* STRESS *P.292* FATIGUE *P.298*

1kg/2lb fresh spinach
2tbs olive oil
1-2 cloves garlic, chopped
1 fresh red or green chilli,
   chopped
a squeeze of fresh lemon juice

Italian greengrocers sell a wide range of greens, ready trimmed and washed. As well as spinach, wild chicory, beetroot tops, and endives can all be cooked in the following way – and even mixed together. When cooking spinach, you don't have to trim off all the stalks – only the very toughest and thickest should be removed.

Wash the spinach thoroughly in several changes of water. Put it while it is still wet into a large pan, cover, and cook over the lowest possible heat. Within 10 minutes the greens will have wilted and become just tender. Drain thoroughly.

At this point, you can choose two ways of serving the spinach. Either heat the oil in a big pan, quickly sauté the garlic and chilli, toss the spinach very quickly in the flavoured oil, and serve. Alternatively, you can dress the drained spinach with a little olive oil and freshly pressed lemon juice, and serve it lukewarm.

Vegetable samosas

CIRCULATORY *P.278* DIGESTIVE *P.284*

2 potatoes, cut into cubes

125g/4oz finely chopped
    vegetables – use
    combinations of favourite
    vegetables, such as carrots,
    beans, peas, spinach,
    cauliflower, and parsnips

1tsp mild curry powder or
    paste

2tbs cream cheese or
    cottage cheese

salt and pepper

1tbs olive oil

30g/1oz butter, melted

8 sheets filo pastry

4tbs poppy seeds or black
    sesame seeds

Preheat the oven to 190°C/375°F/gas 5. Boil the potato cubes in lightly salted water for about 10 minutes, or until soft. Drain well. In a separate pan, bring enough water to the boil to just cover the chopped vegetables and cook them until tender but still crisp. Drain well and put the vegetables and potatoes into a bowl. Add the curry powder or paste, cheese and salt and pepper. Mix everything really well together.

Melt the olive oil and butter in a small saucepan. Lay out one sheet of filo pastry and brush it with the melted butter and oil. Lay another sheet on top and brush again. Now cut the pastry lengthways into strips about 7cm/3in wide. Put a heaped teaspoon of filling at one end of a strip. Fold the pastry diagonally across so that it makes a triangle. Keep folding over along the length of the strip until your triangle is completed. Brush the outside with butter and roll the samosa in poppy or black sesame seeds. Repeat with all your pastry and filling.

Put the samosas on a baking sheet and bake in the oven for 15–20 minutes, until golden. Serve the samosas while they are still warm. Makes about 16.

Sweet potato and nutmeg mash serves 4

DIGESTIVE *P.284* SKIN *P.318*

2 large sweet potatoes,
    scrubbed and cubed
quarter head dark green
    cabbage, finely shredded
juice of a lemon
½tsp ground nutmeg
extra-virgin olive oil
freshly ground black pepper

This quick and easy recipe provides loads of slow release energy, betacarotene, and other essential carotenoids, together with protective vitamin C and anticancer chemicals from the cabbage and plenty of feel-good myristicine from the nutmeg. It's also rich in fibre. Serve as a side dish or top with an organic poached egg for a light supper or Sunday brunch.

Put the sweet potatoes in a large saucepan of cold water and bring to the boil uncovered. After 5 minutes, place the cabbage in a steamer on top and cover. Strain the sweet potatoes, put them back in the saucepan and on the heat, shaking vigorously until completely dry. Drizzle with olive oil, mash, stir in the steamed cabbage, add the nutmeg and pepper, and serve.

New potato and beer salad serves 4

CIRCULATORY *P.278* DIGESTIVE *P.284*

1kg/2lb new potatoes
1 red onion, finely chopped
2 cloves garlic, finely chopped
1tbs fresh thyme, chopped
1tbs flat-leaf parsley, chopped
6tbs extra-virgin olive oil
2tbs cider vinegar
175ml/6fl oz beer
4 spring onions, chopped
1tbs wholegrain mustard
1tsp honey
pepper

Put the unpeeled potatoes in a large saucepan of cold water, bring to boil, and cook uncovered until just soft (about 20 minutes). Drain and leave until cool enough to handle. Cut each potato in half and mix gently with the onion, garlic, thyme, and parsley. To make the dressing, whisk all the other ingredients together to a smooth, creamy consistency. To serve, pour the dressing over the warm potatoes and serve immediately. If you're not going to eat this straight away, refrigerate the potatoes and dressing separately.

★ ★ ★ Snacks – always **nice** but they don't have to be naughty or unhealthy. Here's the pick of the bunch.

Snacks

- ★ Tapenade
- ★ Falafel
- ★ Pitta pizza
- ★ Potato pancakes
- ★ Salade niçoise
- ★ Millet croquettes
- ★ Beef and onion burgers
- ★ Onion wholemeal burgers
- ★ Cress, watercress, and carrot sandwich filling

- ★ Chicken liver and alfalfa sandwich filling
- ★ Sardines tinned in oil sandwich filling
- ★ Banana and almond muffins
- ★ Green tea bread
- ★ Blueberry muffins
- ★ Banana and walnut bread

Tapenade serves 4

CIRCULATORY *P.278* JOINTS *P.304* RESPIRATORY *P.312*

20 pitted black olives
1 tin anchovy fillets, drained
1 heaped tbs capers, rinsed
1tsp lemon juice
1 clove garlic
black pepper
100ml/3½fl oz olive oil

Put all the ingredients except the oil in a blender and blend for a few seconds. Add black pepper to taste, and half a tablespoon of olive oil. Blend again and repeat, adding more oil until the mixture is a smooth, thick purée.

Falafel serves 4

CIRCULATORY *P.278* STRESS *P.292* JOINTS *P.304*

250g/8oz dried chickpeas
2 Spanish onions, finely
    chopped
3tbs fresh parsley,
    finely chopped
2tsp ground coriander
2tsp ground fennel
2tsp ground cumin
½tsp baking powder
4 cloves garlic, crushed
salt and freshly ground
    black pepper
2tbs flour (optional)
3-4tbs sunflower oil
paprika to garnish

Every cookery writer has their own version of falafel: our favourite is that of Paul Laurenson and Ethel Minogue published in *The Taste of Health* (BBC Books).

Soak the chickpeas in water for several hours until they double in size. Change the water as often as you remember during the soaking, as this reduces the likelihood of their causing flatulence. Blend the chickpeas with a little of their cooking water to a smooth paste. Add the onions and parsley to the chickpeas and blend again for a few seconds. Add all the ground spices, baking powder, crushed garlic, and salt and pepper. Knead the mixture for a moment or two to mix the ingredients well, then let it rest in the refrigerator for 30 minutes. Take small pieces and form into little flat cakes about 2 inches across. If they are sticky, roll them in a little flour. Heat the oil and fry for about 2 minutes each side. Drain on kitchen paper, sprinkle with paprika, and serve hot or cold.

Pitta pizza serves 1

CANCER *P.264* FATIGUE *P.298*

1 wholewheat pitta
1 medium-sized tomato, sliced
salt and freshly ground
   black pepper
a good pinch of dried oregano
1 tbs Cheddar cheese, grated
1 tsp olive oil

Made with wholewheat pitta bread, this is a superfast, healthy variation on pizza. Try any of the classic pizza toppings, such as anchovies, black olives, thinly sliced onion, slivers of red or green pepper, thin slices of mushroom, diced ham, or slices of pepperoni.

Heat the grill to red hot. Toast the pitta on one side for a minute or two, and remove from the grill. Turn the bread over, and top with sliced tomatoes, salt and pepper to taste, oregano, and the grated cheese. Dribble the oil over the top, and return to the grill. The pizza will be done in 2–3 minutes. This recipe serves one, but it can easily be multiplied to serve more.

Potato pancakes serves 4

CIRCULATORY *P.278* DIGESTIVE *P.284*

500g/1lb potatoes
1 medium-sized onion
2 eggs
2 tbs plain flour
salt and pepper
3–4 tbs sunflower oil

Peel the potatoes and onion, and grate them into a large bowl. Beat the eggs, and add them, stir in the flour and the salt and pepper. Mix together well. Heat the oil in a frying pan and fry tablespoonfuls of the mixture, flattening them down in the pan, for 5 minutes on each side.

Salade niçoise serves 4 ▶

CANCER *P.264* CIRCULATORY *P.278* STRESS *P.292* FATIGUE *P.298*

1 head cos or iceberg
    lettuce
2 eggs
4 firm tomatoes
1 large red pepper
½ cucumber
4 small boiled potatoes
4 anchovy fillets
2tbs milk
2 cloves garlic, chopped
a pinch of mixed herbs
1½tbs good wine vinegar or
    balsamic vinegar
3tbs extra-virgin olive oil
12 pitted black olives

Wash and dry the lettuce. Hard boil and halve the eggs. Wash and quarter the tomatoes. Deseed the pepper and slice into strips. Peel and slice the cucumber. Halve the boiled potatoes. Soak the anchovy fillets for 30 minutes in the milk, then drain and dry.

Make the dressing by adding the garlic and mixed herbs to the vinegar and oil. Mix thoroughly, and leave to stand while you prepare the salad. Line the salad bowl with the lettuce leaves. Arrange all the other ingredients in the middle, decorate with the olives and anchovy fillets on top, and add the dressing just before you eat. Toss and serve.

Millet croquettes serves 4

CANCER *P.264* DIGESTIVE *P.284* STRESS *P.292*

900ml/1½pt water
300g/10oz millet
4tbs oil
1 onion, finely chopped
2tbs parsley, freshly chopped
250g/8oz grated cheese
salt and pepper
1 egg, beaten
1tbs wholemeal flour

Bring the water to the boil, add the millet, and simmer for about 25 minutes, stirring frequently, until the water is completely absorbed. In another pan, heat 2tbs of the oil, then melt the chopped onion. Add to the millet, together with the parsley and cheese, and season with salt and pepper to taste. Leave the mixture to cool. When cool, shape it into croquettes. Dip the croquettes in the beaten egg, then in the wholemeal flour, and fry in the rest of the oil until golden brown.

Two burgers

The following are recipes for two different burgers, one made with meat, the other with a mixture of breadcrumbs, onions, potatoes, and plenty of seasoning. They are delicious eaten hot, with a sharp green salad; when cold, they can be packed into burger buns with a few onion rings, and a couple of lettuce leaves.

Beef and onion burgers serves 4

FATIGUE *P.298* JOINTS *P.304* RESPIRATORY *P.312* URINARY *P.324*

1 large onion, finely chopped
1tbs sunflower oil
375g/12oz chuck steak or
    shin of beef, with all fat
    removed, minced
250g/8oz carrot, finely grated
1tbs wholemeal breadcrumbs
1tbs each fresh mint and
    parsley, chopped

Soften the onion in a very little oil, and add to all the other ingredients. Mix, shape into burgers, dust with a little flour, and fry.

Onion wholemeal burgers serves 4

CANCER *P.264* CIRCULATORY *P.278* FATIGUE *P.298* RESPIRATORY *P.312*

12 spring onions
2 eggs, lightly beaten
a good pinch grated nutmeg
2 slices wholemeal bread with
    the crusts cut off, crumbed
375g/12oz cold mashed
    potato
sea salt and black pepper
sunflower oil

Wash and cook the spring onions in boiling water until soft. Drain and chop. Mix the eggs, nutmeg, salt and pepper, breadcrumbs, mashed potatoes, and onions thoroughly. Heat the oil in a large frying pan, shape into burgers, and fry until golden brown. Serve with iceberg lettuce, rings of onion and slices of tomato, and a favourite relish.

Three fillings for sandwiches

Three fillings for wholewheat sandwiches, wholewheat or granary rolls, or wholewheat baps. They can be made overnight and stored in the refrigerator, wrapped in foil or clingfilm.

Cress, watercress, and carrot serves 2

STRESS *P.292* FATIGUE *P.298*

1 bunch watercress
1 bunch cress
1 carrot, grated

Chop the watercress and cress and mix with the grated carrot. You can add a little low-fat mayonnaise if desired.

Chicken liver and alfalfa serves 2

FATIGUE *P.298* JOINTS *P.304* SKIN *P.318*

6 chicken livers, preferably from free-range birds
1 tbs olive oil
1 small onion, finely chopped
1 hard-boiled egg, finely chopped
125g/4oz low-fat soft cheese
a handful of alfalfa sprouts

Make the chicken liver pâté the night before. Grill the livers. Heat a little oil in a non-stick frying pan, melt the onion until soft but not brown, and remove from pan with a slotted spoon. Put the livers, onion, egg, low-fat cheese, and alfalfa in a blender or food processor, and blend to a smooth pâté. You may need a little more cheese. Pack into a small dish, cover with foil, and refrigerate overnight.

Sardines tinned in olive oil serves 2

CIRCULATORY *P.278* FATIGUE *P.298*

1 tin of sardines
1 tsp cider vinegar
1 tbs fresh parsley, chopped
black pepper

Drain the sardines, remove tails, mash up with a dash of cider vinegar and a little of their own oil, a sprinkling of chopped parsley, and some black pepper. Put in sandwiches with cucumber slices.

Banana and almond muffins serves 6

CIRCULATORY *P.278* DIGESTIVE *P.284* FATIGUE *P.298*

175g/6oz plain flour
1½tsp baking powder
1½tsp bicarbonate of soda
½tsp salt
2 eggs
6 large ripe bananas,
   thoroughly mashed
250g/8oz dark brown sugar
90ml/2½fl oz sunflower oil
90ml/2½fl oz buttermilk
½tsp vanilla extract
100g/3½oz almonds, toasted
   and chopped

Preheat the oven to 200°C/400°F/gas 6. Lightly grease a 12-cup muffin tin. Put the flour, baking powder, bicarbonate of soda, and salt in a large mixing bowl and mix well together. Mix the eggs, bananas, sugar, oil, buttermilk, and vanilla extract in a separate bowl and then pour them into the dry ingredients. Mix them together until just combined. (Be careful not to overmix or the muffins will be rubbery.) Fold in the almonds. Fill each muffin cup to the rim with batter. Bake for 25–30 minutes, until firm to the touch and golden on top. Cool the muffins for 2–3 minutes and serve them warm or at room temperature.

Green tea bread serves 6

CIRCULATORY *P.278*

375g/12oz seedless raisins
   and sultanas, mixed
300ml/½pt green tea (or
   your favourite tea)
175g/6oz soft brown sugar
250g/8oz wholemeal
   self-raising flour
1 egg
1tsp mixed spice
grated zest of 1 lemon
90g/3oz mixed chopped
   almonds, walnuts, and
   hazelnuts

Put the dried fruit in a large bowl and stir in the tea and sugar. Cover and set aside to soak overnight. Next day, preheat the oven to 180°C/350°F/gas 4. Lightly grease a 1kg/2lb loaf tin. Add the remaining ingredients to the dried-fruit mixture and beat well. Pour into the prepared loaf tin, pushing the mixture into the corners of the tin. Transfer to the preheated oven and bake for 1 hour 15 minutes, or until a skewer inserted into the centre of the bread comes out clean. Turn out of the tin and leave to cool on a wire rack.

Blueberry muffins serves 6

CIRCULATORY *P.278* DIGESTIVE *P.284* FATIGUE *P.298*

100g/3½oz self-raising flour
60g/2oz wholemeal flour
1tsp baking powder
1tsp mixed spice
125ml/4fl oz milk
60g/2oz butter, melted
1 large egg
2tsp lemon juice
90g/3oz soft brown sugar
90g/3oz fresh blueberries

Preheat the oven to 180°C/350°F/gas 4. Put 12 paper muffin cases into a muffin tin. Sift the flours, baking powder, and mixed spice into a mixing bowl, putting the bran in the sieve back into the bowl. Beat together the milk, butter, egg, lemon juice, and sugar in a bowl or wide jug. Make a well in the centre of the flour mixture and pour in half the milk mixture. Gently fold it in, then add the rest and stir it in. Then fold in the blueberries.

Spoon the mixture into the muffin cases and bake in the oven for about 20 minutes, until well risen and golden on top. Take the muffins out of the tin and leave on a wire rack to cool.

Banana and walnut bread serves 6

CIRCULATORY *P.278* DIGESTIVE *P.284* FATIGUE *P.298*

250g/8oz cottage cheese,
    pressed through a sieve
125g/4oz soft brown sugar
3 eggs, beaten
60g/2oz chopped walnuts
2 bananas, mashed
250g/8oz wholemeal
    self-raising flour

Preheat the oven to 180°C/350°F/gas 4. Line a 1kg/2lb loaf tin with greased greaseproof paper or baking parchment. Cream the cottage cheese and sugar together until well blended. Gradually beat in the eggs. Add the chopped nuts and bananas and mix well. Add the flour, mixing it in well. Spoon the mixture into the prepared tin, pressing it into the corners. Bake in the oven for 40-45 minutes, or until a skewer inserted into the centre of the bread comes out clean. Cool on a wire rack and serve in lightly buttered slices.

★ ★ ★ **From Caesar to Waldorf,** iceberg to little gem, mixed or green, dressed or not – salads offer a rainbow of delicious, healthy eating.

Salads

- ★ Mushroom and radicchio salad
- ★ Spinach and mushroom salad
- ★ Watercress salad
- ★ Dutch salad
- ★ Avocado and watercress salad
- ★ Red bean salad in plum sauce
- ★ Tomato salad
- ★ Waldorf salad
- ★ Complete coleslaw

- ★ Celery, radish, and walnut salad
- ★ Winter white salad
- ★ Orange and watercress salad
- ★ Radish and rocket salad
- ★ Frisée salad
- ★ Sprouted seed salad
- ★ Carrot salad
- ★ Tsatsiki
- ★ Sauerkraut salad
- ★ Tricolour coleslaw

Mushroom and radicchio salad serves 4

STRESS *P.292* FATIGUE *P.298*

12 medium-sized field
   mushrooms
3tbs olive oil
salt and pepper
2 cloves garlic, chopped
1 head of radicchio, cleaned
4 tomatoes, sliced
   piece of Parmesan cheese,
   weighing approx.
   125g/4oz
1tbs fresh parsley, chopped

Heat the grill. Wipe the mushrooms clean and grill them for 1 minute or so on each side. Meanwhile, heat the oil. Transfer the grilled mushrooms to the frying pan, season with salt and pepper, add the garlic, and sauté quickly. Arrange the radicchio leaves and tomato slices on 4 plates. Add 3 grilled mushrooms to each plate. Divide the hot, garlicky olive oil between the plates and flake the Parmesan cheese on top. Garnish with chopped parsley.

Spinach and mushroom salad serves 4

CANCER *P.264* STRESS *P.292* FATIGUE *P.298*

250g/8oz young, tender
   spinach leaves
175g/6oz mushrooms
4 rashers streaky bacon
2tbs olive oil
1tbs sunflower seeds
2tsp vinegar
salt and a little freshly ground
   black pepper

Wash and dry the spinach leaves and arrange them in a salad bowl. Wipe and slice the mushrooms and add them to the bowl. Chop the bacon and fry it in a non-stick pan until it is crispy. Remove the bacon pieces with a slotted spoon and add them to the salad. Put the olive oil in the pan, heat it, and add the sunflower seeds. Toss them until they are lightly browned. Add the vinegar, season with salt and pepper, and pour the contents of the pan over the salad. Toss, and serve.

Watercress salad serves 2

CANCER *P.264* CIRCULATORY *P.278* STRESS *P.292* SKIN *P.318*

1 bunch watercress
1 avocado
2 slices streaky bacon
1 tbs olive oil
1 tsp vinegar
salt and freshly ground
    black pepper

Wash, trim, and dry the watercress, and arrange it in a salad bowl. Peel, stone, and slice the avocado, and add it to the bowl. Chop the streaky bacon, heat the oil, and fry the bacon pieces until they are crisp. Add the vinegar to the pan, season with salt and pepper, and pour over the salad.

Dutch salad serves 4

CIRCULATORY *P.278* DIGESTIVE *P.284* FATIGUE *P.298*

6–8 tiny new potatoes
4 eggs, hard-boiled
2 medium-sized apples
4 rollmop herrings
2 medium-sized beetroot
2 pickled dill cucumbers

For the dressing:
125ml/4fl oz natural
    yoghurt
1 tbs olive oil
1 clove garlic, chopped
salt and pepper
1 tbs fresh parsley, chopped

Wash the potatoes and put them in a panful of boiling water until they are cooked, then cool and dice them. Slice the hard-boiled eggs. Wash and dice the apples. Chop the herrings into bite-sized pieces. Peel and dice the beetroot. Slice the cucumbers.

Make a ring of diced beetroot around the edge of the salad bowl, and pile the potatoes, apples, herrings, and cucumbers into the middle of the beetroot ring. Top with the egg slices. Make a dressing with the yoghurt, oil, garlic, and salt and pepper, and pour over the salad. Garnish with a sprinkling of parsley.

Avocado and watercress salad serves 4 ▶

CANCER *P.264* CIRCULATORY *P.278* STRESS *P.292* FATIGUE *P.298* SKIN *P.318*

1 bunch watercress
2 avocados
30g/1oz pine nuts
2tbs walnut oil
juice of half a lemon
salt and pepper

Wash and dry the watercress, discard the bigger stalks, and put the cress in a salad bowl. Add the avocados, sliced thinly, and the pine nuts. Make a dressing with the walnut oil, lemon juice, salt, and pepper and pour over. Toss very gently, then chill, covered with a damp cloth, for an hour or so before eating.

Red bean salad in plum sauce serves 4

CANCER *P.264* CIRCULATORY *P.278* STRESS *P.292* SKIN *P.318*

1 clove garlic
dash cayenne pepper
6 leaves fresh basil, torn
   in pieces
a few sprigs of fresh
   coriander
1tbs red wine vinegar
5tbs damson jam
1tbs olive oil
375g/12oz cooked red kidney
   beans, drained

Nathalie Hambro gives the recipe for this piquant salad in her book *Particular Delights*. Although it sounds a little strange, this traditional dish from Georgia (in the former USSR) is a real taste-treat.

Crush the garlic. Add the cayenne, basil, and some of the coriander leaves, chopped, and mash the mixture to a smooth paste. Combine the vinegar and jam in an enamel or stainless-steel pan and boil over a high heat, stirring constantly, until the jam is dissolved. Rub the mixture through a fine sieve, add the oil, then gradually beat it into the garlic and herb paste. Add the beans and toss gently but thoroughly. Cover and refrigerate overnight. Serve decorated with the remaining coriander leaves.

Tomato salad serves 4

CANCER *P.264*   CIRCULATORY *P.278*   DIGESTIVE *P.284*   FATIGUE *P.298*

4 tomatoes
4 cloves garlic, finely chopped
2tbs fresh basil, chives, or
    parsley, finely chopped
2tbs spring onions, chopped
sea salt and freshly ground
    black pepper
2tbs extra-virgin olive oil

Slice the tomatoes finely. Spread them on a long, flat white china dish. Clean, trim, and chop the spring onions. Strew the chopped garlic across the tomatoes, top with the chopped green herbs and the chopped spring onions, add a little freshly ground pepper and a touch of salt, and drizzle the oil over the surface.

Waldorf salad serves 4

CANCER *P.264*   CIRCULATORY *P.278*   DIGESTIVE *P.284*   JOINTS *P.304*   RESPIRATORY *P.312*

4 sticks celery
2 large eating apples
a handful of raisins
1tbs olive oil
1tsp lemon juice
150g/5oz natural yoghurt
salt and pepper
1tbs parsley, finely chopped
60g/2oz walnuts

Clean and slice the celery into small chunks; wash and core the apples and cut into small slices; wash and dry the raisins. Put celery, apple chunks, and raisins into a salad bowl. Stir the olive oil and lemon juice into the yoghurt, season with salt and pepper, and add to the salad. Toss lightly and garnish with the walnuts and parsley.

Complete coleslaw serves 4

CANCER *P.264*   CIRCULATORY *P.278*   DIGESTIVE *P.284*   FATIGUE *P.298*   JOINTS *P.304*

half small white cabbage
2 carrots
1 small eating apple
juice of half a lemon
1tbs olive oil
150g/5oz natural yoghurt
salt, pepper, and fresh chervil

Wash and shred the cabbage, wash and grate the carrots, and wash and shred the apple, and then put them all in a salad bowl. Sprinkle with the lemon juice. Stir the oil into the yoghurt, season with salt and pepper to taste, and stir into the slaw. Cover and chill for at least an hour. Garnish with chopped chervil before serving.

Celery, radish, and walnut salad serves 4

CANCER *P.264* DIGESTIVE *P284* STRESS *P.292* JOINTS *P.304* SKIN *P.318*

1 bunch radishes
3–4 sticks celery
125g/4oz walnuts
2tbs extra-virgin olive oil
1tsp lemon juice
salt and pepper

Scrub the radishes and cut into fine slices; save the best unwilted bits of the green leafy tops. Clean the celery and slice finely; save some of the feathery fronds. Roughly chop the walnuts. Make a dressing with the oil, lemon, and salt and pepper to taste. Stir thoroughly. Arrange the celery, radishes, and walnuts on a flat dish. Spoon the dressing over and decorate with the radish and celery fronds.

Winter white salad serves 4

CANCER *P.264* CIRCULATORY *P.278* STRESS *P.292* FATIGUE *P.298* JOINTS *P.304*

1 large fennel bulb
a chunk crisp white cabbage
2 sticks celery
2–3 white radishes
2tbs oil
1tbs lemon juice
salt and pepper
1tbs fresh parsley,
    finely chopped

Clean and slice the fennel into strips, saving the feathery fronds; clean and shred the cabbage; clean and slice the celery; clean and slice the radishes. Arrange in the salad bowl. In a separate bowl, mix the oil, lemon juice, and salt and pepper, and pour over. Toss. Garnish with the parsley.

Orange and watercress salad serves 4

CANCER *P.264* CIRCULATORY *P.278* DIGESTIVE *P.284* SKIN *P.318* URINARY *P.324*

1 large bunch watercress
2tbs olive oil
2tsp lemon juice
salt and pepper
2 large ripe oranges
2tbs pumpkin seeds
2tbs fresh parsley, chopped

Wash and dry the watercress thoroughly. Trim off the thicker bits of stalk, and line a white china dish with the leaves. Make a dressing with the oil, lemon juice, and salt and pepper. Scrub one of the oranges, grate the rind, and stir it into the dressing. Toast the pumpkin seeds lightly in a dry frying pan over a moderate heat. Peel both oranges, remove most of the pith, separate into segments, and slice each one in half. Add to the bowl and sprinkle with the parsley and pumpkin seeds. Pour over the dressing and toss just before serving.

Radish and rocket salad serves 4 ▶

CANCER *P.264* CIRCULATORY *P.278* DIGESTIVE *P.284* SKIN *P.318*

1 bunch fresh young
   radishes
2 small bulbs or 1 medium-
   sized fennel bulb
1 bunch rocket
2tbs extra-virgin olive oil
2tsp lemon juice
salt and pepper

Rocket is found in every greengrocer in Italy all year round. Its peppery taste adds piquancy to salads or can be used as a foil for thin slices of prosciutto or rare roast beef.

Clean the radishes and cut them lengthways – including the tops if these are still fresh. Clean the fennel and slice it lengthways into thin slices. Clean the rocket and separate it into smaller stems or leaves. Arrange the radish and fennel slices on a white dish, top with the rocket, dribble the olive oil over, sprinkle with the lemon juice, and season with salt and pepper to taste. Add a serving of ricotta or cottage cheese, and you have the perfect light lunch.

Frisée salad serves 4

CANCER *P.264* CIRCULATORY *P.278* STRESS *P.292* SKIN *P.318* URINARY *P.324*

1 head frisée (frizzy endive)
1 bunch watercress
3tbs olive oil
2tbs sunflower seeds
2tsp lemon juice
1 clove garlic, finely chopped
salt and pepper

Wash and dry the endive, and tear into small pieces. Wash and dry the watercress. Remove the thickest stalks and separate into sprigs. Put the endive and cress in a salad bowl. Heat 1 tablespoon of the olive oil in a non-stick pan, and toss the sunflower seeds until they take a little colour. Remove, drain on kitchen paper, and add to the salad bowl. Mix the rest of the oil, lemon juice, chopped garlic, salt and pepper, add to the salad, and toss. This salad can be kept chilled for up to an hour before you serve it: cover the bowl with clingfilm or a damp tea towel.

Sprouted seed salad serves 4

CANCER *P.264* DIGESTIVE *P.284* STRESS *P.292* FATIGUE *P.298* JOINTS *P.304* SKIN *P.318*

a choice of sprouts – alfalfa,
    mung beans, or aduki beans
1 bunch watercress
60g/2oz walnuts
2tbs olive oil
1tsp lemon juice
salt and pepper

Wash and dry the sprouts and put them in a salad bowl. Wash the watercress, strip off the toughest stalks, and divide into sprigs. Add to the salad bowl with the walnuts, broken up. Mix together the oil, lemon juice, salt and pepper, and add to the salad. Toss and serve.

Carrot salad serves 4

CANCER *P.264* CIRCULATORY *P.278* FATIGUE *P.298* SKIN *P.318*

250g/8oz carrots
1 medium-sized crisp apple
150ml/¼pt natural yoghurt
juice and rind of 1 orange

Scrub the carrots, wash the apple, and grate them both into a plain white china bowl. Mix the yoghurt with the orange juice, stir into the salad, and toss; grate a little of the orange rind on top.

Tsatsiki serves 4

CANCER *P.264* CIRCULATORY *P.278* DIGESTIVE *P.284* JOINTS *P.304* SKIN *P.318*

1 medium-sized cucumber
1 tsp sea salt
3 cloves garlic, crushed
300g/10oz natural yoghurt
1 tbs extra-virgin olive oil
2 tbs fresh mint leaves
freshly ground black pepper

Wash, dry, and cut the cucumber into cubes, sprinkle with salt and place in a colander. Leave to drain for at least an hour. Stir the garlic into the yoghurt, add the oil and most of the mint leaves – save a few to garnish it. Dry the cucumber, put in a bowl, add the yoghurt mixture, and toss. Add the black pepper and garnish with the reserved mint leaves.

Sauerkraut salad serves 4

CANCER *P.264* DIGESTIVE *P.284* JOINTS *P.304* RESPIRATORY *P.312* URINARY *P.324*

500g/1lb natural sauerkraut
2 tbs olive oil
1 medium-sized carrot, grated
1 tsp caraway seeds
1 tbs parsley, finely chopped

Put the sauerkraut in a dish, add the oil, mix in the carrot, and sprinkle the caraway seeds over it. Toss thoroughly, sprinkle with the parsley, cover, and chill for an hour or so.

Tricolour coleslaw serves 4

CANCER *P.264* CIRCULATORY *P.278* DIGESTIVE *P.284* FATIGUE *P.298* JOINTS *P.304*

125g/4oz each of red, white,
    and green cabbage
125g/4oz carrots, grated
2 tbs raisins or sultanas
1 medium-sized onion, finely
    sliced
1 small crisp eating apple
150ml//¼pt natural yoghurt
2 tbs extra-virgin olive oil
1 tbs cider vinegar
1 clove garlic, crushed

Wash, dry, and finely shred the cabbage. Combine with the carrots, sultanas or raisins, and onion; grate in the apple. Mix the dressing ingredients, and pour over the salad. Toss, cover with clingfilm, and chill for half an hour, so that the flavours have time to develop. Sprinkle the coleslaw with 1 teaspoon of caraway seeds and toss well before serving.

★ ★ ★ **Everyone likes to indulge** and you deserve a treat, but even puddings can be low in fat, high in fibre, and full of antioxidants.

Puddings

- ★ Winter compote
- ★ Peach and apricot compote
- ★ Tangerine and apricot pudding
- ★ Almond fruit whip
- ★ Toffee bananas
- ★ Pears cassis
- ★ Apple amaretto
- ★ Banana and mango crumble
- ★ Orange mango fool
- ★ Baked apples
- ★ Buckwheat pancakes
- ★ Fruit dipped in chocolate sauce
- ★ Mont blanc
- ★ Red plum pudding
- ★ Crowdie
- ★ Spicy winter pudding
- ★ Blackcurrant jelly
- ★ Summer pudding
- ★ Ginger fruit pudding
- ★ Stewed apple with mascarpone
- ★ Apricot whip
- ★ Spiced peaches

Winter compote serves 4

DIGESTIVE *P.284* STRESS *P.292* FATIGUE *P.298*

250g/8oz stoned prunes
250g/8oz stoned dried
    apricots
250g/8oz dried pears
250g/8oz dried apples
125g/4oz seedless raisins
125g/4oz seedless sultanas
125g/4oz chopped or flaked
    almonds
half a lemon, sliced thinly
1tsp cinnamon
¼tsp ground nutmeg
4tbs brandy
juice of half a lemon
2tbs soft brown sugar

This is a traditional Jewish winter dessert that is equally good cold for breakfast.

Preheat the oven to 175°C/350°F/gas 4. In a large casserole dish arrange the dried fruit and lemon slices in layers, with the raisins, sultanas, and almonds sprinkled in between. Sprinkle the cinnamon and nutmeg on top. Mix the brandy, lemon juice, and sugar, and pour over the fruit. Add enough boiling water to cover. Bake in the oven for 20 minutes.

Peach and apricot compote serves 4

CANCER *P.264* FATIGUE *P.298* RESPIRATORY *P.312* SKIN *P.318*

500g/1lb small peaches,
    stoned
500g/1lb ripe apricots, stoned
150ml/¼pt white wine
    or apple juice
1 cinnamon stick
1tbs honey

This is a pudding for the summer, when fresh ripe apricots and tiny peaches are cheap and plentiful on every market stall.

Wash the fruit carefully and put it in a pan with the wine or apple juice, the cinnamon stick, and the honey. Bring to the boil, turn the heat right down, and simmer, covered, for about 10–15 minutes, or until the fruit is soft. Chill. Serve with yoghurt, crème fraîche, or ice cream.

Tangerine and apricot pudding serves 4

CANCER *P.264* CIRCULATORY *P.278* DIGESTIVE *P.284* STRESS *P.292* FATIGUE *P.298*

10-12 firm ripe apricots
6 tangerines
250ml/8fl oz fresh
    orange juice
1tsp honey
a few drops vanilla essence

Wash, halve, and stone the apricots; peel the tangerines and divide into segments. Put the apricots in a pan with the orange juice, honey, and vanilla essence. Simmer until soft but still whole – about 10 minutes – then remove from the heat. Transfer to a dish, add the tangerine segments, and chill.

Almond fruit whip serves 4

CANCER *P.264* CIRCULATORY *P.278* STRESS *P.292* FATIGUE *P.298* SKIN *P.318*

150ml/¼pt fresh orange juice
60g/2oz dried apricots
125g/4oz raisins
500g/1lb fresh ripe apricots,
    nectarines, or peaches
juice of 1 lemon
150g/5oz natural yoghurt
60g/2oz flaked almonds
¼tsp cinnamon

Put the orange juice in a pan with the washed, dried apricots and raisins. Simmer gently until the fruit is soft and plumped out. Wash the apricots, nectarines, or peaches, cut into chunks, and purée in a blender or food-processor with the lemon juice. Mix the fresh fruit purée with the dried fruit purée and stir in the yoghurt. Transfer to a dish and sprinkle with flaked almonds and cinnamon. Chill before serving.

Toffee bananas serves 4

STRESS *P.292* FATIGUE *P.298*

4 bananas
2tbs brown sugar
4tbs dark rum

A quick, gooey dessert that goes well with thick yoghurt or crème fraîche.

Heat the grill to red hot. Peel the bananas and lay them in a shallow ovenproof dish. Sprinkle them thickly with the brown sugar and pour the rum around them. Place under the grill until the sugar and rum bubble. Serve immediately.

Pears cassis serves 4

CANCER *P.264* CIRCULATORY *P.278* DIGESTIVE *P.284* FATIGUE *P.298* URINARY *P.324*

4 pears
4 cloves
300ml/½pt unsweetened
   blackcurrant juice
zest of 1 lemon
2tsp honey
a generous pinch of nutmeg

Wash the pears thoroughly, leaving their stalks on. Stick a clove in each one, and if possible, pack them into a casserole or baking dish in which they just fit, stalks uppermost. Add the blackcurrant juice, lemon zest, honey, and a little nutmeg. Simmer, covered, over the lowest possible heat until the pears are tender. Take out very carefully and arrange in a dish. If necessary, reduce the liquid until it is thick and syrupy, pour it over the pears, and chill. Serve with Greek yoghurt.

Apple amaretto serves 4

DIGESTIVE *P.284* FATIGUE *P.298*

4 medium-sized cooking
   apples
125g/4oz ground almonds
2tbs orange juice
¼tsp cinnamon
¼tsp nutmeg

Core the apples. Cut off the bottoms of the cores and stuff them back into the apples as a plug. Mix the ground almonds and orange juice to a paste and stuff the apples with it. Put them in a heatproof dish with a little water, sprinkle with cinnamon and nutmeg, and bake at 150°C/300°F/gas 2 for about 20 minutes. These are delicious hot or cold.

Banana and mango crumble serves 4

CIRCULATORY *P.278* DIGESTIVE *P.284* JOINTS *P.304* URINARY *P.324*

1 large mango, peeled and
   cubed
4 bananas, peeled and sliced
grated rind and juice of
   1 lemon
2tbs soft brown sugar
175g/6oz wholewheat
   breadcrumbs (*p.254*)
75g/3oz butter
2tbs sugar-free muesli

Preheat the oven to 190°C/375°F/gas 5. Mix the mango and banana with the lemon rind, lemon juice, and half the sugar, and pour into a lightly greased pie dish. Knead together the breadcrumbs and the butter, add the remaining sugar and the muesli, and distribute evenly on top of the fruit. Dot with a little more butter. Cook for 20 minutes. Serve with a little single cream.

Orange mango fool serves 4

DIGESTIVE *P.284* FATIGUE *P.298*

2 ripe mangoes
150ml/¼pt Greek yoghurt
grated rind and juice of half
   an orange

Peel the mangoes, remove the flesh, and put it in a blender or food processor. Add the yoghurt and orange juice and process until smooth. Chill. Decorate with the grated orange rind, and serve.

Baked apples serves 4

CANCER *P.264* DIGESTIVE *P.284* FATIGUE *P.298* JOINTS *P.304* RESPIRATORY *P.312*

4 large cooking apples
1tbs butter
2tbs ground almonds
1tbs raisins, washed
1tbs orange juice
8 cloves
1tbs brown sugar
¼tsp nutmeg

Carefully wash and core the apples. Butter an ovenproof dish and stand the apples in it – you may have to slice off their bottoms to keep them upright. Stuff the ground almonds and raisins into the cavities, moisten with the orange juice, and stick a couple of cloves in each apple. Then smear a little butter around the top of each apple and sprinkle with a little sugar. Grind some fresh nutmeg over the tops and bake until the skins are shiny and just ready to burst.

Buckwheat pancakes serves 4

CANCER *P.264* DIGESTIVE *P.284* STRESS *P.292* FATIGUE *P.298* URINARY *P.324*

125g/4oz buckwheat flour
125g/4oz wholewheat flour
½tsp salt
1tbs brown sugar
2tsp baking powder
2 eggs
275ml/9fl oz milk
1tbs sunflower or grapeseed
　　oil, plus extra for brushing
　　the pan

Sieve the flours into a bowl, and add the salt, sugar, and baking powder. Beat the eggs, and add them with the milk. Stir in the oil, and blend or mix in the food processor. Allow to stand for 30 minutes. Heat a non-stick pan, brush with a very little oil, and drop in spoonfuls of the mixture. When bubbles have formed all over the surface, turn the pancakes. Serve with lemon juice, honey, and sesame seeds.

Fruit dipped in chocolate sauce serves 4 ▶

STRESS *P.292* FATIGUE *P.298*

fresh fruit, washed, dried,
　　and chilled for 2–3 hours
250–300g/8–10oz dark
　　chocolate (minimum 70 per
　　cent cocoa solids)

Choose your children's favourite fruit for this fondue – apples, pears, grapes, strawberries, peaches, tangerine segments, chunks of pineapple, bananas, melon – and use organic chocolate, if possible. Have plenty of wooden skewers handy for dipping the fruit into the chocolate.

Cut large fruits into chunks, if necessary, then put all the fruit in a bowl or on a large platter. Break the chocolate into pieces, and put it in a bowl set over a pan of hot, but not boiling, water. Leave it to melt. Keep the chocolate hot in a fondue pot or over a tealight while the children are dipping fruit into it. Don't leave the children unattended while the flame is lit.

Mont blanc serves 4

CIRCULATORY *P.278* FATIGUE *P.298*

500g/1lb tin of unsweetened
    chestnut purée
1tbs brown sugar
rind and juice of 1 orange
6tbs thick cream or
    crème fraîche
1tbs bitter chocolate, grated,
    to garnish

Put the chestnut purée, sugar, and orange juice and rind in a food processor and blend until smooth. Add 4 tablespoons of the cream or crème fraîche and blend again. Serve heaped in a mound on a pretty dish, topped with the rest of the cream or crème fraîche, and sprinkle the grated chocolate on top.

Red plum pudding serves 4

CIRCULATORY *P.278* DIGESTIVE *P.284*

500g/1lb dark red plums,
    washed and stoned
2tsp runny honey
2tbs red wine
4–6 cardamom pods
1tbs cassis or brandy

Put the plums in a pan with the honey, the wine, and the cardamom pods. Simmer over a low heat until the plums are just starting to disintegrate, then add the brandy (alcohol, incidentally, evaporates when heated, leaving only the flavour behind). Heat through again and transfer to a serving dish. Serve with cream, yoghurt, fromage frais, or crème fraîche. This pudding is also delicious served cold.

Crowdie serves 4

STRESS *P.292* FATIGUE *P.298*

125g/4oz coarse oats
60g/2oz flaked almonds
1tbs brown sugar
250g/8oz whipping cream
250g/8oz Greek yoghurt

Spread the oats and flaked almonds on a flat baking tray and sprinkle with the sugar. Place in a hot oven until crispy but not browned. Reserve one tablespoon of this mixture. Whip the cream, fold in the yoghurt, stir in the oat-and-almond mixture, and spoon into glass dishes. Decorate with the reserved oats and almond mix.

Spicy winter pudding serves 4

CANCER *P.264* DIGESTIVE *P.284* FATIGUE *P.298* RESPIRATORY *P.312*

300ml/½pt apple juice
4 cloves
a little freshly grated ginger,
    or ½tsp powdered ginger
½tsp cinnamon
good pinch grated nutmeg
1tbs honey
250g/8oz assorted stoned or
    seedless dried fruit
    – prunes, apricots, raisins,
    apples, pears, washed
twist of lemon peel
8–10 pieces wholewheat
    bread, thinly sliced and
    lightly buttered

Heat up the apple juice with the cloves, ginger, cinnamon, nutmeg, and honey. When it is boiling, add the fruit and the lemon peel and simmer very gently for about 25 minutes or until the fruit is soft. Drain, saving the juices. Meanwhile, grease a heatproof dish, then line with thin slices of wholewheat bread, crusts removed. Fill with the fruit mixture, top with more bread, and pour over it enough of the cooking liquid to saturate the bread. Sprinkle the top with a little brown sugar and cinnamon. Put in a moderate oven for 20–25 minutes. Pour the remaining cooking liquid over it.

Blackcurrant jelly serves 4

DIGESTIVE *P.284* FATIGUE *P.298* RESPIRATORY *P.312*

1kg/2lb blackcurrants
600ml/1pt apple juice
2tsp agar-agar
small red eating apple
honey to taste

Wash and trim the blackcurrants. Heat the apple juice, add the agar-agar, and bring gently to the boil, stirring until all the agar-agar is dissolved. Mix with the blackcurrants, wet a jelly mould, pour all the mixture in, and place in the refrigerator. When just beginning to set, core the apple and cut it into fine slices. Arrange on the half-set jelly and return to the refrigerator until set.

Summer pudding serves 4

CANCER *P.264* DIGESTIVE *P.284* FATIGUE *P.298*

375g/12oz raspberries
175g/6oz red currants
60g/2oz blackcurrants
60g/2oz soft brown sugar
6 thin slices wholemeal bread,
  crusts removed
crème fraîche or Greek
  yoghurt to serve

Classic summer pudding is made with white bread and much more white sugar than this. But the pudding works just as well with wholemeal bread, and the lovely fruity taste comes through much more sharply when it is not overwhelmed by sugar. You may find you want to use even less. Make the pudding at least 6 hours before it is going to be eaten.

Wash the fruit, pull the currants off their stalks with a fork, and put all the fruit in a large saucepan together with the sugar. Set the pan over a very low heat for 2–3 minutes, until the sugar melts and the juices begin to run. Set the pan aside.

Use 5 slices of the bread to line a 1kg/2lb pudding basin, making sure there are no gaps that could spoil the pudding's appearance. Add the fruit, reserving a good half-cup of the juice. Roof over the pudding with the remaining slice of bread, then put a plate on top with a weight on it to press it down into the basin. Chill the pudding for at least 6 hours.

To serve, up-end the basin over a pretty china dish so that the pudding slides on to the middle of it. Pour over the reserved juice and serve, on its own or, alternatively, with a little crème fraîche or Greek yoghurt.

Ginger fruit pudding serves 4

DIGESTIVE *P.284* STRESS *P.292*

125g/4oz wholemeal self-
   raising flour
2tsp cinnamon
½tsp grated nutmeg
1tsp ground ginger
1tsp bicarbonate of soda
125g/4oz soft dark
   brown sugar
1 egg
60g/2oz butter
90g/3oz black treacle
300ml/½pt milk
60g/2oz sultanas
4 pieces (more if you like)
   preserved ginger, chopped
whipped cream to serve

Preheat the oven to 180°C/350°F/gas 4. Lightly butter a 1.2 litre/2 pint capacity deep ovenproof dish. Sieve the flour, cinnamon, nutmeg, ginger, bicarbonate of soda, and sugar into a bowl, tipping the bran left in the sieve into the mix. Mix in the egg. Melt the butter in a small saucepan and add the treacle to warm through. Add this to the flour-and-egg mixture, then pour in the milk. Using a balloon whisk, mix thoroughly so there are no lumps. Stir in the sultanas and preserved ginger.

Pour the mixture into the prepared dish. Bake in the oven for 30–35 minutes. Don't overcook and don't worry if it subsides a bit in the middle; this gives a nice sticky centre to the pudding. Serve hot with chilled whipped cream. You can add some of the syrup from the preserved ginger to the whipped cream, if you wish.

Stewed apple with mascarpone serves 4

CIRCULATORY *P.278* DIGESTIVE *P.284* JOINTS *P.304*

60ml/2fl oz water
30g/1oz caster sugar
500g/1lb cooking apples, such
   as Bramleys, peeled, cored,
   and sliced
250g/8oz mascarpone cheese

Put the water into a saucepan. Add the sugar and heat gently until the sugar has dissolved. Add the apple slices to the sugar mixture, cooking very gently. When the apples have cooked to a smooth purée, fold in the mascarpone. Put into individual dishes and chill in the refrigerator.

Apricot whip serves 4

CANCER *P.264* CIRCULATORY *P.278* DIGESTIVE *P.284* FATIGUE *P.298* JOINTS *P.304*

250g/8oz dried apricots
300ml/½pt water
1tbs apple juice concentrate
1tbs lemon juice
1–2tbs honey
4tbs Greek yoghurt
¼tsp nutmeg
1tbs flaked almonds

Wash the apricots. Mix the water with the apple juice concentrate, lemon juice, and honey. Pour the mixture over the apricots and leave to soak, covered, overnight. Next day, put the apricots in a pan with the liquid, bring to the boil, and simmer until soft – about 5–10 minutes. Leave to cool, then purée. Spoon into individual glass dishes; top with a spoonful of Greek yoghurt, a dusting of nutmeg, and a few flaked almonds.

Spiced peaches serves 4 ▶

DIGESTIVE *P.284* STRESS *P.292* FATIGUE *P.298* RESPIRATORY *P.312* SKIN *P.318*

8 small peaches
8 cloves
enough red or white wine
    to cover
peel of 1 lemon
1tbs honey
¼tsp nutmeg or cinnamon

A clever cook we know invented this all-purpose pudding on holiday in Spain, profiting by a glut of tiny peaches at give-away prices and cheap local wine. It is highly adaptable; we have cooked hard little apricots or nectarines the same way, or used up oddments of brandy, whisky, apple, or grape juice instead. Chilled and piled up in a dish with the syrupy remains of the juice poured over, and with Greek yoghurt or cream served separately, it can be a grand party pudding. Any leftovers never survive breakfast time.

Wash the peaches, stick a clove in each one, and put in a pan with the wine. Add the peel of a well-scrubbed lemon, honey, and nutmeg or cinnamon to taste. Bring to the boil, lower the heat, and simmer, covered, until the peaches are tender and almost at bursting point.

★ ★ ★ Juices, smoothies, herbal teas – there are no rules about what goes with what. Spread out your palate and build your own food rainbow.

Drinks

- ★ Lime-apple tea
- ★ Banana milkshake
- ★ Summer special
- ★ Ginger punch
- ★ Highland fling

- ★ Black-jack
- ★ Green apple
- ★ Pineapple julep
- ★ Cold borscht
- ★ Dandelion and mint julep

Lime-apple tea serves 1

STRESS *P.292* RESPIRATORY *P.312*

1 limeflower teabag
2tsp apple juice concentrate
a dash of freshly squeezed
    lemon juice

Make a cup of limeflower tea with boiling water and the teabag. Allow to infuse for 6 minutes. Add the apple juice concentrate and the lemon juice and stir. Serves 1, but can be multiplied to make more.

Banana milkshake serves 1

CIRCULATORY *P.278* STRESS *P.292*

1 banana, peeled
200ml/7fl oz milk
1tbs natural yoghurt
1tsp honey
2tsp brewer's yeast

This is a protein-rich drink that makes a good substitute for breakfast when you're too busy to cook.

Put all the ingredients in the blender and liquidize. Serves 1, but can be multiplied to make more.

Summer special serves 1

CANCER *P.264* URINARY *P.324*

1tbs raspberries
1tbs blackcurrants
150ml/¼pt natural yoghurt
1tbs crème fraîche

You could also make this drink in winter, using frozen summer fruit. If you use frozen fruit, put it in a pan and warm through over a low heat for 2–3 minutes.

Wash the fruit and put all the ingredients in a blender or food processor and liquidize. Serves 1, but can be multiplied to make more.

Ginger punch serves 1

CANCER *P.264* RESPIRATORY *P.312*

2.5cm/1in piece fresh ginger,
   peeled and grated
300ml/½pt water
1tbs honey

Drink this at the first sign of a cold or flu. Add the ginger to the water, bring to the boil, simmer until it has reduced by half, stir in the honey, simmer until it is dissolved, and then drink it as hot as possible just before you go to bed. You should sweat the bugs out overnight. Serves 1, but can be multiplied to make more.

Highland fling serves 4

CIRCULATORY *P.278* STRESS *P.292* FATIGUE *P.298*

60g/2oz fine oatmeal
1tsp honey
juice of 1 lemon
2.5cm/1in piece fresh ginger,
   peeled and grated
1.2litres/2½pt water

Put the oatmeal and a large spoonful of honey into your largest pan. Add a little warm water, the juice of a lemon, and the ginger. Bring 1.2 litres (2½ pints) of water to the boil and add it slowly to the oatmeal mixture, stirring all the time. Bring back to the boil and continue stirring for 3 minutes. Strain into a large jug, chill, and keep in the fridge – for not more than 3 days.

Black-jack serves 2

RESPIRATORY *P.312*

250g/8oz blackcurrants
2 cloves
500ml/16fl oz apple juice
1tbs honey

Add the blackcurrants and 2 cloves to the apple juice in a pan. Simmer for 10 minutes, then strain. Add 1 tablespoon honey and drink hot. If blackcurrants are not in season, use a dessertspoonful of blackcurrant jelly. Comforting for coughs, colds, and sore throats. Serves 2, but can be multiplied to make more.

Green apple serves 1

JOINTS *P.304* RESPIRATORY *P.312* SKIN *P.318*

a sprig of mint
1 small bunch parsley
2-3 dandelion leaves
1 small green eating apple
125ml/4fl oz apple juice
1 tsp apple juice concentrate
1 tsp honey
1 tsp lemon juice

Chill all the ingredients before making. Wash the greens and the apple. Put the apple juice, apple juice concentrate, honey, and lemon juice in a blender. Slice in the apple, add the green leaves, and blend. Drink at once. You can use spinach instead of dandelion if you prefer. Serves 1, but can be multiplied to serve more.

Pineapple julep serves 1

DIGESTIVE *P.284* FATIGUE *P.298*

1 peppermint teabag
50ml/2fl oz boiling water
125ml/4fl oz pineapple juice
a sprig of fresh mint, crushed

Put the teabag in a cup and add the water. Let infuse for 6 minutes, then strain and cool. When cold, add the pineapple juice, mint leaves, and serve over ice. Serves 1, but can be multiplied to serve more.

Dandelion and mint julep serves 1

DIGESTIVE *P.284* RESPIRATORY *P.312* SKIN *P.318* URINARY *P.324*

200ml/7fl oz white grape juice
1 slice of lemon
a sprig of mint
2 young dandelion leaves

Pour white grape juice over crushed ice, add a slice of lemon, a sprig of mint, and 2 young dandelion leaves. For extra flavour, slice in a couple of ripe strawberries or some fresh peach. Serves 1, but can be multiplied to serve more.

Cold borscht serves 1

DIGESTIVE *P.284* JOINTS *P.304* RESPIRATORY *P.312* SKIN *P.318* URINARY *P.324*

1 medium-sized beetroot
4-5 sprigs of parsley
150g/5oz natural yoghurt
1 tsp lemon juice

Cook, peel, and slice the beetroot. Put all the ingredients in the blender and liquidize. Serves 1, but can be multiplied to serve more.

★ ★ ★ Basic doesn't have to mean boring. It's just the starting point for the very best soups, stews, casseroles, sauces, and salads.

Basic recipes

- ★ Mean dressing
- ★ Yoghurt and garlic dressing
- ★ Wholemeal garlic croutons
- ★ Mean cheese sauce
- ★ Tomato sauce
- ★ Garlic mayonnaise
- ★ Anton Mosimann's sauce
- ★ Basic brown rice
- ★ Basic barley
- ★ Mozzarella and tomato sauce

- ★ Tomato and anchovy sauce
- ★ Quick tomato and olive sauce
- ★ Tomato and lemon salsa
- ★ Spicy tomato and onion sauce
- ★ Sauce Mornay
- ★ Michael's millet and buckwheat
- ★ Vegetable stock

Mean dressing serves 4

DIGESTIVE *P.284* URINARY *P.324*

1 small carton low-fat
   natural yoghurt
1 tsp lemon juice
1 pinch dried mixed herbs or
   dried basil
freshly ground black pepper

Mix all ingredients together well and serve over salad leaves.

Yoghurt and garlic dressing serves 4

URINARY *P.324*

1 small carton low-fat
   natural yoghurt
1 clove garlic, crushed
1 tsp olive oil
1 tsp cider vinegar
a pinch of black pepper

Mix well together and use instead of mayonnaise or salad dressing. Flavour according to taste with fresh mint, chives, finely chopped cucumber, a little chilli, or a teaspoon of curry powder.

Wholemeal garlic croutons serves 4

STRESS *P.292* FATIGUE *P.298* RESPIRATORY *P.312*

2 thick slices wholemeal
   bread – not too fresh
2 tbs olive oil
2 cloves garlic, crushed

Add the crushed garlic to the oil and leave for at least an hour. Then cut and discard the bread-crusts, cut the slices into cubes, strain the olive oil into a baking dish, turn the cubes into it and turn them around in the garlicky oil. Bake in a hot oven until they are crispy brown – about 20 minutes. For plain wholemeal croutons, simply omit the garlic.

Mean cheese sauce serves 2

FATIGUE *P.298*

1 small onion
150ml/¼pt skimmed milk
1 bay leaf
2tsp butter
2tsp white flour
¼tsp mustard powder
60g/2oz low-fat Cheddar
   cheese, grated

Peel and quarter the onion, put in a pan with the milk and bay leaf, heat the milk to near-boiling point, and leave to infuse for half an hour. Melt the butter in a small pan, add the flour and the mustard powder, stirring briskly. Remove from the heat. Strain and reheat the milk, stir into the flour-butter mixture and beat over a low heat until smooth. Stir in the cheese. Pour over any vegetables – steamed until tender – and put under a hot grill for 2-3 minutes.

Tomato sauce serves 4

CANCER *P.264* CIRCULATORY *P.278*

2tbs olive oil
2 cloves garlic, finely chopped
1 medium-sized onion,
   chopped
2 425g/14oz tins of Italian
   plum tomatoes
salt and pepper
2tbs fresh parsley, chopped

Heat the oil, put in the finely chopped garlic and onion, and fry gently without browning. Add the tomatoes and their juice and cook briskly, uncovered, stirring occasionally, for about 20 minutes. When the sauce thickens, purée it in a blender or food processor, reheat, season with salt and pepper to taste, and stir in the parsley.

Serve with plain grilled fish, meat, or pasta. Add a small finely chopped chilli pepper or a half a teaspoon cayenne pepper and this becomes the traditionally fiery arrabbiata – literally "raging" – tomato sauce beloved of the Italians, and served with pasta – usually the big tubes of penne. It goes superbly with any dried pasta.

Garlic mayonnaise *serves 4*

CIRCULATORY *P.278* STRESS *P.292* FATIGUE *P.298*

2 egg yolks
2 cloves garlic, crushed
a pinch of salt
200ml/7fl oz extra-virgin
    olive oil
1 tbs lemon juice

Break the yolks into a small bowl, crush, and add the garlic and salt and beat together. Start beating in the oil a drop or two at a time. Once the mayonnaise has begun to thicken, the oil can be added in a steady trickle, then a thin stream. From time to time, add a squirt of lemon juice. When all the oil and lemon juice have been added, the mayonnaise should be a thick, shiny mix. Cover the bowl with clingfilm and refrigerate until you are ready to use it. If you would like it a little thinner, stir in a teaspoon or two of boiling water.

If the mix suddenly thins as you work, this means it has begun to curdle. You may be able to rescue it by adding a few drops of boiling water and stirring hard. If not, take a clean bowl, another egg yolk, and start again with more oil. When the mayonnaise is safely under way, start adding the curdled mixture.

NOTE: Both eggs and oil should be at room temperature. If your eggs have been stored in the fridge, warm them up in a basin of hot water for a minute or two before you start. To stop the bowl rocking about as you make the mayonnaise, rest it on a damp cloth as you stir. Stir with a small wooden spoon.

Anton Mosimann's sauce serves 4

FATIGUE *P.298* URINARY *P.324*

300g/10oz low-fat natural
  yoghurt
1tsp caster sugar
1tsp powdered cinnamon
grated zest of half a lemon

A low-calorie sauce for stewed fruits, fresh berries, and other fresh or dried fruit. You can also use it instead of cream or custard. Combine all ingredients and whisk to a smooth, creamy consistency.

Basic brown rice serves 4

CIRCULATORY *P.278* DIGESTIVE *P.284* STRESS *P.292* FATIGUE *P.298*

250g/8oz brown rice
water
½tsp sea salt

Wash the rice in a sieve, letting cold water run through for a couple of minutes and shaking it. Drain, put in a heavy casserole, and add enough boiling water to come to the depth of a thumbnail above the surface of the rice. Add half a teaspoon of sea salt, cover tightly, and put in a low oven: 170°C/325°F/gas 3. Cook for about 40 minutes. If it is still inclined to be wet, turn the oven off, remove the lid, and return to the oven for another 5–10 minutes.

Basic barley serves 4

CIRCULATORY *P.278* DIGESTIVE *P.284* FATIGUE *P.298* URINARY *P.324*

250g/8oz pot barley
750ml/1¼pt water

Wash the barley thoroughly. Put it in a pan with the water and bring to the boil. Lower the heat and simmer, covered, for 45 minutes, or until the barley is tender. Drain the barley, but don't throw away the water: it is nutritionally rich. Add to soups or stews, or drink it on its own.

Mozzarella and tomato sauce serves 4

CANCER *P.264* FATIGUE *P.298*

375g/12oz ripe fresh
    tomatoes
6tbs olive oil
a handful of fresh basil leaves,
    roughly torn
a sprig of fresh oregano
3tbs Parmesan cheese,
    freshly grated
150g/5oz mozzarella
    cheese, cubed

A couple of hours before you plan to eat, skin and finely chop the tomatoes. Put them in a bowl with the olive oil, basil leaves, oregano, and grated Parmesan. Leave to macerate for 2 hours. Put the cubes of mozzarella into the dish in which you plan to serve the pasta. Cook your chosen pasta until it is *al dente* (just tender). Drain it well and tip it on top of the mozzarella cubes, stirring very quickly so that the melting cheese disperses throughout the pasta. Add the tomato mixture, stir again, and serve.

Tomato and anchovy sauce serves 4

CANCER *P.264* CIRCULATORY *P.278*

100ml/3½fl oz olive oil
3 cloves garlic, finely chopped
200g/7oz tinned chopped
    tomatoes
60g/2oz soft pitted black
    olives, chopped
a pinch of dried oregano
3-4 anchovy fillets, well
    rinsed, dried and finely
    chopped
2tbs fresh parsley, finely
    chopped
freshly ground black pepper

Older children will enjoy this Italian classic. But the first time you make it, add just a touch of anchovy – perhaps a blob of anchovy paste from a tube. The sauce can be made in advance and reheated to serve with your chosen pasta.

Heat the oil in a small saucepan, add the garlic, and cook gently for 2-3 minutes. Add the tomatoes, olives, and oregano. Simmer very gently for a few minutes, then add the chopped anchovies. Cook a few minutes longer, until the anchovies have softened and blended with the sauce. Add the parsley and a twist or two of fresh black pepper. The anchovies will give the sauce all the salt it needs.

Quick tomato and olive sauce serves 2

CANCER *P.264* STRESS *P.292*

2tbs olive oil
1 onion, chopped
400g/13oz tinned tomatoes,
  chopped
3tbs black olive tapenade
  (*p.212*) or ready-made
2tbs sun-dried tomatoes, cut
  into strips
freshly ground black pepper

This unusual tomato sauce goes beautifully with pasta, or you can serve it with grilled fish or chicken. Black olive tapenade and sun-dried tomatoes can be bought from most large supermarkets. They impart a rich texture and flavour to an otherwise simple sauce.

Heat the oil, fry the onion until it is golden, then add the tomatoes. Stir and heat through for a few minutes. Stir in the tapenade and the sun-dried tomatoes, heat for a minute or two, and season to taste with pepper.

Tomato and lemon salsa serves 4

CANCER *P.264* DIGESTIVE *P.284*

500g/1lb ripe red tomatoes,
  skinned and chopped
2–3 cloves garlic, finely
  chopped
2tbs fresh coriander, basil, or
  parsley, chopped
8tbs extra-virgin olive oil
2tbs fresh lemon juice
4–5 spring onions, finely
  chopped
fresh red or green chilli, to
  taste, deseeded and chopped

This wonderful fresh sauce with a sharp chilli tang is good with grilled fish or chicken, rice, or pasta.

Mix all the ingredients together in a bowl, cover with clingfilm, and chill for at least 1 hour. You can store the salsa in the refrigerator for 2–3 days.

Spicy tomato and onion sauce serves 6-8

CANCER *P.264* RESPIRATORY *P.312*

60g/2oz butter
1 onion, finely chopped
2 cloves garlic, crushed
2tbs vinegar
150ml/¼pt water
1tbs English mustard
2tbs demerara sugar
a thick slice of lemon
a pinch of cayenne pepper
2tbs Worcestershire sauce
6tbs tomato ketchup
2tbs tomato purée
salt and freshly ground
   black pepper

Serve this sauce with pasta, grilled chicken, or fish. You can make a large amount, divide it into smaller quantities, and keep it in the freezer.

Melt the butter in a pan and sauté the onion and garlic gently for 2-3 minutes. Stir in the vinegar, water, mustard, sugar, lemon, and cayenne. Bring to the boil, cover, and simmer for 15 minutes. Stir in the remaining ingredients, season to taste with salt and pepper, and cook for a further 5 minutes. Remove the lemon from the sauce before serving.

Sauce Mornay serves 2

FATIGUE *P.298*

2tbs butter
2tbs flour
300ml/½pt milk, heated
salt and white pepper
60g/2oz hard, strongly
   flavoured cheese, such as
   Cheddar, grated
a pinch of crushed dried chilli
a good pinch of nutmeg

This simple, quick sauce is the basis for delicious gratin dishes. Vegetables lend themselves particularly well to the Sauce Mornay treatment – courgettes, cauliflower, broccoli, and young turnips can be cooked until just tender, then transferred to an ovenproof dish, covered in Sauce Mornay, and topped with a little grated cheese. Five minutes in a hot oven will produce a delicious dish with a golden-brown topping.

Melt the butter in a saucepan. Stir in the flour and add the hot milk a little at a time, stirring to keep the sauce smooth. Season with salt and pepper, add the cheese, chilli, and nutmeg, and cook over the lowest possible heat for 5 minutes.

Michael's millet and buckwheat serves 4

CANCER *P.264* DIGESTIVE *P.284* FATIGUE *P.298* JOINTS *P.304*
RESPIRATORY *P.312* SKIN *P.318*

2 large carrots
1 large onion
2 sticks celery
2 cloves garlic
2tbs oil
250g/8oz millet
250g/8oz buckwheat
900ml/1½pt vegetable stock
   (*see below*)
1 green pepper
1 red pepper
1tsp yeast extract
a pinch of paprika
a few fronds of fennel tops
2 bay leaves
250g/8oz mushrooms

Grate 1 carrot and finely chop the onion, celery, and garlic. Heat the oil in a heavy-bottomed pan, add the carrot, onion, celery, and garlic, and sweat together, stirring constantly, over a high heat, until softened. Add the millet and buckwheat, stir for 2–3 minutes, then add the stock and all the other vegetables, sliced, except the mushrooms. Add the yeast extract, paprika, fennel, and bay leaves, then bring to the boil. Simmer, stirring occasionally, until the vegetables and grains are soft, about 45–60 minutes. Add more stock if necessary. Ten minutes before serving, add the mushrooms, wiped and sliced. Stir the mixture until warmed through.

This will serve four very hungry people and there will be enough left over for the next day, when it's good served cold with a green salad.

Vegetable stock serves 4

DIGESTIVE *P.284* FATIGUE *P.298* JOINTS *P.304* RESPIRATORY *P.312*

2 large carrots
1 large onion
2–3 cloves garlic
2 sticks celery, including tops
2tbs olive oil
1 bay leaf
1tbs each fresh thyme and
   marjoram, chopped
900ml/1½pt water

Peel and slice the carrots, peel and chop the onion and garlic, and clean and chop the celery. Heat the oil in a big saucepan, melt the onion and garlic, add the carrot and celery, stir and cook gently for about 5 minutes. Add the herbs and water, bring to the boil, and simmer for about an hour, covered.

Protect your health

* Cancer
* Circulatory problems
* Digestive problems
* Stress
* Fatigue
* Joint problems
* Respiratory problems
* Skin problems
* Urinary problems
* Weight control
* Harmonious eating

Cancer

It is no longer possible to doubt that there is a direct link between diet and cancer. For years, orthodox medicine denied the possibility, let alone the existence, of such a simple cause and effect. The handful of doctors working with nutrition to fight cancer, among them Max Gerson, Kristine Nolfi, Josef Issels, C. Moerman, Henry Bieler, and Hans Nieper, were not simply derided but were actively persecuted. Now, however, the scientific evidence is piling up.

In 1982, the US National Cancer Institute (NCI) published a watershed report summarizing the evidence for the diet–cancer link. The report also made recommendations that included eating more fruits, vegetables, and wholegrains, and cutting down on fats and smoked, salt-cured, and pickled food, as well as alcohol. This report made it respectable for scientists and doctors all over the world to study the diet–cancer link. A couple of years later, a study was begun that involved nearly 30,000 women. They were given nine recommendations, including those made by the US NCI, and were then followed by scientists from the Mayo Clinic for 13 years. This study concluded in July 2004 that lifestyle and dietary changes could reduce the risk of cancer by up to an astonishing 42 per cent.

There is less and less doubt that eating plenty of fresh fruit, vegetables, and wholegrains and reducing the refined carbohydrates and processed

"Lifestyle and dietary changes could reduce cancer risk by 42 per cent."

foods in your diet will have a serious impact on your vulnerability to cancer. Researchers now believe that for some cancers, such as colorectal cancer, differences in dietary habits may account for up 90 per cent of the differences in incidence around the world. In other words, the healthy eating being advocated more than 50 years ago by great nutritional pioneers such as Bircher-Benner, Max Gerson, Henry Bieler, Gayelord Hauser, and Robert McCarrison was not so cranky after all.

Follow the general advice given here, and you will enormously enhance your body's natural defences against cancer, or indeed, against any disease. Apart from a poor diet, there are other well-known risk factors for cancer: heavy smoking; exposure at work to toxic chemicals in the agriculture and pharmaceutical industries, or in the manufacture of rubber, plastics, dyes, paints, furniture treatments, and so forth; heavy alcohol consumption; obesity; a family history of cancer; radiation exposure in industry or medicine; chronic gastritis; long periods of bad eating habits; and high levels of stress, unhappiness, or frustration. If any of these factors apply to you, or to other members of your family, then you will need to follow the anti-cancer diet far more faithfully.

If you have cancer, or are recovering from it, this should be your basic diet for life, and you should read and put into practice all the recommendations of the eating plan.

THE FOUR-STAR SUPERFOODS
★ Apricots ★ Carrots ★ Beetroot ★ Cabbage ★ Garlic

The Superfoods

Fruits Apples, apricots, bananas, all citrus fruits (oranges, lemons, limes, and especially grapefruits), all berries (particularly cranberries), all currants (especially blackcurrants), canteloupe melons and watermelons, yellow peaches, strawberries, persimmons

Vegetables Asparagus, avocados, endives, all crucifers – cabbage, broccoli, Brussels sprouts, cauliflower, collard greens, horseradish, kale, leeks, kohlrabi, mustard, radishes, turnips and turnip greens, tomatoes, watercress, lettuce, mushrooms, red, yellow, and green peppers, potatoes, pumpkins, sweet potatoes or yams

Dried fruits Apricots and prunes, in particular

Grains Barley, brown rice, buckwheat, millet, whole wheat, wheatgerm

Pulses Lentils, chickpeas, all beans

Seeds, nuts Almonds, hazelnuts, pumpkin, sesame seeds and sunflower seeds, walnuts

Herbs Parsley, garlic, camomile, thyme, cloves, sage, tarragon, rosemary

Others Extra-virgin olive oil, fermented foods and liquids – yoghurt, Quark, sauerkraut

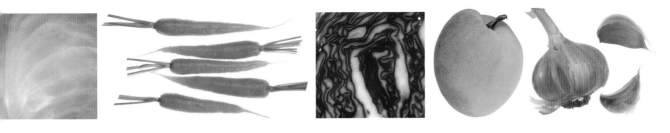

Drinks Fermented fruit and vegetable juices, especially beetroot, cabbage, carrot, and potato juices, papaya juice and pineapple juice

The danger foods

Animal protein In population studies, high meat intake has been associated with a high incidence of cancer, particularly of the bowel, pancreas, and prostate. The myth that people need lots of protein had encouraged the consumption of vast quantities of animal proteins, which are not only surplus to the body's needs, but impose a heavy tax on its energy resources. Additionally, most meat sold today is contaminated with hormones, tenderizers, antibiotics, pesticide residues, and other undesirable substances.

Trans-fats Trans-fats are a particular type of fat created during the hydrogenation of oils. They're usually found in fast and processed foods and are now being singled out as the most dangerous type of fat in our diets today.

Rancid fats, oils, and nuts When oily foods oxidize or turn rancid, harmful chemicals called free radicals are produced. These are irritant to the stomach, affect our bodies' absorption of vitamins A, C, and E, and can be carcinogenic. This is one of the many reasons why we need to eat foods rich in antioxidants, which combat

free radical activity. Wholegrain flour, cereals, and wheatgerm should be stored in covered containers in the fridge and thrown away when they lose their first freshness. Nuts are best eaten fresh from their shells.

High glycaemic index (GI) foods The GI diet is not just a daft fad diet. In fact, the glycaemic index of our foods and our diets plays a key role in our health. When we eat refined carbohydrates, or high-GI foods, such as white flour or white sugar, the explosive impact on our blood sugar levels means that the adrenal system needs to work extra hard to maintain its balance. And that, scientists increasingly believe, can have major implications on our long-term health.

A study published in the Journal of the National Cancer Institute in 2004 that followed nearly 40,000 women for seven years found that the group eating the highest-GI diet were nearly twice as likely to develop colorectal cancer as the group eating the lowest-GI diet. Refined carbohydrates have also been stripped of fibre, vitamins, minerals, trace elements, and enzymes.

Smoked, barbecued, and salt-cured foods Bacon, kippers, pickled herrings, vegetables in brine, and "chargrilled" steaks all contain carcinogenic (cancer-causing) substances. Studies in countries where the diet is high in pickled and smoked foods, where salt

intake is excessive, and where vitamin C intake is very low, show a high incidence of stomach cancer.

Processed meat Products preserved with nitrates and high in salt and saturated fat, such as salami, sausages, ham, and luncheon meat, should definitely be avoided, because nitrates are converted in the stomach into nitrosamines, which are carcinogenic.

Food additives All additives, particularly coal-tar dyes and artificial sweeteners, should be avoided.

Mouldy foods The moulds that form on some foods are carcinogenic. A famous example is aflatoxin, which comes from mould found in some peanuts. Since microtoxins migrate from the mould itself into the food beneath, it is not safe simply to scrape mould off cheese or a jar of jam and eat the rest – alas, the food should all be thrown away.

Overheated oils If you allow cooking oil to get too hot, or use the same oil over and over, you will be dishing up a plateful of toxic chemicals likely to cause damage to the stomach, kidneys, liver, or heart. Any oil heated to smoking or foaming point is without doubt toxic.

Alcohol As well as having high sugar levels, most wines are laced with a cocktail of chemicals and may also be contaminated with traces of the pesticides used in grape production. The cheaper the wine, the higher its

chemical load is likely to be. Alcohol itself depletes body levels of important nutrients, such as the B vitamins.

Caffeine This also depletes nutrient levels, particularly by increasing their elimination in urine, since caffeine is irritant to the kidneys. If you drink tea or coffee at, or soon after, meals that supply your daily source of iron (meat, green vegetables, and so on), your body's ability to absorb that iron will be greatly reduced.

The eating plan

The recommendations in this eating plan are based on a mixture of respectable scientific research, unorthodox concepts with a proven success rate, and population studies. The foods advocated here are included because they are particularly rich in nutrients known to be of key importance in fighting cancer: vitamin A (and particularly its precursor beta-carotene), the B vitamins riboflavin and folic acid, vitamin C, vitamin E, selenium, and foods especially high in fibre.

Fresh fruit and vegetables Your best allies in the war against cancer are fruit and vegetables. Five portions a day is the quantity recommended by most governments, but many experts consider nine portions to be closer to the ideal. Fruit and vegetables contain powerful weapons, such as antioxidants, which scientists are only now coming to understand. A wonderful piece of research in Illinois found that rats who were fed on tomatoes and broccoli together were far less likely to show prostate tumour growth than rats fed a supplement of lycopene (the antioxidant in tomatoes that is believed to fight prostate cancer).

The rats on Finasteride, a drug used to treat benign prostate growths, did worst of all.

For this reason, since plants clearly contain more natural goodness than we currently understand, those threatened by or afflicted with cancer should eat from the widest possible range of plant-food sources, including fruits, vegetables, herbs, and cereals. Every effort should be made to ensure that these foods are fresh, whole, and organically grown. Any vitamin supplements should be from natural sources rather than synthetic wherever possible.

Vitamin A and beta-carotene Beta-carotene is a precursor of vitamin A. It is the pigment found in yellow, orange, and dark green fruits and vegetables, so the brighter the natural colour of a food, the better. Vitamin A, and beta-carotene in particular, are effective against cancer because they are potent antioxidants.

The best food sources of vitamin A and beta-carotene are the dark green, yellow, and orange fruits and vegetables: carrots, apricots, pumpkins, spinach, and watercress. In addition, vitamin A is present in full-cream milk, cheese, and butter.

Vitamin C Apart from its importance to the immune system and its tremendous antioxidant powers, vitamin C is also a potent anti-toxin. The richest food sources of vitamin C are blackcurrants, strawberries, kiwifruits, watercress, mustard and cress, green peppers, raw cabbage, cauliflower, spinach, and parsley, together with all of the citrus fruits.

Vitamin E A 6- and 10-year follow-up study of 20,000 men in Finland, published in the American Journal of Epidemiology in 1988, found that

"men with higher serum alpha-tocopherol levels had a lower risk of cancer than did other men". This was particularly noticeable in cancers other than those related to smoking.

The richest sources of vitamin E are extra-virgin olive oil, cold-pressed sunflower and safflower oils, nuts (especially almonds), wholegrain cereals, wholemeal bread, wheatgerm, dark green vegetables, and eggs.

Selenium Like vitamin E, this essential trace element is an efficient antioxidant, which is vital for the defence mechanisms of each cell. Selenium enhances the activity of vitamin E and protects against chromosome damage.

Like most trace elements, selenium is toxic in excess, and supplementation without professional guidance can be risky. It is much better to rely on food sources for your supply. The richest sources are garlic, brewer's yeast, eggs, shellfish, mushrooms, sesame seeds, herring and mackerel, brazil and cashew nuts, and asparagus.

Folate Lung and colon cancers were the first cancers to be linked to folate deficiency. Evidence is growing of the vital role this B-vitamin plays in cancer prevention. Good sources include green vegetables, beans, broccoli, cauliflower, citrus fruits, and sweet potatoes.

Raw food Try to eat as much of your diet as possible raw, because raw food is food at its nutritional best. This does not mean that all foods can safely be eaten raw, nor does it mean that cooked foods are worthless – but all forms of cooking reduce some of the nutritional qualities of any food, and in some, cooking produces potentially harmful substances.

For over 150 years, practitioners of Natural Cure have successfully used raw food diets to treat cancer and other diseases.

You should aim to consume about one-third of each day's food in raw form. A weekly raw food day is of great value for people in cancer high-risk groups, but total raw food therapy should be undertaken only with professional guidance.

High-fibre foods An adequate intake of cereal fibre is vital for the correct functioning of the bowel. Vegetable and fruit fibre also plays an important role in digestion and elimination, combining with certain toxins and carcinogens to carry them safely out of the body. Studies worldwide show that the higher the intake of fibre, the lower the rate of cancer in the bowel. Although it emerged a few years ago that sufferers from colorectal cancer who took fibre supplements could be worsening their condition, the same study found no such problems with fibre consumed in a natural form. In other words, you can't just turn fruit and vegetables into tablets without losing some of their natural goodness.

The richest sources of fibre are oats, wholewheat bread, wholegrain breakfast cereals, barley, brown rice and other wholegrain cereals, cabbage, peas, beans, lentils, berries, and dried fruits. There is some fibre in nearly all vegetables, and in most fruits.

Oily fish The role of omega-3 fatty acids in cancer prevention is now being proven – so far, studies have shown that they can help protect against breast and colorectal cancers. The best sources are herring, pilchards, sardines, sprats, and whitebait.

Sprouted seeds, grains, nuts, and pulses Sprouts are a cheap, easily accessible, and unpolluted source of vitamin C, a little protein, trace-elements, and B-group vitamins. They are also a true organic food, since they can be grown on your own windowsill, without chemicals. You can grow them any day of the year, whatever the weather, and harvest them fresh just days later. They don't need cooking, cleaning, or preparing – just put them in a sandwich, toss them in a salad, or eat them as a vegetable. However, make sure you buy your seed and grains for sprouting from a reliable source that can guarantee them free from fungicides.

Fermented foods Lacto-fermented foods, such as sauerkraut and yoghurt, have been staples in the diets of some of the healthiest and longest-lived people in the world. Fruit and vegetable juices can also be fermented, eliminating the need for destructive heat treatment.

"Try to eat as much of your diet as possible raw...at its nutritional best."

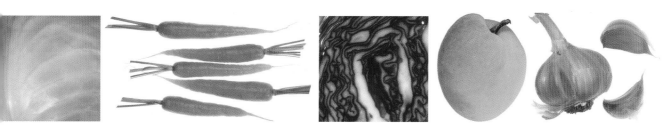

MENUS FOR A WEEK

Fluid intake is important. You should drink a minimum of 1.5 litres/4 pints of liquid each day. Juices should be freshly pressed or lacto-fermented; if you must, use bottled juices free from sugar, salt, and additives. On no account use tinned juices. Drink herb teas and plain but not artificially carbonated mineral waters. Do not drink tea or coffee, even if it's decaffeinated. Ideally, juice should be drunk half an hour before a meal.

Monday

Breakfast Beetroot juice; muesli with dried apricots, almonds, and natural yoghurt.

Light meal or snack Beetroot juice; Classic crudités (*p.150*); wholegrain toast.

Main meal Beetroot juice; Onion and wholemeal burgers (*p.216*); Orange and chicory salad.

Tuesday

Breakfast Beetroot juice; grilled mushrooms and tomatoes on toasted wholegrain bread.

Light meal or snack Beetroot juice; baked potato with Quark; Sprouted seed salad (*p.230*).

Main meal Beetroot juice; Michael's millet and buckwheat (*p.261*). Baked apples (*p.237*).

Wednesday

Breakfast Carrot juice; porridge.

Light meal or snack Carrot juice; Brown rice and celery soup (*p.142*). A bowl of raisins and nuts.

Main meal Carrot juice; Bean casserole (*p.193*); green salad; potato salad. Pears cassis (*p.236*).

Thursday

Breakfast Carrot juice; muesli with fresh fruit and natural yoghurt.

Light meal or snack Carrot juice; Ratatouille (*p.202*). A big bunch of grapes.

Main meal Carrot juice; Marinated mushrooms (*p.153*); Celery, radish, and walnut salad (*p.227*). A ripe, sweet pear.

Friday

Breakfast Orange and grapefruit juice; mixed berries with kiwifruit and some sunflower and sesame seeds.

Light meal or snack Orange juice; Sardines with mustard sauce (*p.168*); Radish and rocket salad (*p.228*).

Main meal Grapefruit juice; Rainbow peppers (*p.196*); salad of raw mushrooms, parsley, spring onions, and garlic with extra-virgin olive oil. Apricot whip (*p.244*).

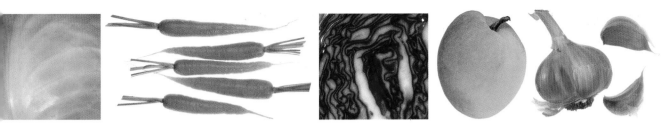

Saturday

Breakfast Carrot juice; muesli with fresh fruit and natural yoghurt.

Light meal or snack Grapefruit juice; Tricolour coleslaw (*p.231*).

Main meal Orange juice; Herb-coated sea bass (*p.168*) with steamed broccoli; Radish and rocket salad (*p.228*).

Sunday

Breakfast Tomato juice with a squeeze of lemon; porridge or kasha; papaya, grapes, fresh or dried figs.

Light meal or snack Tomato juice, Vegetable and barley soup (*p.147*); goat's or feta cheese with rice or rye crackers; celery and radishes.

Main meal Tomato juice with lemon; steamed, baked, or poached salmon or other oily fish; broccoli. Spicy winter pudding (*p.241*).

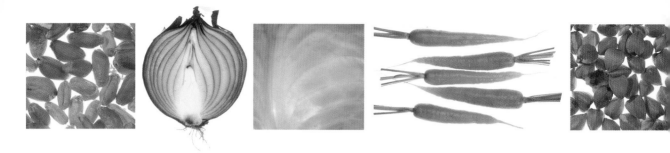

Circulatory problems

Heart disease, in spite of worldwide health education programmes, is still the number one cause of premature death. Despite millions of pounds, euros, and dollars being thrown at the problem, a new factor is now coming into play that may see heart disease rates rising yet further.

An obesity epidemic is sweeping the developed world, along with steadily rising numbers of people developing type 2 (adult-onset) diabetes. Both obesity and type 2 diabetes carry a high risk of coronary artery disease. The percentage of deaths attributable to circulatory illness worldwide is, on average, 29 per cent. In developed countries that number rises to an awful 45.6 per cent.

Medical research into a "cure" for heart disease, in the form of newer and better drugs, is focusing increasingly on common fruits and vegetables, in which several compounds with exciting potential are being found. However, those who hope for "miracle drugs" in the form of active plant principles will surely be disappointed. When food is your medicine, the prescription is for whole foods, not extracts. We should consume less fat, sugar, salt, and alcohol, and more fruits, vegetables, and wholegrain cereals. Eat plenty of these foods; no other medicine for the heart will be so effective.

"Heart disease is still
the number one cause
of premature death."

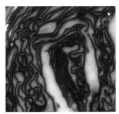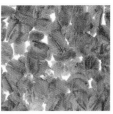

THE FOUR-STAR SUPERFOODS

★ Carrots ★ Onions ★ Cabbage ★ Barley ★ Buckwheat ★ Oats ★ Garlic ★ Oily fish (herring, mackerel, sardines) ★ Extra-virgin olive oil

The Superfoods

Fruit Apples, blackcurrants, cherries, grapes, lemons, plums, melon, pineapple, strawberries, figs, grapefruit

Vegetables Artichoke, broccoli, dandelion, chicory, lamb's lettuce, leeks, sweet peppers (red, yellow, or green), potatoes, pumpkins, seaweed, squash, tomatoes, turnips, watercress

Grains Whole wheat, brown rice

Seeds, nuts, pulses Nuts, sesame and sunflower seeds, walnuts, dried beans

Herbs Coriander, juniper, thyme, ginger, marjoram, chervil, chilli peppers

In moderation Alcohol, butter, eggs, and cheeses can be eaten, but in moderation only. Remember that the harder the cheese, the higher the fat content. Low-fat hard cheeses or soft cheeses, such as Brie, are the ones to choose. Similarly, game, free-range chicken and eggs, lean unprocessed meats, and shellfish are fine in moderation. Trim off skin and visible fat.

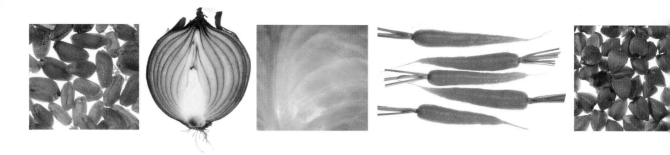

The danger foods

Trans-fats Trans-fats are emerging as the real bad guys of the fat world. Partial hydrogenation is an industrial process used on vegetable oils to prolong their shelf life and make them more solid, and trans-fats are created as by-products. Trans-fats have numerous serious effects, including clogging of the arteries, increases in LDL cholesterol, and insulin resistance. Margarine, in particular, is a source of trans-fats.

Saturated fats A diet high in saturated fat would not be a good idea, but trans-fats (*see above*) are far worse for us. Saturated fats, in moderation and from healthy sources such as grass-fed cattle, can be fine – just don't go overboard. Trim meat of all visible fat and keep your intake of dairy products low. Avoid animal-based oils.

Polyunsaturated fats In excess, these can actually endanger the heart. Without sufficient vitamin E – and many fats are low in this precious antioxidant – they may generate dangerous free-radical activity.

Caffeine Tea, coffee, chocolate, and cola drinks all contain caffeine. An occasional cup of tea or coffee is fine, but six or more a day will push up both blood pressure and cholesterol.

Excess alcohol There is some reason to believe that a daily glass or two of a good red wine, or a small Scotch,

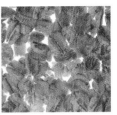

can be beneficial to the heart, but any more than this is definitely not.

Refined carbohydrates Refined sugar (sucrose) has been shown to raise cholesterol levels and blood pressure in some people; sucrose consumption is also linked with atherosclerosis. Unrefined sugar and honey, both of which contain small amounts of trace elements, may be used very sparingly instead. High-GI foods, such as white bread or sugary pastries, do you no good either.

Excess salt A diet high in salt leads to high blood pressure. Salt crops up in surprising places, such as in many wholegrain breakfast cereals. But in moderation, an occasional pinch of salt in cooking should do no harm.

The eating plan

If you suffer from heart disease, or if you are in a high-risk group, whether from smoking or drinking, excess weight, stress, little or no exercise, or a hereditary disposition, you need to be particularly aware of the dangers in our Western diet. You should be eating generous amounts of cereal fibre, which helps your body break down and eliminate cholesterol. Oats, beans, barley, and the pectin in apples are known to be the most effective. Plenty of other wholegrain cereals should figure on the menu. Like nuts and seeds, they supply vitamin E, which is vital for the heart and circulation.

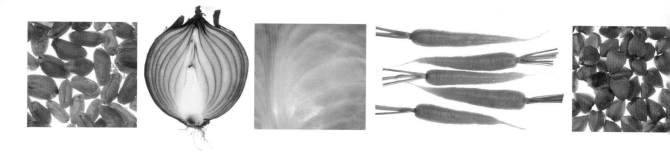

Eat plenty of all types of fresh fruit and vegetables. They provide potassium, which is vital to the health of the heart. Eat more fish, especially oily fish; the oil they contain has been shown to be beneficial to the heart. If you suffer from varicose veins or haemorrhoids, eat plenty of buckwheat: the bioflavonoids in brightly coloured fruits, such as oranges and lemons, are also beneficial. Eat plenty of them. Instead of red meat, eat more poultry and game. Instead of sugar, use dried fruits and pure fruit juices. Instead of salt, use herbs, spices, and lemon juice. Use natural yoghurt in place of cream.

MENUS FOR A WEEK

Monday
Breakfast Porridge; a slice of wholemeal toast.
Light meal or snack Onion wholemeal burger (*p.216*).
Main meal Onion soup (*p.138*); Orange and watercress salad (*p.228*). Fresh fruit.

Tuesday
Breakfast Sardines on wholemeal toast with grilled tomatoes and mushrooms.
Light meal or snack Onion soup (*p.138*), with a chunk of bread. Dried fruit, seeds, and nuts.
Main meal Frisée salad (*p.230*); Bean casserole (*p.193*).

Wednesday
Breakfast Muesli with grated apple.
Light meal or snack Falafel (*p.212*); Carrot Salad (*p.230*).

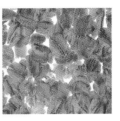

Main meal Artichoke vinaigrette (*p.148*); Devilled chicken (*p.182*); brown rice; salad. Pears cassis (*p.236*).

Thursday

Breakfast Porridge; a slice of wholemeal toast.

Light meal or snack Sardines with mustard sauce (*p.168*).

Main meal Tofu and vegetable stir-fry (*p.200*). Apricot whip (*p.244*).

Friday

Breakfast Porridge or wholegrain cereal.

Light meal or snack Big Macks (*p.166*) with Tricolour coleslaw (*p.231*); rye crispbread or crackers.

Main meal Salmon; Sun-dried tomato risotto (*p.192*).

Saturday

Breakfast Fresh fruit salad.

Light meal or snack Herrings in oatmeal (*p.169*); salad.

Main meal Citrus chicken (*p.185*) with chicory. Tangerine and apricot pudding (*p.235*).

Sunday

Breakfast Omelette with 1 egg and an extra white; wholemeal toast.

Light meal or snack Slice of melon.

Main meal Guinea fowl casserole (*p.188*) with potatoes; Red bean salad in plum sauce (*p.224*); rye crackers.

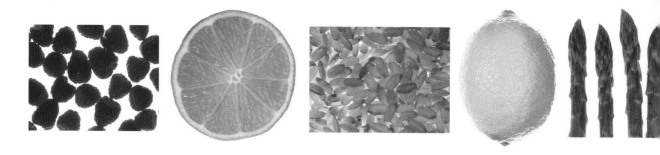

Digestive problems

Most digestive problems start in the kitchen, and the kitchen is also the place where they can be dealt with most effectively. If you have a clear understanding of the relationship between specific foods and digestion, a well-stocked spice rack, and a collection of fresh herbs, you'll be able to dish up an effective prescription for digestive restoration and health.

It is only in the last few years that we have begun to really appreciate the delicate balance that should exist inside our gut. The credo that all bacteria are bad is finally being shifted towards an understanding that the bacteria of our gut are both necessary and hardworking. A good diet should help maintain the balance of bacteria in our intestines, but instead our digestive systems are often expected to cope with fats, caffeine, alcohol, and chemicals, while being deprived of the fibre and nutrients they need. This mismanagement results in a spectacular array of maladies, ranging from mild dyspepsia and irritating symptoms of recurrent malaise to chronic constipation, ulcers, gallstones, irritable bowel syndrome, ulcerative colitis, diverticulitis, and fatal cancers. Diseases as diverse as arthritis and cancer, as well as problems of the gut itself, are now seen as having their roots in the poor absorption of nutrients and the inefficient elimination of toxic wastes, which accompany almost all digestive problems.

Despite the diversity of these conditions, and the battery of treatments used to overcome each one, there is one treatment that could prevent and cure them all. This treatment is simple, safe, cheap, and above all, effective, but is often depressingly overlooked by the vast majority of doctors. That treatment is correct diet.

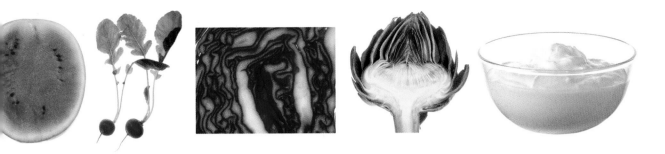

THE FOUR-STAR SUPERFOODS

Apples ★ All citrus fruit ★ Raspberries ★ Melons ★ Pineapples ★ Raw vegetable juices (in small quantities, sipped slowly) ★ Radishes ★ Potatoes ★ Artichokes ★ Asparagus ★ Cabbage ★ Sauerkraut ★ Brown rice ★ Yoghurt ★ Dandelion ★ Extra-virgin olive oil

The Superfoods

Fruits Bananas, blueberries, blackberries, blackcurrants, grapes, figs, mangos, papayas, pears

Vegetables Carrots, celery, celeriac, cress, lamb's lettuce, nettles, onions, spinach, turnips

Grains Barley, buckwheat, maize, millet, oats, rye, wheat

Seeds and nuts Sweet almonds, coconut, linseed, pine nuts, sesame seeds, sunflower seeds, walnuts

Herbs and spices To name only a few beneficial herbs: mint and peppermint, dill, caraway, horseradish, bay, coriander, chervil, tarragon, chives, garlic, marjoram, cinnamon, ginger, sweet paprika, cumin, fenugreek, fennel, cardamom, slippery elm, camomile, and lime. The idea that highly spiced foods should be avoided is generally unfounded; in moderation, many spices are in fact a help to the digestive process.

Fermented foods Live yoghurt and probiotic drinks such as Yakult are one particularly fine way of helping out the benevolent bacteria in your gut. They contain

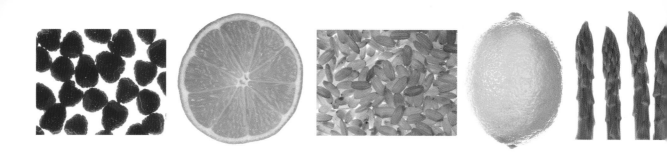

the good bacteria that our gut needs, so provide useful top-ups. Other sources include organic cottage cheese, miso soup, and sourdough bread.

Others Fish, shellfish, poultry, game, and eggs can be good for the digestion. So can pasta with cooked or raw vegetable sauces; wholegrain and mixed-grain bread; rye breads; crispbreads; and pumpernickel. Cold-pressed vegetable oils, particularly sunflower and grapeseed, can help; keep them in the refrigerator and out of direct light. Use them quickly; if they taste "off", discard them.

The danger foods

Refined Carbohydrates White sugar and white flour are used in cakes, biscuits and convenience foods that are often high in fat as well. Too much wheat – bread or pasta with every meal, for instance – can make your digestive system feel clogged up.

Fat and all deep-fried foods

Red meat Particularly risky meats are pork in any form, including ham, bacon, salami, luncheon meat, and other processed meat products such as pies and burgers.

Artificial colourings, flavourings, and preservatives Many of these can be gastric irritants. Artificial sweeteners also seem to irritate the gut.

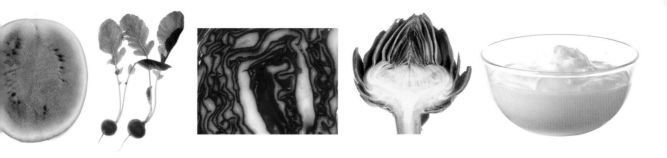

Coffee If you drink lots of coffee, try cutting it out before making other dietary changes, but be prepared for withdrawal symptoms, including headaches, nausea, irritability, and tremor. Caffeine is highly addictive, and it could take time to recover when you go "cold turkey". Check that there is no caffeine in any over-the-counter medicine you may be taking. Avoid fizzy drinks.

Acidic foods You should particularly avoid malt vinegars, pickles, and NBC (non-brewed condiment), which is a vinegar substitute.

Alcohol and digestive problems do not mix, not even in the form of digestive bitters. Excessive alcohol intake is definitely a serious factor in many digestive problems.

The seven-day alimentary plan

This plan helps clear out toxic wastes. It starts with two "fasting days", when you will be drinking plenty of cleansing fruit and vegetable juices and eating little more than salads and fresh fruit. After that come five days of healthy eating with the emphasis on fruit and vegetables. But this is no starvation diet. After the first two strict days of cleansing you won't feel hungry because the calories seldom total less than 1500 daily. For these seven days, forget about coffee or alcohol, but weak China tea is allowed after day two, with lemon or a little milk. The diet follows the rules of Harmonious Eating (*p.344*). Among its many advantages, Harmonious Eating cures many people of a craving for snacks between meals and sweet treats, which cause so many digestive problems.

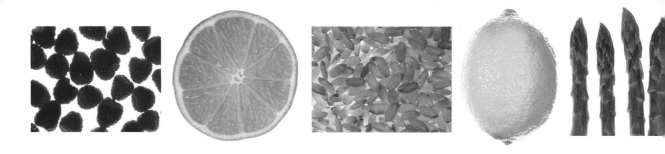

In the first couple of days of this regime, you may have flatulence and diarrhoea. But by the end of the week, most people will experience an improvement in a wide range of digestive disturbances, and as a bonus, there will be an overall improvement in wellbeing and particularly in the complexion. Those who need to lose weight may find that they have shed up to half a stone.

MENUS FOR A WEEK

Day one

Breakfast Juice of half a grapefruit in half a glass of hot water, topped up with apple juice, and a dessertspoon of honey. A bunch of grapes; an apple.

Mid-morning A glass of hot water and honey; grapes.

Light meal A large glass of vegetable juice spiked with a squeeze of lemon juice. A large bowl of dried fruit soaked overnight.

Mid-afternoon Hot blackcurrant and apple juice with a little honey added.

Main meal A mixed salad of raw fresh vegetables: celery, finely grated cabbage, chicory, any of the wide range of green and red salad leaves now available, chunks of fennel, watercress, and any other fresh salad vegetables; Mean dressing (*p.254*). An apple.

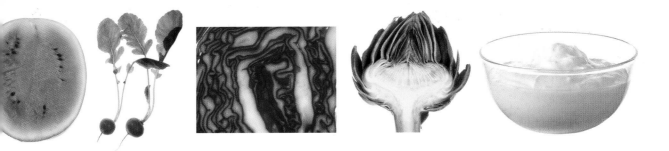

Day two

Same as day one until evening.
Main meal Celery, radish, and walnut salad (*p.227*), plus a baked potato and sugar-free baked beans.

Day three

Breakfast Start preparing this the night before. Put a couple of spoonfuls of oatflakes in a cereal bowl, add a tablespoon of water, and leave to soak overnight. In the morning, stir in a teaspoon of fresh lemon juice, a spoonful of single cream or a little soya milk, and either slice a small banana into it or grate a pear on top.
Mid-morning A big glass of vegetable juice.
Light meal A big mixed salad. Finely shredded cabbage and a selection of the following: dandelion leaves, grated beetroot or carrot, watercress, red, yellow, or green peppers, avocado, and spring onions. Make the dressing as above. A moderate serving of tuna, salmon, or mackerel in brine, or sardines in olive oil. Finish with a piece of your favourite fruit.
Mid-afternoon A glass of grapefruit and apple or vegetable juice or a cup of weak tea.
Main meal Make a large pan of Vegetable and barley soup (*p.147*), enough for lunchtime the next day as

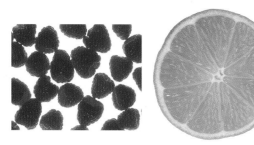

well. Eat a big bowl of this with a chunk of crusty wholemeal bread. Follow with some fresh dates, or a small bowlful of dried fruit, or a ripe pear.

Day four

Breakfast Half a grapefruit, an apple, or grapes. An egg, boiled, poached, or scrambled in a very little butter.

Mid-morning If you have a juicer, a glassful of freshly pressed carrot, celery, and apple juice; if not, tomato juice spiked with lemon and fresh herbs.

Light meal A big bowl of yesterday's soup; a wholemeal roll or bread; Tricolour coleslaw (*p.231*).

Mid-afternoon Fruit or vegetable juice or weak tea.

Main meal Your favourite fish, grilled or steamed, or a piece of chicken, grilled or casseroled; a green vegetable steamed or cooked in a very small amount of water and tossed with nut butter and a little lemon juice. A piece of your favourite fresh fruit or sugar-free yoghurt.

Day five

Breakfast As for day three.

Mid-morning A glass of freshly-pressed vegetable juice.

Light meal Michael's millet and buckwheat (*p.261*); a small mixed salad of raw vegetables.

Mid-afternoon Fruit or vegetable juice or weak tea.

Main meal A big salad of raw vegetables, sprinkled with

roasted sesame and sunflower seed; Devilled chicken (*p.182*). A plain low-fat yoghurt with a little honey.

Day six

Breakfast A fresh fruit salad; a helping of plain yoghurt. A glass of hot water with a little honey.

Mid-morning A glass of freshly pressed vegetable juice.

Light meal Tomato and herb omelette (*p.156*) made in a non-stick pan with the faintest trace of oil or butter; a big mixed raw vegetable salad. Some fresh fruit.

Mid-afternoon Fruit juice or a cup of weak tea.

Main meal Cook enough brown rice for two meals and add one helping to a casserole of root vegetables. Follow with a small raw vegetable salad, and a banana or pear.

Day seven

Breakfast As for day four.

Mid-morning A glass of fresh vegetable juice.

Light meal A salad using the rice from yesterday, with a few raisins, sultanas, nuts, pine nuts, sweetcorn, peas, peppers, spring onions; sprinkle with herbs and a little salad dressing with fresh garlic. Follow with a banana.

Mid-afternoon Fruit juice or a cup of weak tea.

Main meal A whole avocado, sliced, with cress, grated carrot, celeriac, or celery, grated beetroot, and a small dollop of cottage cheese, Quark, or ricotta. Fruit.

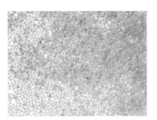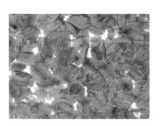

Stress

Since the dawn of time, man has understood that food and drink can have profound effects on mental and emotional states. When primitive tribes sought euphoria or oblivion, they had no man-made drugs; instead, they fermented foodstuffs to make alcohol, chewed the coca leaf or the betel nut, and harvested opium poppies and magic mushrooms.

In today's society, we seem to have forgotten what we once knew. Doctors prescribe ever-increasing numbers of drugs, such as Ritalin or Prozac, for conditions that could possibly be caused by simple nutrional deficiencies or food or environmental sensitivities. In the US, more than one child in every 35 is on Ritalin, while Ritalin abuse soars - in one survey in Massachusetts, it was second only to marijuana as drug of choice for most young people. Tranquillizers and antidepressants are also prescribed more and more freely, to the despair of anyone who has seen the improvements that a few simple dietary adjustments can bring.

Some children given doses of cod liver oil (which is rich in omega-3 essential fatty acids) have shown rapid improvements in concentration and temperament. And some children suffering from ADHD (attention deficit hyperactivity disorder, the modern syndrome for which Ritalin is now routinely prescribed) also improved when certain food additives were excluded from their diets. In another study at King's College Hospital in

"The Western diet is catastrophically bad at providing the nutrients we need."

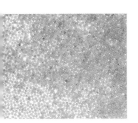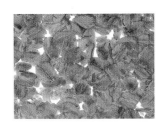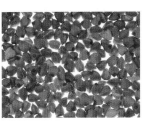

London, patients suffering from depression and schizophrenia who were shown to have low folate levels were given folic acid supplements every day, and improved significantly faster than a control group given nothing. And zinc supplements have helped sufferers of anorexia nervosa, who frequently display zinc deficiency to start with.

In almost every study of essential nutrients - particularly of iron, magnesium, and the B complex vitamins - mental disorders or malfunctions have been prominent among the symptoms of deficiency. Studies have shown that the Western diet is catastrophically bad at providing all the nutrients our bodies need. In fact, in some cases, we may be getting only one-half to one-tenth of the nutrients we need.

It seems extraordinary. The Western world is finally coming to understand that good nutrition is necessary for healthy bodies, but the realisation that we also need good nutrition for good mental health lags far behind. Even stress and a general state of feeling blue can be food-related. If you think that your problems are all in the mind, don't feel that you have to limp through the rest of your life on the crutch of tranquillizers, antidepressants, or sleeping pills. Many of the answers lie in your own hands, the hands that purchase, prepare, and put food on your plate.

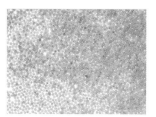    

THE FOUR-STAR SUPERFOODS

★ Grapes ★ Buckwheat ★ Millet ★ Oats ★ Wheat ★ Brewer's yeast ★ Molasses

The superfoods

Fruit Apricots, bananas, dates, oranges, apples, pears, plums, grapes, peaches, blackcurrants, lemons, figs, strawberries, raspberries, raisins, mangos

Vegetables Asparagus, avocados, aubergines, beetroot, cabbage, carrots, celery, chicory, watercress, French beans, lettuce, turnips, onion, leeks, mushrooms

Grains Oats, barley, rye, wheat, brown rice, buckwheat

Seeds and nuts Almonds, pecans, walnuts, hazelnuts, peanuts, sunflower seeds, pumpkin seeds, sprouted seeds

Legumes All dried beans, especially soybeans, dried peas, sprouted beans

Herbs and spices Garlic, parsley, lemon balm, lemon verbena, basil, rosemary, camomile, fresh ginger, marjoram, thyme, nutmeg, juniper berries, liquorice

Others Cockles, winkles, shrimps, oysters, sardines, liver, kidney, lean beef, egg yolks, brewer's yeast, dark chocolate

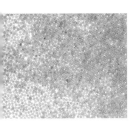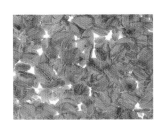

The danger foods

Refined and processed foods Avoid white flour, white sugar, white rice, confectionary, and bakery products. If you often feel down or stressed at a certain time of day, consider what you are eating: peaks and troughs in blood sugar can lead to mood swings. Dr Joseph Mercola and Patrick Holford both believe that depression sufferers should eliminate it from their diets. Even natural fruit juices, if taken undiluted and in excess, can destabilize blood sugar levels.

Food additives, colourings, preservatives, and artificial flavourings. Many people find they are sensitive to different additives, and it's worth keeping a food diary to find out what may be causing you problems. Things such as ready meals can contain surprising amounts of sugar, food additives, and salt, so once you are aware of your sensitivities, always read the label.

Alcohol, a depressant, is more destructive of vital brain nutrients than any other commonly consumed substance: it breaks down the vitamin B complex and depletes the body's stores of magnesium, zinc, and calcium, which are all vital to normal brain function.

Tea and coffee In excess, they can actually provoke anxiety, nervousness, depression, and insomnia. They can also inhibit zinc and iron absorption.

The eating plan

Food and chemical sensitivities are at the root of many mental and emotional problems. Depression, anxiety, and a range of other mental problems can be triggered by food sensitivities, as well as by the 3000 permitted chemicals that go into our foods. This eating plan will provide an abundance of the nutrients known to be crucial for mental health, since they influence both intellectual and emotional function.

MENUS FOR A WEEK

Monday

Breakfast Porridge.
Light meal or snack Sprouted seed salad (*p.230*); wholemeal roll with tahini.
Main meal Grilled aubergines; Rosemary chicken (*p.188*); carrots; runner beans. Stewed plums.

Tuesday

Breakfast Grapefruit; poached eggs on wholemeal toast.
Light meal or snack Cold chicken with garlic mayonnaise (*p.256*) and slices of tomato and cucumber.
Main meal Winter white salad (*p.227*); Herrings in oatmeal (*p.169*). Yoghurt with apple and peaches.

Wednesday

Breakfast Orange juice. Crowdie (*p.240*).
Light meal or snack Falafel (*p.212*); Watercress salad (*p.223*).

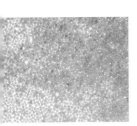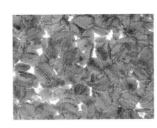

Main meal Carrot, leek, and ginger soup (*p.147*);
Grilled garlicky gambas (*p.167*) on Chinese leaves.

Thursday

Breakfast Chopped dried fruit in yoghurt with seeds.
Light meal or snack Cress, watercress, and carrot
sandwich (*p.217*).
Main meal Avocado and watercress salad (*p.224*);
Warm bulgur with aubergines (*p.194*). Fresh fruit salad.

Friday

Breakfast Orange juice; boiled egg; wholewheat toast.
Light meal or snack Cold bulgur with a green salad.
Main meal Vegetable and barley soup (*p.147*); Sardines
with mustard sauce (*p.168*); tomato and onion salad.
Fromage frais and damson purée.

Saturday

Breakfast Citrus fruit; Buckwheat pancakes (*p.238*).
Light meal or snack Salade niçoise (*p.214*).
Main meal Braised fennel (*p.207*); Hearty beef stew
(*p.178*); baked potato; watercress salad. Goat's cheese.

Sunday

Breakfast Orange juice; kipper; tomatoes; mushrooms.
Light meal or snack Vegetable risotto (*p.194*).
Main meal A green salad. Ginger lamb stir-fry (*p.180*),
broccoli. Almond fruit whip (*p.235*).

Fatigue

Millions of people the world over wake up every morning wondering how on earth they'll get through the day ahead. "TATT" – "Tired All The Time" – syndrome is reported to GPs in Britain all the time: it's estimated that between 20 and 30 per cent of the population feel this way all year round. When exhaustion strikes, it's easy to feel that there's nothing to do but make another cup of coffee and struggle on through. But in fact, once a thorough check with your doctor has established that there is no serious underlying illness to cause it, the cure for fatigue is often in your own hands, and self-help can be remarkably successful.

Fatigue may have a psychological or a physical cause, and is often a combination of the two. Among common psychological causes are stress, anxiety, depression, dissatisfaction, relationship problems, anger, frustration, or just plain boredom. Physically, there are specific illnesses that can cause chronic fatigue, such as thyroid and hormone problems, or heart disease. Viral infections and their lingering after-effects, surgery, and all major illnesses inevitably result in fatigue. Post-Viral Fatigue Syndrome, sometimes known as ME, is now recognized as a genuine physical problem. So, too, is chronic pain, which may result from back problems, arthritis, rheumatism, tension headaches, and migraines. Your diet and your lifestyle can also play a huge part in this syndrome. For

"Diet and lifestyle can play a huge part in causing or curing fatigue."

example, a diet full of high-GI foods such as white bread, sweets, sugary snacks, and white rice will have your blood sugar and energy levels constantly fluctuating. This fluctuation is the first step to what used to be called hypoglycemia but is now known as dysglycemia, another step on the way to diabetes. Eating complex carbohydrates such as oats, wholewheat bread, and brown rice will smoothe out your blood sugar levels and keep energy levels much steadier throughout the day.

Allergy or sensitivity to foods and environmental pollutants is another major, and increasingly common, cause of fatigue. According to Dr Stephen Davies, Chairman of the British Society of Nutritional Medicine, "waking tired" is one of the classic symptoms of a food or chemical sensitivity. Finally, fatigue can be a symptom of something else, not a syndrome in itself. Deficiency in B vitamins (particularly folic acid) and iron both show up as fatigue. To make matters worse, your body can't absorb iron properly if you also suffer from vitamin C deficiency or are not getting enough exercise. It's easy to see how this can become a vicious circle and can even lead to anaemia (low levels of iron in the blood), which is especially common among careless vegetarians who stop eating meat and don't substitute other good sources of iron.

Our eating plan will teach you how to reverse this downward spiral. Follow it in order to rebuild your energies and physical resources with vitality-rich Superfoods.

THE FOUR-STAR SUPERFOODS

Apricots ★ Spinach ★ Broccoli ★ Brown rice ★ Wheat ★ Oats ★ Almonds ★ Sesame seeds ★ Sprouted seeds

The Superfoods

Fruit Apples, bananas, dates, figs, grapes, lemon, oranges, pears, plums, raspberries, rhubarb, strawberries

Vegetables Asparagus, Jerusalem artichokes, beetroot, broccoli, cabbage, carrots, celery, chicory, endive, dandelion, nettles, onions, salsify, seaweed, tomatoes

Grains Barley, buckwheat, maize, millet, oats, wheat, and wheatgerm

Seeds and nuts Most nuts and seeds, particularly walnuts, sunflower seeds, sprouted seeds

Legumes Lentils, soybeans

Herbs and spices Parsley, juniper, thyme, rosemary, fenugreek, mint, sage, marjoram, horseradish, cinnamon

Others Brewer's yeast

The danger foods

High-GI foods White sugar, white flour, and processed foods made with them cause energy spikes and then energy lows, destabilizing your blood sugar levels and leading to cravings and mood swings.

Fats in excess are a drain on the body's resources. Hidden fats are found in processed foods and fast foods.

Alcohol Its most pernicious effect is the destruction of nutrients, in particular the B vitamins needed for stamina and for the health of your nervous system in general.

Caffeine in tea, coffee, colas, and chocolate inhibits the uptake of iron. Don't drink caffeinated beverages at meals featuring good sources of iron.

Red meat itself, although supplying valuable iron, is a drain on your digestive energies: you're better off getting your iron from other sources for the time being.

High-energy drinks, marketed as giving energy to the listless, are rich in glucose. They may give you a deceptive lift, but they contain nothing of real value.

The eating plan

Rule one Eat regularly and eat properly. Little and often is better than starving and bingeing.

Rule two Eat high-quality foods rich in nutrients. The Superfoods for this section provide optimum nutrition and ease of digestion.

Rule three No matter how desperate you get for instant energy, don't fall into the sugar trap: stick to the Superfoods for a permanent lift.

Rule four Eat plenty of raw foods. They should be a major feature in your regime.

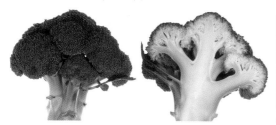

MENUS FOR A WEEK

Monday

Breakfast Porridge with honey and cream or milk; wholewheat toast. A banana.

Light meal or snack Red and yellow eggs (*p.158*); salad.

Main meal Classic crudités (*p.150*); Michael's millet and buckwheat (*p.261*). Fresh figs and cream.

Tuesday

Breakfast Compote of soft fresh fruit with natural yoghurt; boiled egg; a slice of wholemeal toast.

Light meal or snack Hummus plus (*p.153*) with wholemeal pitta bread; Sprouted seed salad (*p.230*)

Main meal Jerusalem artichoke soup (*p.140*); Potato galette (*p.201*) with a salad. Pears cassis (*p.236*).

Wednesday

Breakfast Soaked and dried apricots with yoghurt; sardines and sliced tomatoes on toast.

Light meal or snack Chicken liver and alfalfa sandwich (*p.217*). Yoghurt with fresh fruit.

Main meal Fresh asparagus; Warm bulgur with aubergines (*p.194*); peas and broccoli. An orange.

Thursday

Breakfast Muesli with yoghurt and seeds, wheatgerm, and dried fruits, especially apricots and sultanas.

Light meal or snack Sugar-free baked beans with wholewheat toast; Sprouted seed salad (*p.230*).

Main meal Tomato salad (*p.226*); Guinea fowl casserole (*p.188*); Almond fruit whip (*p.235*).

Friday

Breakfast Scrambled eggs with smoked salmon, served on wholewheat toast.

Light meal or snack Complete coleslaw (*p.226*); cottage cheese and chives on rye bread or rye crackers.

Main meal Haddock and broccoli au gratin (*p.166*); Avocado and watercress salad (*p.224*); rye crackers and goat's cheese.

Saturday

Breakfast Buckwheat pancakes (*p.238*)

Light meal or snack White bean soup (*p.145*) served with wholewheat bread. A banana.

Main meal Classic crudités (*p.150*); Italian pan-fried liver (*p.179*); potatoes boiled in their skins, baby sweetcorns. Peach and apricot compote (*p.234*).

Sunday

Breakfast Muesli with yoghurt, seeds, and dried fruit.

Light meal or snack Chicken liver and alfalfa sandwich (*p.217*). A ripe pear.

Main meal Citrus chicken (*p.185*) with brown rice and carrots. Summer pudding (*p.242*).

Joint problems

People who never know what it is to have aching joints, muscles, or bones are the lucky few – these problems are nearly universal. There's nothing new about joint disease, either; even ancient skeletons uncovered by archaeologists often show signs of arthritis. As man was not designed to stand on two feet, our structure is not ideal for the upright posture. Consequently, our skeleton bears the brunt of excessive wear and tear on its weight-bearing joints, and our modern sedentary lifestyles and diets have only added to those problems.

An improved diet is not, on its own, a panacea for these problems. Stone Age man, after all, lived on game, roots, nuts, and berries rather than refined foods, and he still had joint problems. But it is certainly true that these problems can be exacerbated by the wrong diet, and alleviated, or even resolved altogether, by the right foods.

In traditional medicines, poor digestion and constipation are seen as the root cause of many health problems. They interfere with the body's ability to eliminate waste products. Toxins build up in the system leading to, and aggravating, a host of illnesses, of which arthritis and rheumatism are a prime example. (*See Digestive problems, p.284.*) This is one of the reasons that scientists are now looking into the benefits of fruits and vegetables that are rich in antioxidants. It has already been observed that arthritis sufferers who eat plenty of vitamin C and E can slow the progress of the disease, perhaps because the antioxidants battle the free radicals that may be causing the joint problems in the first place. Omega-3 fatty acids have also (as usual) been shown to play a useful role as anti-inflammatory agents. In addition, ginger has been found to help ease arthritis. A small study in India, in which arthritis sufferers were

given ginger every day, showed remarkable results, in that ginger seemed to have a pronounced anti-inflammatory effect on the joints.

Rheumatoid arthritis, which is an acute inflammatory disease, sometimes results from an intolerance to certain foods or chemicals. If you have a family history of asthma, hay fever, rhinitis, or eczema, this could be significant to your case. Like other allergy-related ailments, many joint problems are improved following a switch from normal eating habits to the pattern explained in the Harmonious Eating section (*p.344*). We recommend that you give this a trial. Like rheumatoid arthritis, fibrositis and other conditions of muscular inflammation also respond well to dietary change. Even gout, which is a form of arthritis, can be successfully controlled by very careful eating.

Many cases of rheumatoid and osteoarthritis and gout respond dramatically to a two-day fast followed by a raw food diet for some weeks. Details of how to carry out a two-day fast follow in this section. If you find the idea daunting but think it might help you, try the less dramatic regime on p.287. Any improvement will give you the encouragement to follow the full eating plan.

The list of foods to avoid may seem rather restrictive at first, but anyone who has severe rheumatoid arthritis or osteoarthritis will find it well worth following for a few weeks at leasts. Even modest improvement will encourage you to adopt new eating habits that will bring you increasing relief from pain and discomfort.

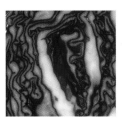

THE FOUR-STAR SUPERFOODS

Lemons ★ Pineapple ★ Celery ★ Turnips ★ Cabbage ★
Dandelion ★ Ginger ★ Oily fish

The Superfoods

Fruit Cherries, strawberries, raspberries, apples, plums, blackcurrants, pomegranates, gooseberries, melon, pears, grapes, bananas, lemon

Vegetables Artichokes, carrots, cabbage, onion, leek, celery, chicory, olives, dandelion, Jerusalem artichokes, fennel, radish, potatoes, turnips, nettles

Grains Rye, soy, brown rice, millet, buckwheat

Nuts seeds pulses Walnuts, hazelnuts, sprouted alfalfa, sprouted mung beans, beansprouts, pumpkin seeds

Herbs Chervil, parsley, garlic, juniper, thyme, sage, camomile, rosemary, marjoram, coriander

The danger foods

Alcohol Alcohol is a terrible inflammatory agent. In the joints, eyes, and skin, it's easy to see the effect that alcohol has on your system if you avoid it for just a couple of days. For gout sufferers in particular, alcohol is lethal because it inhibits excretion of uric acid.

High fat foods and refined carbohydrates These sorts of foods offer no nutrients and won't help you lose

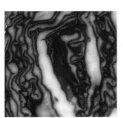

weight either. In addition, some sufferers are sensitive to dairy products and wheat. Gout sufferers in particular should also try to avoid the following foods: offal, yeast and meat extracts, chicken, beef, pork, tea, coffee, chocolate, cocoa, cola drinks, sardines, anchovies, whitebait, sprats, herring, mackerel, mussels, scallops, all fish roe, partridge, and guineafowl.

The Nightshade Family Avoiding potatoes, aubergines, peppers, and paprika has brought relief to some suffers from joint problems.

The eating plan

No two sets of joints are identical. Reactions can be idiosyncratic. If you find by experience that any food, however warmly recommended here, has an adverse effect on your complaint, omit it from your diet.

The first priority in the successful management of joint problems is to reduce excessive weight. Carrying extra weight causes wear and tear on the joint surfaces, which in turn causes pain, which in turn restricts activity, and adds to the initial weight problem. It is interesting to note that many gout sufferers are overweight.

Traditional medicine for these problems has always included foods that assist cleansing and improve digestion. An eating plan that achieves this is vital. The best possible introduction to your new way of eating is a cleaning two-day fast, details of which follow this section. This is not recommended for anyone who is suffering from or has had gout, as it may trigger a fresh attack. Gout sufferers should try the diet on p.287.

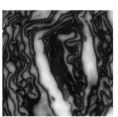

Any diet based on Dr Max Bircher-Benner's principles of mainly raw food will improve digestion and elimination, reduce inflammation, and raise resistance and vitality. The menus below are filled with raw foods.

Joint problems often have an allergic component. Just about every clinical ecologist can recount case histories where symptoms were either triggered or severely aggravated when patients ate such common culprit foods as wheat, oranges, pork, or bananas. It's well worth making the effort to try an elimination diet if you think this could apply to you.

Traditionally, strawberries and raspberries have been forbidden for the arthritic. However, French research shows that both help to eliminate uric acid and have a beneficial effect on gout, osteoarthritis, and rheumatoid arthritis. For this reason we have included them here.

The two-day fast It is not wise to smoke or take drugs while fasting, but do not stop any prescription drugs without first consulting your doctor. Have two days of preparation, during which you should not eat any meat. You should also restrict your tea and coffee intake to no more than two cups of either per day. Avoid chocolate, cocoa, and cola drinks. Eat only eat fresh fruit, raw or lightly cooked vegetables, and small quantities of grilled, poached, or steamed fish on the first day, and nuts, seeds, beans, or grains on the second. Drink plenty of filtered or bottled spring water. Avoid dairy and alcohol.

For the fast itself, pick two days when you don't have to be active physically or mentally. You may feel well, but you will have no energy to spare. Headaches, a furred tongue, bad breath, lower back pain, and general aches and pains have all been reported during a fast. The improvement in wellbeing that you will experience after will make it

worthwhile. During the two fast days, eat absolutely nothing, and drink only bottled spring water, at room temperature. Stop any vitamin and mineral pills and non-prescription remedies you usually take.

Break your fast with freshly pressed fruit juice and a few grapes; mid-morning, have a little fresh fruit. At midday, eat a couple of rye crispbreads without butter, with a raw vegetable salad. Mid-afternoon, drink herb tea with some dried fruit. In the evening, have a baked potato with cooked vegetables, followed by fresh fruit. On the second day, breakfast should be herb tea, fresh fruit, and a plain yoghurt with honey and nuts or seeds. At midday, eat muesli or a baked potato with a fresh salad and some dried fruit. For a snack, have herb tea and a slice of wholemeal bread and honey or peanut butter. In the evening, eat vegetable soup with an omelette or some grilled fish with salad and vegetables. For the rest of the week, avoid meat, keep tea and coffee intake low, and eat as much of your food raw as you can.

MENUS FOR A WEEK

Monday
Breakfast Banana; rye crispbread and peanut butter.
Light meal or snack Pear and celery almondaise (*p.152*).
Main meal Verdant broth (*p.142*). Beef and onion burger (*p.216*); Complete coleslaw (*p.226*). Fresh fruit.

Tuesday
Breakfast Stewed apples with goat's milk yoghurt.
Light meal or snack Waldorf salad (*p.226*).

Main meal Cucumber salad. Tuna and fennel pasta (*p.158*). Apricot whip (*p.244*).

Wednesday

Breakfast Poached haddock; rye crispbread or bread.

Light meal or snack Crudités with Tsatsiki (*p.231*), made with goat's milk yoghurt. Rye crispbread.

Main meal Spanish white garlic soup (*p.139*). Vegetable risotto (*p.194*). Lettuce and watercress salad. Fresh fruit salad.

Thursday

Breakfast Millet muesli with nuts and honey.

Light meal or snack Leftover risotto salad with cucumber, radishes, celery, and spring onions. A pear.

Main meal

Vegetable platter: leeks, courgettes, carrots, cabbage, onions, lightly cooked and tossed with sunflower oil, sesame seeds, and parsley. Grapes.

Friday

Breakfast Millet muesli with nuts and honey.

Light meal or snack Winter white salad (*p.227*).

Main meal Grilled red radicchio (*p.202*); Big Macks (*p.166*) and spinach. Baked apple (*p.237*).

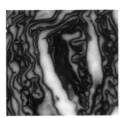

Saturday

Breakfast Scrambled eggs and rye toast.

Light meal or snack Sardines with mustard sauce (*p.168*) and a mixed beansprout salad.

Main meal Avocado vinaigrette made with lemon juice; Rainbow peppers (*p.196*).

Sunday

Breakfast Fresh grapes or berries – whichever fruit is in season.

Light meal or snack Sardines on toast. Winter white salad (*p.227*). Fresh fruit.

Main meal Verdant broth (*p.142*). Tofu and vegetable stir-fry (*p.200*); salad. A slice of fresh pineapple.

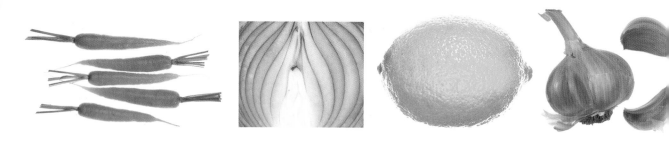

Respiratory problems

There are two kinds of respiratory problems: acute and chronic. Among the acute problems are chest, throat, nose, and ear infections, such as tonsillitis, whooping cough, bronchitis, sinusitis, sore throat, earache, flu, and the common cold. Chronic non-infective conditions range from asthma, hay fever, and other localized allergies to catarrh, voice problems – common among those who depend professionally upon a speaking or singing voice – bronchitis, and emphysema. Their origins are many and varied and may include an unhealthy lifestyle, not enough fresh air and exercise, poor breathing and posture, smoking, polluted air, working in an atmosphere polluted by dust or fluff, and chemicals in the shape of sprays, paints, or insecticides that irritate the lungs. All of these can create the perfect breeding ground for acute, and eventually chronic, respiratory problems.

Allergies are one important cause of respiratory problems, and adverse food reactions are also implicated. Another hazard to respiratory health is abuse of all the commercially available inhalants for nasal congestion. Constant use of these products damages the mucous membranes and eventually produces a "rebound effect", so that as soon as you stop using them, the condition returns in an aggravated form because the mucous membranes now become so highly irritated. Although some of the causes of these illnesses are out of your control, you can improve your chances of avoiding them by beefing up your immune system, helping out the bacteria and intestinal flora in your gut, and making sure you get lots and lots of fresh air.

Your immune system will be forever grateful to you for eating as much garlic as you possibly can. Garlic does not just vanquish vampires, but

bacteria as well. There are other foods that contain antioxidants such as vitamins A, C, and E that are equally useful – kiwifruit and avocados are both good immune system boosters. Salads in the summer, and wonderful home-made vegetable soups in winter, are what you should be eating. Put lots of herbs and spices into your foods too: rosemary, thyme, and oregano are particularly helpful, as is ginger, which gives your circulation a boost. Remember that catarrh, which afflicts literally millions of people, is often caused by years of eating too much sugar, too many refined carbohydrates, and too much dairy produce. It may seem worse at first when you change your diet, but that is the eliminative effect.

In the cases of some respiratory illnesses, such as asthma (which is now beginning to reach epidemic proportions), the gut may be just as important. Our appreciation of the complexity of the system of bacteria that live in our gut is increasing enormously. A recent study into probiotic drinks, which top up the beneficial bacteria in our intestines, found that workers who took one of these drinks daily were two and half times less likely to call in sick for work. There is now great interest in the effect of probiotics on asthma in children. Will it be shown, as has happened in the case of eczema (another atopic condition), that taking probiotics early in life can drastically reduce the probability of developing this condition?

Finally, get outside in the fresh air as much as you possibly can. Research in the 1920s showed that in a stuffy, stagnant atmosphere the mucous membranes of the nose and sinuses become swollen, congested, and eventually covered with a thick secretion, the perfect breeding ground for bacteria. But remember to wrap up warm, because it turns out Mum was right (isn't she always?) – getting chilled really can make your cold worse.

THE FOUR STAR SUPERFOODS
★ Lemons ★ Carrots ★ Onions ★ Garlic

The Superfoods

Fruits Almonds, apples, blackberries, cherries, dates, figs, lemons, rosehips, limes, papaya

Dried fruit Especially figs

Vegetables Turnip, carrots, onion, garlic, cabbage, asparagus, radishes, fennel, leeks, celery, lettuce, watercress, sweet potatoes

Herbs and spices Rosemary, thyme, parsley, chervil, horseradish, liquorice, cloves, mint, sage, savory, oregano, anis, cinnamon, marjoram

Grains Barley

Others Honey

The danger foods

Dairy products These encourage the production of mucus, which adds to any existing congestion.

Sweet, fat, and stodgy food Buns, chocolate bars, Danish pastries, and so forth also encourage the body's production of mucus and aggravate congestion.

Artificial colourings, flavourings, and preservatives These can be particularly harmful to people with asthma and hayfever.

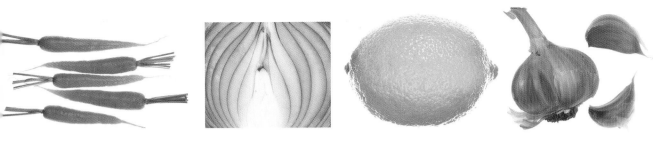

The eating plan

The week's eating plan we suggest will be beneficial for people with respiratory problems because it avoids mucus-forming foods, is very low in sugars, and is relatively low in carbohydrates.

We prefer natural products wherever possible, and for this reason we do not like margarine. However, there are situations where a drastic reduction in intake of dairy products is advisable, and this is one of them. Throughout this section, use a good sunflower oil or margarine free from additives and hydrogenated oils. Milk intake should be minimal and skimmed, but low-fat yoghurts can be used sparingly instead of cream. There is no cheese in this week's eating.

Throughout the week, at breakfast time, you could have a little milk in an occasional cup of tea, but avoid milk in coffee. Instead, have hot lemon and honey, herb teas, lemon teas, weak China tea, one of the good coffee substitutes, or homemade ginger punch (*p.249*).

Fenugreek is a herb you should get to know well. Its little golden seeds produce a delicious tea with a long reputation in traditional medicine for countering all catarrhal conditions, both in the respiratory tract and in the gut. Fennel tea, which is equally delicious, also helps clear excess catarrh. It is important to maintain a fluid intake of around one and a half litres/two to three pints a day, which encourages the body's elimination of mucus. The myth that a cold winter calls for rich, fatty foods and pounds of stodge is probably responsible for more runny noses than the weather. If your annual bronchitis has struck again, many of the Superfoods for respiratory problems are available even in the winter.

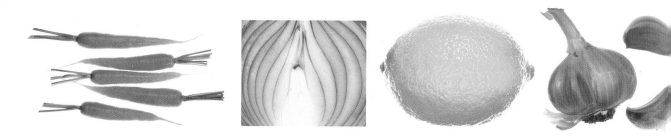

MENUS FOR A WEEK

Monday
Breakfast Apple purée; toast and honey.
Light meal or snack Tomato and herb omelette (*p.156*); orange and raw onion salad. Fresh fruit.
Main meal Spanish white garlic soup (*p.139*). Blackcurrant jelly (*p.241*).

Tuesday
Breakfast Muesli with low-fat yoghurt and fruit.
Light meal or snack Beef and onion burger (*p.216*) with salad.
Main meal Verdant broth (*p.142*); Waldorf salad (*p.226*).

Wednesday
Breakfast Half a grapefruit; two eggs; toast and honey.
Light meal or snack Tuna and bean salad.
Main meal Sauerkraut salad (*p.231*); Vegetable risotto (*p.194*). Spicy winter pudding (*p.241*).

Thursday
Breakfast Dried fruit compote; toast and honey.
Light meal or snack Cold vegetable risotto (*p.194*); salad.
Main meal Roasted vegetables (*p.204*); Ginger lamb stir-fry (*p.180*); steamed carrots. Spiced peaches (*p.244*).

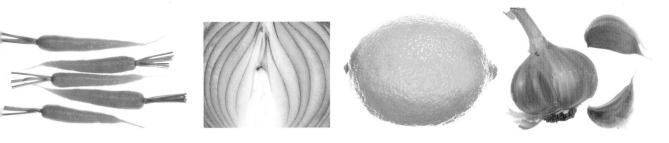

Friday

Breakfast Grilled herring with wholewheat toast.

Light meal or snack Beef and onion burger (*p.216*); watercress, fennel, and radish salad – including the radish leaves, too.

Main meal Sauerkraut salad (*p.231*); Peppered fish with vinaigrette (*p.171*) and steamed cabbage with caraway seeds. Baked apple (*p.237*).

Saturday

Breakfast Muesli with low-fat yoghurt and fruit.

Light meal or snack Beef and onion burgers (*p.216*) with tomato sauce and a baked potato.

Main meal Bedouin chicken (*p.186*); green salad. Spicy winter pudding (*p.241*).

Sunday

Breakfast Grilled bacon and mushrooms; poached or scrambled eggs; wholemeal toast.

Light meal or snack Carrot soup (*p.140*) with wholemeal bread. Selection of fresh fruit.

Main meal Classic crudités (*p.150*); Lamb burgers (*p.180*) with mashed potato and mangetout. Fresh pineapple.

Skin problems

The psychological importance of skin is incalculable. It's what we present to the outside world. It's how others see us. A skin disfigured by pimples, pustules, cratered scars, and scaly, flaky patches undermines confidence and self-esteem. It affects relationships with others, both social and sexual. If you are unhappy with your skin, you won't enjoy having it looked at, let alone caressed, and your partner is likely to feel the same way.

Skin is not just a protective covering. Like the lungs, the kidneys, and the bowel, it is also a major organ of elimination, helping the body rid itself of waste products. It is estimated that 10 billion dead cells are sloughed off our bodies every 24 hours, totalling a whopping 18kg/40lb in an average lifetime. These outer cells are made of a dead, horny material that easily absorbs waster excreted through the skin and is shed along with it.

The concept of this book is that we are what we eat. This is nowhere more relevant than when considering skin problems. No matter what the skin condition, no treatment can ever be complete without careful attention to diet. Creams, lotions, potions, masks, cleansers, and exfoliants may have their place, but a poor diet deprives the skin of the vitamins, minerals, and trace elements essential to its health. A junk-food diet produces irritating toxic wastes that, as they are eliminated through the skin, will exacerbate existing conditions and frequently trigger further problems.

Anyone who suffers from eczema or psoriasis and has experimented with diet will know that certain foods instantly make the condition worse. These are commonly animal fats, citrus fruits, highly spiced dishes, and

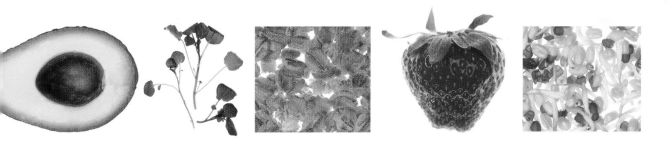

dairy products. Happily, the converse is equally true – eating the right foods can bring about a real, often startling, improvement in your skin, no matter what the problem. However, nutritional therapy seldom works with great speed and sometimes it may take weeks or months before you see a defininte improvement.

Skin is a mirror of general health, and deficiencies in any nutrient are likely to be reflected in its condition sooner or later. Low levels of three nutrients in particular tend to show up fast: vitamin A, vital to the general health of your skin; vitamin C, without which your skin cannot carry out its unceasing work of self-renewal; and zinc, which promotes repair and healing (the stretch-marks of pregnancy are usually due to a lack of this mineral, which is gradually depleted by pregnancy). It's also vital to have plenty of antioxidants in your diet, from foods such as avocados, strawberries, carrots, and watercress, which are fantastic for helping fight the free radicals that cause much skin damage, and are also very cleansing foods. The diuretic effects of grapes and dandelion are also useful for cleaning up your system. Once again, oily fish and the omega-3 fatty acids they contain play an important role in keeping skin healthy.

One way to discover which foods might be causing problems for your skin is to keep a food diary for a week. On the lefthand page, write down every single morsel that passes your lips, and on the right hand page, note down all symptoms. This technique can be very useful for other problems too.

Whatever the problem with your skin, the following chapter will help. It recommends all the foods that provide essential nourishment for the skin and encourage more efficient elimination of waste products through other channels.

 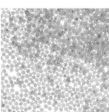   

THE FOUR STAR SUPERFOODS

★ Strawberries ★ Melon ★ Avocado ★ Watercress ★ Carrots ★ Millet ★ Oats ★ Pumpkin seeds ★ Sprouted seeds ★ Oily fish ★ Dandelion

The Superfoods

Fruit Apricots, oranges, grapes, kiwifruit, peaches, nectarines, papaya

Vegetables Cabbage, broccoli, kale, celery, nettles, spinach, watercress, tomatoes, Oriental greens, swede

Grains Wholewheat, wheatgerm, millet, buckwheat

Nuts, seeds, etc. Hazelnuts, walnuts and walnut oil

Herbs Parsley, dandelion, sage, thyme, celery seeds

The danger foods

Dairy products and eggs Dairy products are often implicated in skin disorders. Choose recipes that exclude them, or use non-dairy substitutes. Eggs may trigger eczema. If you follow a dairy-free regime long-term, take care to supplement your diet with calcium and vitamin D. Consult your doctor before cutting dairy products out of a child's diet. Yoghurt, especially goat's milk yoghurt, is generally good for skin problems.

Meat and animal fats These, especially pork and all processed meats, tend to exacerbate skin problems.

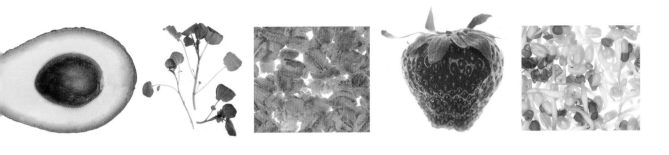

If you cannot avoid eating meat, trim off every scrap of fat, since it is in fat that the chemicals are stored. Wherever possible, choose organically produced eggs and poultry.

Sugar Sugar is particularly bad for acne sufferers. For sweeteners, use honey or molasses in small quantities, dried fruits, or concentrated fruit juices.

Coffee and tea There are more than 650 different chemicals in coffee, apart from caffeine, and none of them seems to do any good at all to your skin. The coffee substitute roasted dandelion root is beneficial in any skin problem. Tea can be drunk, in small amounts and not too strong.

Alcohol The skin is the first place where the effects of alcohol can be observed in a tell-tale flush. It is best avoided in all skin complaints.

Shellfish Fish and shellfish may trigger eczema.

The eating plan

Skin problems can result from eating the wrong foods or from allergic reactions or poor digestion and absorption of nutrients. Most frequently, poor elimination is the cause. Constipation is mirrored in a dull, clogged skin. There are many other factors involved in skin complaints, such as stress, anxiety, depression, environmental pollution, menstruation, pregnancy, and menopause. Whatever the cause of your problem, start your skin revolution with the Three-Day

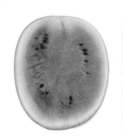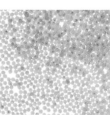

Elimination Diet. This consists of the first three days of the Seven-Day Alimentary Plan (*see p.287*).

As toxins are eliminated through your skin, your skin problems may be aggravated to start with. However, persevere with the eating plan and improvement will come.

MENUS FOR A WEEK

Avoid strong tea and coffee and drastically reduce or eliminate milk.

Monday

Breakfast Porridge; a banana. Weak tea or herbal tea.
Light meal or snack Avocado and watercress salad (*p.224*); mixed dried fruits, seeds and nuts.
Main meal Verdant broth (*p.142*); Citrus chicken (*p.185*) and salad. A piece of fresh fruit.

Tuesday

Breakfast Soaked dried fruits with natural yoghurt, followed by rice cakes and honey.
Light meal or snack Verdant broth (*p.142*) with wholewheat crispbread; radishes and celery. Fruit.
Main meal Green pasta salad (*p.162*); Herrings in oatmeal (*p.169*) with carrots and a baked potato.

Wednesday

Breakfast A fresh fruit salad; wholemeal toast.
Light meal or snack Watercress salad (*p.223*).

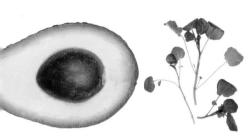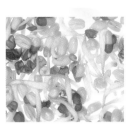

Main meal Vegetable and barley soup (*p.147*) with wholemeal rolls; Sprouted seed salad (*p.230*).

Thursday

Breakfast Muesli with fresh fruit.

Light meal or snack Hummus plus (*p.153*) with salad.

Main meal A slice of melon. Michael's millet and buckwheat (*p.261*); a green salad. Nuts and dried fruits.

Friday

Breakfast A fresh fruit salad; wholemeal toast.

Light meal or snack Sprouted seed salad (*p.230*).

Main meal Artichoke vinaigrette (*p.148*); Grilled red mullet (*p.173*). Green salad.

Saturday

Breakfast Pineapple; a grilled kipper; wholewheat toast.

Light meal or snack Pumpkin soup (*p.138*).

Main meal Half an avocado; Tofu and vegetable stir-fry (*p.200*). Spiced peaches (*p.244*).

Sunday

Breakfast Cold spiced peaches; wholemeal rolls.

Light meal or snack Carrot soup (*p.140*).

Main meal Classic crudités (*p.150*); Citrus chicken (*p.185*); braised chicory. Sliced fresh kiwifruit.

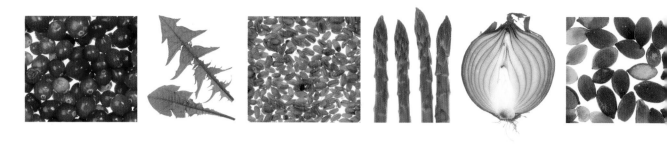

Urinary problems

The kidneys and bladder manufacture and store urine prior to passing it out of the body. This eliminative action is vital to our health, since it rids the body of surplus water and filters out the waste by-products of metabolism. It is a mistake to consider the urinary system merely as a bit of sophisticated plumbing. The kidneys also help in the metabolism of vitamin D and in the production of some essential hormones, particularly those responsible for the control of blood pressure.

There is a whole range of problems that can affect the urinary system, including kidney and bladder stones, cystitis, prostate problems, thrush, urethritis and non-specific urethritis, and many more. Even apparently minor urinary problems may be a sign of more serious underlying illness. You must seek professional help if you are aware of any abnormality in kidney and bladder function. This becomes urgent if you pass blood in your urine, if you have severe pain in the kidney region or when passing urine, if you have difficulty passing urine, or if your ankles become swollen.

Even the treatment of the more serious problems will be more effective when combined with healthy eating. Many of the less dramatic problems are much better treated in the kitchen than the surgery. Kidney stones, which tend to be a recurring problem, can be kept in check with the right diet. The misery of cystitis, which is the blight of so many women's lives, can respond dramatically to the omission of the Danger foods and an abundance of Superfoods. Prostate conditions respond magically to a prescription for pumpkin seeds.

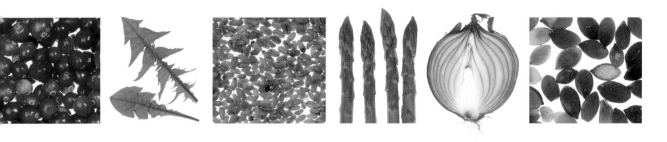

THE FOUR-STAR SUPERFOODS

Cranberries ★ Tomatoes ★ Asparagus ★ Onions ★
Barley ★ Pumpkin seeds ★ Dandelion

The Superfoods

Fruit Raspberries, green and red gooseberries,
watermelon, grapes, apples, figs, redcurrants,
blackcurrants

Vegetables Cabbage, pumpkin, potatoes, carrots,
aubergines, globe artichokes, horseradish, watercress
cucumber, celery, lettuce, runner beans, leeks, all leafy
green vegetables

Grains Barley, soybeans

Herbs Juniper berries, parsley, thyme, garlic, sage,
rosemary, celery seeds, camomile, candelion

Nuts and seeds All nuts except peanuts, pumpkin seeds

Others Shrimp

Drinks Barley water, dandelion coffee

The danger foods

Animal protein Far fewer vegetarians than meat-eaters
have kidney stones. The digestive breakdown of meat
produces uric and oxalic acids, both of which may
contribute to the formation of stones.

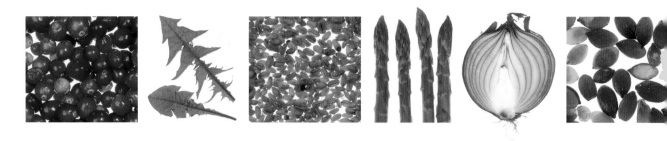

Dairy products These are high in calcium, so people with a tendency to form stones should eat dairy sparingly; yoghurt, however, is very important in the treatment of cystitis and thrush.

Sugar All sugar, including honey and molasses, encourages the proliferation of microorganisms. Avoid sugar, particularly if you have recurrent infectious conditions such as thrush or cystitis. Sugars may also increase the absorption of calcium during digestion, which is not good news for stone-formers.

Salt encourages fluid retention and should be avoided by anyone with problems of the urinary system.

Coffee contains substances highly irritant and damaging to the kidneys.

Oxalic acid is found in tea, coffee, chocolate, rhubarb, peanuts, spinach, beetroot, and strawberries. In certain susceptible people, the oxalic acid content of these foods will promote the formation of stones.

Citrus juice drunk in excess will increase the acidity of the urine and add to inflammatory discomfort.

Malt vinegar and commercial pickles Eat these sparingly for your own comfort, as they are very acidic.

Alcohol should be avoided by anyone with kidney or bladder disorders, since, in excessive quantities, it can interfere with the normal function of the kidneys.

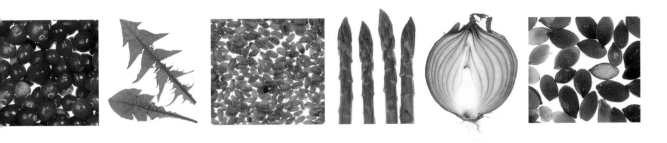

The eating plan

In experiments carried out in London by Professor John Yudkin and Dr R.G.Price, animals fed sugar-containing diets developed early signs of kidney damage and the swollen kidneys seen in diabetic patients. The exclusion of all refined sugars from the diet is good advice for everybody, but for people with kidney problems, it is rule number one.

Salt is a major danger to the modern diet, and nowhere is this more the case than the urinary system. Salt encourages fluid retention, and this diametrically opposes the flushing action of the kidneys. A daily intake of salt in excess of 5g (one level teaspoon) can have a serious effect on blood pressure, but the average person consumes 5-10g of salt a day, even without using the salt cellar. Steam your vegetables without salt, and use lemon and herbs for seasoning. The herbs listed as Superfoods will speed recovery and protect against recurrence, which is one of the worst features of many urinary problems.

An increased fluid intake will improve and maintain urinary health. It is important to dilute the concentration of the urine and to ensure a steady "flushing-through" of the whole urinary tract. Aim for one litre/three pints a day, preferably bottled pure spring water. If stones are a problem, don't drink tap water in hard water areas. Eat as little meat as possible, or exclude it altogether. It's also important to keep dairy consumption low because of its high calcium content, which can encourage the formation of kidney stones in susceptible people. Cottage cheese, soured cream, and Quark are all low in calcium. The value of yoghurt cannot be overemphasized, as it provides bacteria that aid elimination.

MENUS FOR A WEEK

When following this Eating Plan, it is essential to drink at least one litre/three pints of liquid daily. Avoid tea, coffee, and large quantities of citrus juice.

Monday

Breakfast All the watermelon you can eat!
Light meal or snack Toast; Frisée salad (*p.230*).
Main meal Asparagus citronette (*p.150*). Pasta with spicy tomato and onion sauce (*p.260*). Baked apple with cranberries.

Tuesday

Breakfast Porridge; stewed fruit
Light meal or snack Beef and onion burgers (*p.216*).
Main meal A selection of steamed vegetables; fruit.

Wednesday

Breakfast Two boiled eggs; wholewheat toast.
Light meal or snack Brown rice and celery soup (*p.142*).
Main meal Ratatouille (*p.202*); Salmon with green sauce (*p.167*) with rice. A big bunch of grapes.

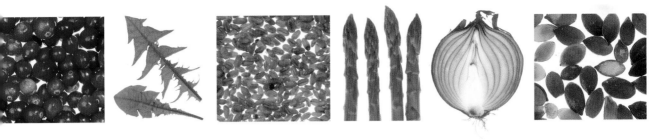

Thursday

Breakfast All the watermelon you can eat.

Light meal or snack Rice salad with parsley.

Main meal Vegetable and barley soup (*p.147*); Tofu and vegetable stir-fry (*p.200*).

Friday

Breakfast Blackcurrants stewed in apple juice; yoghurt.

Light meal or snack Tapenade with wholewheat toast.

Main meal Orange and watercress salad (*p.228*). Cod with sesame and spinach (*p.174*) with rice. Some figs.

Saturday

Breakfast Selection of fruit purées.

Light meal or snack Red and yellow eggs (*p.158*); cucumber salad.

Main meal Tagliatelle with artichokes (*p.160*); Sauerkraut salad (*p.231*). Peach and apricot compote (*p.234*).

Sunday

Breakfast Croissants.

Light meal or snack Onion soup (*p.138*); chicory salad.

Main meal Asparagus citronette (*p.150*); Eggs Mornay (*p.159*) with steamed runner beans. Stewed apples with cranberries.

Weight control

Dieting doesn't work. We've all been through the diet mill dozens of times. Starting on Monday – after a weekend spent stoking up against the lean days ahead, and having a final fling with our friends – and stopping on Wednesday, when our self-control finally snaps at the sight of a crusty well-buttered roll, or a bar of chocolate. The humiliation, the battered self-esteem – and the resolve to start again in earnest, from next Monday. Who hasn't done it?

There are dozens of diets. They claim miraculous results with very little effort. Most of them are useless, and some of them are dangerous. The Drinking Man's Diet – high-fat, high-alcohol, high-protein, and practically devoid of fruits, vegetables, and carbohydrate – is a certain recipe for liver, heart, and nervous system disease. The very-low calorie diets, meal replacements, Atkins, or steak and black coffee diets can damage the heart muscle, increase blood cholesterol, and permanently affect the kidneys. These diets are doomed to failure, since they make no attempt to change eating patterns, and boredom, fatigue, and cravings lead to the inevitable binge-and-collapse familiar to most habitual dieters.

Other recipes for disaster include low-carbohydrate diets, which eliminate the healthy, starchy foods such as wholemeal bread, potatoes, pasta, rice, and other cereals that are essential sources of fibre and

> "Fad diets are doomed to failure and many of them are also dangerous."

nutrients; all-fruit diets, which can have a catastrophic effect on your teeth, and by their very nature do not offer a balanced food intake; and finally, the high-fibre, bran-with-everything diet. Sprinkling a few spoonfuls of bran onto everything you eat, and consuming vast quantities of baked beans and All-Bran, may keep your bowels regular, but can also seriously reduce your absorption of calcium, magnesium, iron, and zinc.

People who follow the rules of Harmonious Eating (*p.344*) for a variety of health problems almost invariably report weight loss as a delightful side-effect. They find, too, that eating this way, the urge to binge or to snack between meals gradually disappears as the digestion improves. If, however, your prime concern is to lose weight, the Superfoods Harmonious Diet is a unique mix of Harmonious Eating and reducing fat intake that will work for everyone. The Harmonious Diet is not a "diet" as such. It's a way of eating that you can adapt to suit your tastes, your work schedule, and your social life. It is not a burden – you will never have to count a calorie; you will never have to weigh a portion of food; you will never have to refuse an invitation. You can start it at your next meal.

According to state-of-the-art research, the most successful – as well as the healthiest – way to lose weight is to restrict fat intake. However, if you cut it right out of your diet, you will not only lose weight, you will also suffer a variety of health problems. Moreover, a diet devoid of fats and oils is a kill-joy diet for masochists, and is more likely than not to lead to rebound bingeing and failure. The Harmonious Diet Nutrition Score-Card is not based solely on whether foods are "fattening" or "slimming". Like every other section in this book, the goal is good health, and good food is the means by which this is achieved.

So in this eating plan, calories don't really count. By following the Harmonious Diet, not only will your general health improve, but surplus weight will shed slowly and steadily. Remember too that exercise is vital, and the Harmonious Diet works best when combined with regular exercise.

The eating plan
The ten commandments for the overweight

1) Before you even think of changing your eating habits, buy a notebook, keep it under lock and key, and write down faithfully, for seven days, every single thing that goes into your mouth, liquid or solid. At the end of the week, study your diary carefully, underlining the black spots, which you will identify without difficulty. You will now know your greatest temptations, and you can start planning a strategy that takes these weak spots into account.

2) Your diary will certainly record moments when, despite your good intentions, a box of chocolates disappears, a tin of biscuits miraculously empties, a pound of cheese, half a pound of butter, and a fresh crusty loaf vanish without you even noticing. It is interesting how often people binge on foods to which they may be allergic, and to which they have become as addicted as any junkie. There's an obvious solution: stop buying your binge foods, even if it does mean the rest of the family going without for a while. The urge to binge or snack is diminished, and often disappears, when you switch to the Harmonious Eating Plan.

3) When you go out, don't use social pressures as an excuse to be diverted from the straight and narrow. You don't have to drink just

because everybody else is. Don't be intimidated by hosts or waiters. If you were a diabetic, you would not accept a slice of chocolate cake, and obesity is just as much an illness as diabetes.

4) If as a child you were brought up to believe it is wicked to leave food on your plate, it's time to put away such childish notions. Always try to leave something on your plate. Always leave the table feeling you could eat a little more. When you're dishing up a meal at home, serve it on smaller plates than usual.

5) If everyone in the family has a weight problem it is easier to tackle it as a family. It's disastrous to provide separate meals for one individual, while everybody else at the dinner table is scoffing fast food and chocolate pudding.

6) Learning the mechanics of proper eating is a skill that can be acquired, just like a good backhand at tennis. Lesson one: even when eating alone, lay the table; light a candle if you feel like it, use a bunch of flowers, or even a few wild grasses from the garden. Prepare your food, serve it elegantly, sit down, and enjoy it. Lesson two: chew! Digestion starts in the mouth: bolting leads to bingeing. Lesson three: when you've finished your meal, clear away and get out of the kitchen.

7) Western social life revolves around alcohol, which is very high in calories, and often displaces the more nutritious foods. If you find it hard to cut it right out, make yourself an allowance of one glass in an evening and stick to it.

8) The golden rule is to choose nutritious foods that give you healthy bulk as well as vitamins, minerals, and proteins. Many foods widely regarded as bad for slimming are in fact the best. These include good carbohydrates, such as potatoes baked in their skins, bread made from whole grains, brown rice and other whole grain cereals, root vegetables, and beans and other pulses. Generous amounts of these foods, with lots of fruits, vegetables, and salads, and more fish, less meat and animal fat, make you leaner but not hungry.

9) Nobody's perfect. However determined, at some point you'll slip. Do not quit. The occasional lapse can so easily become an excuse for just giving up the whole plan. Exorcise your binge the following day by being extra careful. You'll be back on course in no time.

10) Lock the bathroom scales in the attic. Who needs the daily purgatory of the weigh-in? Nobody loses weight every day. The ideal average loss is 1–2lb/½–1kg weekly. Weigh yourself in your local chemist shop the day you start, and try to go back at the same time on the same day and in the same clothes each week. Keep a chart and revel in the falling numbers!

The Harmonious Diet

We have listed all food in the three groups of Harmonious Eating. "A" Foods are the proteins, "B" Foods are neutral, and "C" foods are the starches.

The Nutrition Score-Card
There are five simple rules:

1) Do not exceed 12 points a day (*= 1 point).
2) You can eat A Foods with B Foods, or B Foods with C Foods, at the same meal, but not A Foods with C Foods.
3) Five-point foods should be saved for special treats.
4) Make sure you eat a wide range of foods, with five portions of fruit and vegetables and a salad each day.
5) If you exceed 12 points a day, don't give up. Have only fresh fruit for breakfast next morning, or the juice of a lemon in a glass of hot water, and keep that day's points below 10.

Quantities

The following table allows for average portions, about the size of a helping you'd get in a restaurant, as opposed to the generous slab of cheese or the lavish carving of roast lamb you might serve yourself.

A Foods (Proteins)

5★★★★★

All meat – beef, lamb, veal, or pork – roasted and served
    with its fat. Roast duck or roast goose with skin.
    Cooked mince.
Scrambled or fried eggs.
Taramasalata.

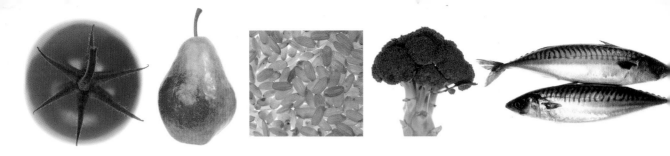

Stilton, Parmesan, Gruyere, Roquefort, mature Cheddar, and real cream cheese.

All sauces made with cheese.

4★★★★

Grilled, roast, braised, or casseroled beef, lamb, veal, or pork with all visible fat removed.

Lean minced beef.

Roast chicken with its skin.

Fish canned in oil.

A 2-egg omelette.

3★★★

Grilled, braised or casseroled liver, kidneys, or heart.

All oily fish grilled, baked, or steamed

Boiled or poached eggs.

Soft cheeses: Brie, Camembert, St Paulin, Edam, Gouda, Wensleydale, Cheshire, etc.

2★★

Roast turkey without skin.

All game birds. Hare and rabbit. Chicken – roast, grilled or casseroled without its skin.

Cottage cheese.

Whole cow's milk.

Greek yoghurt.

1*

All white fish – baked, steamed, grilled, or casseroled.

All shellfish.

Semi-skimmed milk.

Quark. Natural yoghurt. Low-fat cottage cheese.

Natural fromage frais, very low-fat yoghurt, and skimmed milk all have near-zero fat and calorie counts so – within reason! – you can use these on their own as snacks, or incorporated into recipes without increasing your point-count.

Mean dressing (*p.254*).

All fruits.

One glass (150ml/6oz) dry red or white wine, or dry cider. (Not port, sherry, Madeira or malmsey.) Not more than one of these a day.

Half a point drinks

Half a glass (75ml/3oz) dry red or white wine topped up with still or sparkling mineral water: not more than two of these a day.

A glass of fruit juice (150ml/6oz) mixed half-and-half with plain or sparkling mineral water.

B Foods (Neutral)

5★★★★★

1 tablespoon butter, margarine, double cream, clotted cream, or whipping cream.
1 tablespoon mayonnaise.
All sauces made with butter, margarine, or cream.

4★★★★

1 tablespoon single cream, sour cream, or pouring cream.

3★★★

1 egg yolk.
1 tablespoon desiccated coconut.

2★★

All nuts except chestnuts, hazelnuts, and desiccated coconut. Pumpkin, sesame, and sunflower seeds. Nuts and seeds are highly nutritious, but very high in fat, so a 2★★ allowance is only a heaped tablespoon for nuts, a level tablespoon for seeds.
1 tablespoon extra-virgin olive oil, or other vegetable oil, preferably cold-pressed.

1★

Chestnuts. Hazelnuts.

No points

All vegetables, as long as they are raw, steamed, baked, or boiled. If you fry them, add 3 points. Vegetable juice – as much as you like, providing it's salt- and sugar-free. Tea or coffee without sugar, and with a dash of semi-skimmed or skimmed milk: not more than three a day. Herbal teas without milk, sugar or honey, and water – as much as you like.

C Foods (Starches)

1*

Potatoes: 1 medium-sized potato in its skin. 1 serving of boiled or steamed potatoes.

1 large wholewheat roll.

1 wholewheat pitta bread.

1 serving pasta, brown rice, or other wholegrain cereal; or unsweetened breakfast cereal, served with skimmed milk.

1 banana.

1 slice of wholewheat, rye, or other wholegrain bread.

2 crispbreads.

1 serving of porridge.

1 serving of potatoes mashed in their own or other vegetable cooking water.

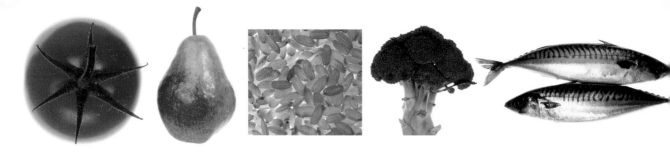

1 serving cooked dried beans – butter, soy, chickpeas.
1 small bunch of very sweet grapes; 1 very ripe papaya;
  4–5 fresh figs.
1 tablespoon of raisin, sultanas, or currants.
A serving of prunes or dried apricots, unsweetened.
2 dried figs or dates (very high in natural sugar!)
½ pint beer or lager.

Treats

A scrape of jam, honey, marmalade, or nut butters: use very sparingly and charge yourself a point each time. If you use sugar in your tea, charge yourself half a point for each teaspoon.

Putting the Harmonious Diet to work

To begin with, make your own ready reckoner on a postcard and carry it with you for quick reference when you're eating out or shopping. Try to plan your daily menus in advance. This makes shopping easier and cheaper, and you won't have any excuse for running out of low-point foods. When you are the cook, working out the point-count of a given dish is easy. If you are eating out, in a restaurant, or with friends, it can be tricky. Here is our rule-of-thumb guide.

1) Any fried food, all dishes with cream sauces, all dishes with butter, anything with cheese – reckon 5 points.

2) All vegetables – 2 points for added butter, 3 points if they're fried.

3) All meat or fish dishes where you can see what you're eating – 3 points. Add 2 for crackling, crispy skin, or visible fat – even if you don't eat it.

4) Any pudding including cream, chocolate, pastry, ice-cream, or lots of sugar – 5 points.

None of the following foods belong in the Harmonious Diet, either because they don't harmonize or because they are very high in fat, and often both.

1) Any form of processed meat – sausages, salami, etc.

2) Combinations of meat and pastry – steak-and-kidney pie, pork pie, Cornish pasty, quiche lorraine, etc.

3) Any combination of meat and cheese – lasagne, moussaka, pasta served with a meat sauce and cheese.

4) Battered, breadcrumbed, or just plain fried food.

5) Sugar's empty calories have no place in the Harmonious Diet, and the combination of poor-quality fats used in made-up cakes and confectionery – especially chocolate – is particularly deadly.

MENUS FOR A WEEK

Monday (total: 10 points)
Breakfast A *roll with a little *butter.
Light meal or snack **Tricolour coleslaw (*p.231*), with low-fat cottage cheese. *Any fresh fruit.
Main meal **Citrus chicken (*p.185*), with *mashed parsnips and carrots. **Apple amaretto (*p.236*).

Tuesday (total: 12 points)
Breakfast *Porridge with *1 dessertspoon of single cream. *1 slice wholewheat toast with *a little butter.
Light meal or snack **Verdant broth (*p.142*); green salad with Mean dressing (*p.254*).
Main meal ***Sardines with mustard sauce (*p.168*). Camembert or other ***cheese, with celery.

Wednesday (total: 11 points)
Breakfast *Half a grapefruit; ****a 2-egg omelette.
Light meal or snack Grilled mushrooms on **lightly buttered toast; green salad with *French dressing.
Main meal *Michael's millet and buckwheat (*p.261*); Steamed mangetout in *olive oil. *Dried fruits.

Thursday (total: 12 points)
Breakfast *Fruit salad with **Greek yoghurt and a dribble of honey. Tea, coffee, or herbal tea.
Light meal or snack Sandwich made with *a slice of

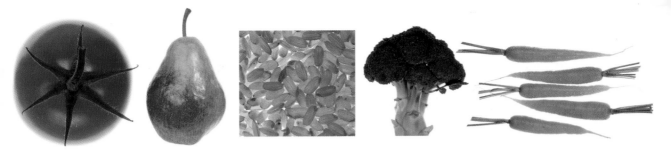

wholewheat bread; **a banana mixed with 2 chopped dates, sesame seeds, and lemon juice. Celery. *A pear.

Main meal **Tandoori chicken (*p.185*); *Tsatsiki (*p.231*). **Spicy winter pudding (*p.241*).

Friday (total: 10 points)

Breakfast *Banana on **toast – 2 slices.

Light meal or snack *Verdant broth (*p.142*); *roll.

Main meal **Baked fish provençal (*p.170*) with spinach; Tomato salad (*p.226*). *Grapes and **Brie.

Saturday (total: 10 points)

Breakfast *As much fresh fruit as you like.

Light meal or snack **Toast; salad with chopped ripe tomato and a few black olives.

Main meal **Guinea fowl casserole (*p.188*); *Braised red cabbage (*p.200*). *Strawberries with **Greek yoghurt and honey. *A glass of wine.

Sunday (total: 12 points)

Breakfast A *roll with a little *butter.

Light meal or snack **Green pasta salad (*p.162*). *A papaya or a ripe pear.

Main meal *****Carpaccio (*p.178*). *Tangerine and apricot pudding (*p.235*). *A glass of wine.

Harmonious eating

For people in the industrialized world, particularly in the affluent West, eating habits have changed more dramatically over the last century than in the thousands of years before. For example, we no longer eat foods grown in our neighbourhood, or even in our own country; instead, we eat food from all over the world. We no longer eat what is in season; thanks to aeroplanes, freezing, and tinning, we eat strawberries at Christmas, Brussels sprouts in mid-summer, and baby peas and avocados all year round.

We may eat meat as often as three times a day, with bacon or sausage for breakfast, roast beef sandwiches for lunch, and meat and two veg for dinner. We also eat denatured food – white flour, white rice, white sugar, chemically refined oils, dehydrated vegetables – from which fibre and important trace minerals have been removed.

Along with our food, we ingest dozens of different chemicals in the form of artificial additives, as well as traces of the tons of chemicals used in Western-style agriculture to ensure a perfect-looking product and a high yield. With all this, it's hardly surprising that our digestive systems, which have been programmed by thousands of years of far simpler eating, can't take the strain and begin to function badly. These days, digestive problems are almost endemic in Western countries. It's a fact

"Eating habits have changed more in the past century than in the last thousand years."

that if our digestive systems are not working at 100 per cent efficiency, the whole body suffers as a result. Absorption of essential nutrients is impaired. Toxic wastes are not eliminated. The gate is then opened to myriad health problems.

When Dr William Howard Hay cured himself of chronic ill health in the 1920s simply by changing the way he ate, after all his medical colleagues had failed to help him with conventional medicine, he stumbled on the answer to many people's problems. He called it Fundamental Eating, and it formed the basis of what is now known as the Hay Diet. The fundamental rule of the Hay Diet is that concentrated starches and proteins are not eaten at the same meal. Thus, if you eat cheese, you don't eat bread; you can eat roast beef, but no roast potatoes; you can have chips, but not fish. According to Dr Hay, the human digestive system is not adapted to the simultaneous digestion of starches and proteins. When it is challenged repeatedly with such combinations, digestive problems result. The nutrients in food are poorly absorbed. Other more serious health problems arise.

The Hay Diet has improved the health of millions throughout the world who have learned how to combine foods in the right way, avoiding mixtures of food that fight. Not just digestive problems but diseases respond to Hay's concept, since the well-nourished, self-cleansing body has the increased resistance and raised vitality essential for nature's own healing processes.

It's not our recommendation that everybody should stick rigidly to Hay's Fundamental Eating plan, but the pulse of Hay can be felt throughout this book. The majority of the recipes given in each section use the healthy combinations of foods he recommended. In most cases, the menus reflect these principles of Harmonious Eating, as we have called it. Even if you feel perfectly healthy, try Harmonious Eating for a

few weeks. You may well be surprised by how much better you feel. If you are not well – and particularly if you have a digestive or bowel or weight problem – Harmonious Eating will produce significant long-term benefits.

What to eat with what

In Harmonious Eating, all foods belong in one of three groups: Protein, Neutral, and Starch (*see p.335*). Starch foods can be combined with Neutral Foods, and so can Protein foods, but Starch and Protein foods should never be eaten at the same meal. Allow at least four hours between meals, and snack on Neutral foods only.

Following Harmonious guidelines, you will be eating in a new pattern, but you will quickly find that you don't need to discard all of your favourite foods. To show you how the plan works in practice, here is a week's menu.

MENUS FOR A WEEK

Monday

Breakfast Fresh peaches; natural yoghurt with honey.
Light meal or snack Jacket potato with sour cream and chives; a mixed vegetable salad.
Main meal Cold roast beef with a green vegetable and a large mixed salad. Cheese and celery.

Tuesday

Breakfast Porridge; wholewheat toast and butter.
Light meal or snack Salade niçoise (*p.214*) (omit the potatoes). An apple or an orange.
Main meal Vegetable risotto (*p.194*). Dates and figs.

Wednesday

Breakfast Orange juice. Scrambled eggs; mushrooms.
Light meal or snack Verdant broth (*p.142*); rye crispbread or a crusty wholewheat roll.
Main meal Rosemary chicken (*p.188*); Ratatouille (*p.202*); a green salad. A baked apple with almonds.

Thursday

Breakfast Orange, grapefruit, and tangerine segments.
Light meal or snack Tuna; Complete coleslaw (*p.226*).
Main meal Spaghetti con aglio e olio (*p.162*). A banana.

Friday

Breakfast Greek yoghurt with honey and chopped nuts.
Light meal or snack Cheese omelette; spinach salad.
Main meal Vegetable risotto (*p.194*). Fruit salad.

Saturday

Breakfast Poached eggs with bacon and mushrooms.
Light meal or snack Wholemeal pitta with salad.
Main meal Grilled lamb chops with root vegetables and broccoli. Apples stewed with lemon juice and honey.

Sunday

Breakfast Compote of dried fruit; toast and butter.
Light meal or snack A bowl of muesli; sliced banana.
Main meal Grilled red mullet (*p.173*); spinach. Pears cassis (*p.236*).

Index

Acknowledgments

★★★★

ABOUT THE AUTHORS

One of the leading authorities on complementary health, Michael van Straten is a former president of the British Naturopathic and Osteopathic Association and a past governor of the British College of Naturopathy and Osteopathy. A practising osteopath, naturopath, acupuncturist, and nutritional consultant and a well-known medical broadcaster and writer, he also contributes regularly to television shows.

Michael has more than 20 health titles to his name, including the best-selling books from DK's *Superfoods* series, and the phenomenally successful *Foods That Harm, Foods That Heal*, for which he was a Consultant Editor. A colourful personality and an enthusiastic cook, his hobby is making jams and chutneys from the produce he grows on his organic farm.

He relieves stress by beating dough during his weekend bread making sessions.

Barbara Griggs has been researching, writing, and lecturing about health and herbal medicine for more than 30 years. She is the author of a number of books on nutrition and herbal medicine, and as a journalist she is well known for the articles she contributed regularly to *Country Living*, where she was Health Editor for 20 years.

PUBLISHER'S ACKNOWLEDGMENTS

Dorling Kindersley would like to thank Sîan Irvine for photography; home economist Pippin Britz; Alyson Lacewing, Katie John, and Helen Murray for editorial assistance; Iona Hoyle for design assistance; Christine Heilman and Jennifer Williams for editing the North American edition, and Kathie Gill for compiling the index.

★★

AUTHORS' ACKNOWLEDGMENTS

The authors would like to thank the DK team for all their hard work, especially: editors, Shannon Beatty and Kathy Fahey and designers, Anne Fisher and Ruth Hope. They would also like to thank the following authors and publishers for their permission to quote excerpts from their work:

Marcella Hazan (White bean soup) from *Essentials of Classic Italian Cooking* (Macmillan London Ltd.); Rosemary Man and Robin Weir (Devilled chicken) from *The Compleat Mustard* (Constable); Pat Chapman (Chicken jalfrezi) from *Favourite Restaurant Curries* (Judy Piatkus Publishers); Paul Laurenson and Ethel Minogue (Falafel) from *The Taste of Health* (BBC Books); Nathalie Hambro (Red bean salad in plum sauce) from *Particular Delights* (Ebury). They would also like to thank J. Sainsbury plc for permission to reproduce a recipe (Peppered fish with vinaigrette) from one of their leaflets.

Some text from the Superfoods section first appeared in *Superfeast* by Michael van Straten published in 2005 by Little Books, Inc. and is reproduced by kind permission of the publisher.

PICTURE CREDITS
All images © DK Images